GOOD LIFE IN HARD TIMES

San Francisco's '20s and '30s

Good Life in Hard Times

Jerry Flamm

CHRONICLE BOOKS   SAN FRANCISCO

To Esther,
David A., Danny, Sammy, David S.
and the other Flamms.

Printed in the United States of America.

Library of Congress Cataloging in Publication Data

Flamm, Jerry.
   Good life in hard times.

   1. San Francisco—Social life and customs.
2. San Francisco—Biography.   3. Journalists—
California—San Francisco—Biography.   4. Flamm, Jerry
I. Title.
F869.S3F58   979.4'61'05   76-30524
ISBN 0-87701-092-7

Cover photograph by Gabriel Moulin courtesy of Station KNBR.

Chronicle Books
870 Market Street
San Francisco, CA 94102

CONTENTS

Introduction

You might call them the Golden Decades if you were young and growing up in San Francisco in those years —from about 1920 to 1940. There was a short, cloudy span of years in there, of course—the Great Depression in the early 1930s. Apples were sold on the streets for a nickel then by men and women with grim lines around their mouths. The WPA make-work projects were launched by FDR. College graduates with every qualification were in the clusters of young and old who rendezvoused every day at the ocean beach in bathing suits for sun and talk—often just for talk. There were no jobs around of any kind—let alone jobs that might match up with university degrees. No matter who you were, you applied at the Post Office at Christmastime for the usual extra work available in the holiday season —things like that. But overall, it's easiest to recall the pleasant, unhurried, and orderly pace of things in a city that everyone agreed was a very nice place in which to live.

Golden Gate Park had a donkey ride then at the Children's Playground. The saddled donkeys, with youngsters strapped to their backs, stoically and almost automatically followed a winding, wire-fenced course. They were started on their way by the slap of the starter who lifted kids on if they were that small, and collected the five-cent tickets. Or kids could ride a goat cart around the course, with an attendant walking alongside.

The Sunset District was still being built up during those years. As kids we went out beyond Twentieth Avenue and made believe we were in the French Foreign Legion, charging up and down sand dunes that stretched all the way to the beach.

You could take a No. 40 Iron Monster streetcar, privately owned by the Market Street Railway Company, and ride for twenty-five cents all the way down to San Mateo on the Peninsula where the line ended. On that trip you would pass over raised rails from

Colma. Stops included the Tanforan Race Track in San Bruno. The round-trip fare was forty cents.

Lone Mountain was a monstrous bare sand dune which towered over the rear of rickety Ewing Field on Masonic Avenue. All the major football games in the city, including the first Shrine East-West contest, were played at Ewing until Kezar Stadium opened in 1926 on the edge of Golden Gate Park. One of our adventures was to plod slowly up through the loose, deep sand to the top of Lone Mountain and then roll down the steep hill.

When I was in grammar school, the big weekend events for many of us were the Saturday and Sunday baseball games of the Pacific Coast League Seals and Missions teams in the Recreation Park stadium. During high school, the Friday night church dances at St. Monica's or St. Anne's were the weekend highlights. Occasional fist fights broke out on the sidewalks outside of the churches, and rumor had it that bloodstains had to be scrubbed off the pavement early on Sunday mornings before services began. On Saturday nights we went to the movies or, in the summertime, to the dances at the Rose Bowl in Larkspur. Oh, we had schoolmates who took dates dancing at the downtown hotels on the weekends, but they were usually the "rich kids," who often had their own cars. Our only contact with the music of Ted Fiorita at the St. Francis, Anson Weeks at the Mark Hopkins, and Paul Pendarvis at the Palace was through the late night radio broadcasts.

In the 1920s most of our families didn't have cars or garages. Often the most luxurious entertainment spot members of our set had visited was the plush, elaborate, and brightly lit Agua Caliente miniature golf course at the southeast corner of Eighth and Market streets.

No bridges crossed the Bay from San Francisco until 1936. Before the Golden Gate Bridge opened in

A 1925 parade on Market Street during the celebration of California's Diamond Jubilee of statehood.

Courtesy of San Francisco Department of Public Works

1937, on weekends in Sausalito cars waiting for the auto ferryboats would back up outside of town and around the curves of the corkscrew road serrating the mountain between Sausalito and Corte Madera. Late on Sunday nights, the headlights of the cars formed an incandescent daisy chain up the side of the mountain.

The vaudeville and stage shows downtown in the City, and even in the outer neighborhoods, made live entertainment perhaps more accessible to everyone than it is now. It was cheaper, for one thing, and had a more general appeal. The neighborhood movie theaters featured a Country Store show at least one night a week, usually Friday. Bags of groceries would be donated by local merchants and given out to lucky ticket holders and to the winners of amateur talent contests. In the latter, the prodigies of stage-struck mothers put on robot-like performances in elaborate

Ghirardelli was a chocolate factory only, not a tourist attraction, in 1919. And Aquatic Park did not exist yet. This photograph is taken from the foot of Van Ness Avenue.

Courtesy of San Francisco Department of Public Works

Sunday at the beach in San Francisco drew a lot of people and cars in 1922.

Courtesy of San Francisco Department of Public Works

Beyond Twentieth Avenue, much of the land was still sand dunes in 1931. This is Sunset Boulevard, looking north from Santiago Street.

Courtesy of San Francisco Department of Public Works

homemade costumes. At Thanksgiving time, turkeys were among the prizes.

When the United States finally entered World War II in 1941 as a participant rather than a nervous neutral, everything changed. San Francisco was not the same—ever again. Hordes of servicemen came flowing into the City on passes from their bases or ships or on a last fling before they took off for combat in the Pacific. Later they came back on furloughs or when they were being mustered out. They all had cash burning a hole in their pockets, and they were all looking for an outlet to live it up. These transient visitors were early targets; they could be overcharged, deceived, and fleeced. "Quick buck operators" and confidence men proliferated throughout the City to take advantage of the heavy cash flow. Caution replaced trust in many aspects of the City's up-to-now easygoing daily life— not only in bars, restaurants, and nightclubs, but also in other channels of the City's normal life style. San

Franciscans' warm hospitality and pleasure in helping puzzled strangers on the streets gradually shaded into impatience. City dwellers began to hurry by strangers needing directions in the famous manner of New Yorkers.

San Francisco is still a fine city in which to live and work, perhaps still the best major city in the United States for the good life. However, I miss the way the City was prior to Pearl Harbor Day. My memories of the 1920s and 1930s have mellowed and been coated with the patina of age. Undoubtedly my recollections have taken on a rosier glow than the actual time had when I was growing up. Readers of this book who lived in San Francisco or the surrounding counties then, will have their own personal reflections on pleasures and events—images they return to and savor occasionally. Hopefully, some of my own impressions, recorded in the following pages, will blend into their own or inspire others.

These are San Francisco unemployed lining up during the Great Depression at Rich and Clara Streets, south of Market, for a free meal (1932).

Courtesy of San Francisco Department of Public Works

The unemployed being fed in a "soup kitchen" at Rich and Clara Streets, south of Market, in 1932 during the Great Depression.

Courtesy of San Francisco Department of Public Works

1

Front Page Days

Hildy Johnson, a fictional star reporter, lived and worked in Chicago in Ben Hecht and Charles Mac-Arthur's 1928 stage play *The Front Page*. The play presented a romanticized version of the Windy City's fiercely competitive press scene. However, Hildy would have been right at home in San Francisco in that era.

Until 1929, five biting, scratching major daily newspapers battled to get out the news first to eager readers in San Francisco and its suburbs. Two of the three afternoon dailies merged that year when *Call and Post* owner William Randolph Hearst was talked into buying the decaying *Bulletin*. When he learned that he had paid more than a million dollars for a "turkey" with little more to its name than some antiquated presses and yellowed library clippings, Hearst fired the hireling who had recommended the purchase to him.

But the merger of the *Call and Post* and the *Bulletin* did not reduce the intensity of the race for stories. The City remained a stage for the scrambling, scheming, and zestful reporters and photographers of the four daily newspapers. Hearst's new *Call Bulletin* and the *Daily News*, a Scripps-Howard chain paper, came out on the streets before noon every day but Sunday. The two morning papers were the *Chronicle*, owned by the de Young family, and Hearst's beloved *Examiner*, the original cornerstone of his publishing empire.

Several short-lived attempts at starting other daily newspapers had been made in the early Twenties. The *San Francisco Journal*, converted from a commercial weekly, lasted for only a couple of years in its bid to compete with the *Examiner* and *Chronicle* in the morning field. This bold endeavor was undertaken by Andrew Lawrence, a former top Hearst organization man from Chicago. Lawrence raised money from some well-heeled San Franciscans and opened editorial offices over Breen's saloon on Third Street, a few steps away from the *Examiner*. But Lawrence's valiant and stormy efforts at keeping the *Journal* alive were punctuated by some rough episodes. One night, for example, the notorious Dago Louis, a tough *Chronicle* circulation boss, invaded the *Journal's* composing room shortly after midnight and spilled all the next edition's page forms filled with type onto the floor. Under pressure of this sort, the *Journal* tossed in the financial towel in 1923. (Dago Louis made headlines a short time later when he was shot and killed in the basement of the Chronicle Building on Kearny and Market Streets, following a personal argument.)

Circulation wars were an accepted part of the highly competitive newspaper business in those years. Burly toughs roamed the City, occasionally beating up rival newsboys and tearing up stacks of papers. Joe Cauthorn, the *Daily News* business manager, solved his paper's headaches by importing his own gang of bruisers to retaliate in true Hollywood-movie style.

Just before Christmas in 1923, another attempt to start a daily newspaper was launched. The trappings of glamour and a splurge of largesse that accompanied this effort promised more than just a transient phenomenon. Young Cornelius Vanderbilt, Jr., no less, invaded the City with grandiose and ambitious plans to bring a one-cent daily tabloid into the exciting San Francisco news arena. The eager scion leased a building for the plant on Twelfth Street between Market and Mission, and began operations with all the trappings—and the money—that the name Vanderbilt conjured up.

The Chronicle *was in the de Young Building at Market and Kearny Streets from 1888 to 1923, one of the few Market Street buildings to survive the fire and earthquake in 1906. This picture was taken in 1918.*

Courtesy of the San Francisco Examiner

8

The entrance to the Examiner *offices at Third and Market Streets in 1936.*

Courtesy of San Francisco Department of Public Works

He opened offices for what he named the *Illustrated Daily Herald* in the Phelan Building downtown in San Francisco, and in Oakland, Berkeley, Richmond, Sacramento, Watsonville, Eureka, and Fresno. Vanderbilt hired a staff, offering and paying reporters and photographers astronomical wages for those days.

The plant building was modernized, two new presses were installed along with no less than five darkrooms and two enlargement rooms for the photography staff, and, the paper boasted, "the most up-to-date composing room in the U.S."

On the night the first edition of the paper was to be printed, a gala birthday party was held at the Twelfth Street plant. Mayor James Rolph, Jr. pressed the button to start the presses rolling. Mrs. Cornelius Vanderbilt cut a huge birthday cake which had been baked in Los Angeles. (Vanderbilt had already started another ambitious tabloid in that city called *Los Angeles Illustrated Daily News.*) An early evening parade through San Francisco's downtown streets flowed past the St. Francis Hotel and Union Square and the Palace Hotel on Market Street. Star shells and skyrockets were sent up in the evening sky.

"Your Paper Starts; Circulation Is 125,000," the first headline said. Vanderbilt claimed that an intensive subscription campaign had netted 90,000 home-delivery customers. Later, advertisements were published inviting investments in a proposed coast-to-coast chain of Vanderbilt newspapers to be published in seven U.S. cities. Los Angeles and San Francisco were only to be starters.

It didn't work. On May 15, 1926, not quite two and a half years later, a front-page story in the *Illustrated Daily Herald* carried the heading, "*Herald* Employees Thank You." The few paragraphs that followed advised readers that the paper's employees had "carried on for three days with hopes," but that Vanderbilt had been unable to either refinance the paper or sell it. "Today's issue exhausts the last of the paper stock," the short notice said. "The *Herald* employees can continue no longer." It was the end of an ambitious journalism experiment in the Bay Area. A day earlier, the Vanderbilt tabloid in Los Angeles had petitioned the court for appointment of a receiver. A third Vanderbilt tabloid in Miami also succumbed. Vanderbilt returned to New York and later settled in Reno. The presses and equipment at the Twelfth Street plant in San Francisco were sold at auction.

In addition to the four City papers, two major daily newspapers thrived across the Bay in Oakland. One was Joe Knowland's *Tribune*. The other was Hearst's *Post Enquirer*, formed in 1922 by his purchase of the *Enquirer* and the *Post*. The *Post Enquirer* was housed in an abandoned telephone building across from the Leamington Hotel. However, Hearst treated the *Post Enquirer* like a stepchild, never doing more for it than keeping it alive. It provided some competition for the *Tribune*, but the latter's large staff made it no-contest. The liveliest competition ensued when a big East Bay story drew the San Francisco reporters and photographers across the Bay; this occurred ever more frequently after the Bay Bridge opened in 1936. The Hearst paper in Oakland was of some value in providing Hearst's International News Service with coverage of the area, and occasionally it provided dupes of local stories to the Hearst-owned *Examiner*, *Call and Post*, and, later, the *Call Bulletin* in San Francisco.

The *Post Enquirer* management hurried that paper's demise when it decided to cut out its Saturday edition, which did fairly well with street sales and the results of the football games, in favor of a Sunday paper. "It turned out to be the world's worst Sunday paper," former staff member Bill Brown said, "with lousy color supplements, lousy comics—a real fiasco. You could say it choked to death on its own Sunday edition." The *Enquirer* finally turned toes up in 1950 with its circulation down to less than 74,000. The *Tribune* figure was just short of 160,000.

All through the Twenties and Thirties, the newspapers were the chief source of news. "Extras" were put out regularly with the results of important events and happenings. These included elections, heavyweight championship fights, disasters, and historic episodes such as Lindbergh's solo flight across the Atlantic. San Franciscans would be eating dinner when suddenly they would hear several voices yelling outside. A group of vendors, both men and boys, would come sweeping through the neighborhood shouting, "Extra, extra! Tunney beats Dempsey! Extra! Read all about it. Extra!"

Cornelius Vanderbilt, Jr., and his wife in the early Twenties when he was opening up newspapers around the country, including the Daily Illustrated Herald *in San Francisco.*

Courtesy of the San Francisco Examiner

The father would give one of the kids a nickel to run downstairs and buy a paper from the shouting news vendor who was walking rapidly and carrying a huge stack under one arm. He never had change if you asked him. The extra usually carried a blaring headline across the top of the front page and a few paragraphs of type in a box at the lower right-hand corner. The *Call*, *News*, and *Bulletin*, the afternoon papers, all used red, blue, or green colored ink for the headlines and in the box. For a fight, the text usually was a brief round-by-round summary.

Ever since the Gold Rush days in the bawdy port City, "freedom of the press" had been interpreted by San Francisco editors, reporters, and photographers as a carte blanche pass to get the story by any means possible. The race for exclusive stories by aggressive reporters and photographers, who supposedly always wore hats with rakishly turned-up brims and reeked of sarcasm and worldly ways, attracted bright young men to the newspapers. Also, a very few women managed to find their way onto newspaper staffs. They were automatically labeled "sob sisters" because they so often were assigned to do sympathetic interviews with female victims, criminals, or relatives. Even college graduates sought places on city room staffs, although relatively few actually landed jobs, and those who did had to overcome a cynical and sometimes scornful attitude by the majority of jaded veterans.

GOOD LIFE IN HARD TIMES

The Call and Post *was at New Montgomery and Jessie Streets in the late Twenties.*

The Bulletin *was on Mission near Fourth Street until 1929, the year this picture was taken.*

The fierce competition for news led reporters and photographers to gather up and hide principal figures and witnesses, sometimes even victims, who were being sought by the police. These newsworthy figures were then held until the paper in possession had published "exclusive" stories and photographs. Cordons of security guards, and even of city policemen, were thrown around newspaper plants to prevent anyone from going in or out until the edition with the story was ready for distribution and the circulation trucks had left on their routes.

In 1920, commercial radio had not even been hatched yet and television was an idea considered a proper subject only for Jules Verne-type visionary fiction. Even when radio broadcasting appeared with some impact in the late Twenties, the average newspaper owner was not really frightened, although this development actually foreshadowed a decline in the

traditional power of the printed daily. When radio seriously moved into the news field, San Francisco newspapers started to lose circulation. People didn't have to depend on the dailies to find out what was happening outside of their homes and apartments. Street sales were affected and the number of corners where boys sold papers dwindled. "The party was over but most newspapermen didn't know it for the next twenty years," is how one veteran news executive phrased it. "That's when young people lost the ability to read. It was during those years."

Several publishers soon began to revise their opinions concerning the effects of radio. They could see what was coming. The *Examiner* opened station

From 1923 to 1926, there were six competing daily newspapers in San Francisco

San Francisco Chronicle

LEADING NEWSPAPER of the PACIFIC COAST   REG US PAT OFF

THE SAN FRANCISCO CALL

AN INDEPENDENT AND POST NEWSPAPER

The San Francisco News

San Francisco Examiner

AMERICA FIRST

Monarch of   the Dailies   REG. U.S PAT. OFF.

EVENING MEMBER ASSOCIATED PRESS

SAN FRANCISCO BULLETIN

A NEWSPAPER IN PUBLIC SERVICE

Illustrated Daily Herald

The Hall of Justice press gang have their Thanksgiving Dinner upstairs at the City Prison with Lieutenant Jim Boland. (Early Thirties.)

Courtesy of Bob Hall

KUO and later acquired KYA. The *Chronicle* bought into radio station KPO.

But at the height of the newspapers' power, the police-beat reporters at the old Hall of Justice, on Kearny Street across from Portsmouth Square and the lower part of Chinatown, lived out the best traditions of the *Front Page* image. While none of the San Francisco reporters went as far as Willie Hale of the *Oakland Tribune*, who covered crime stories armed with a revolver, the press room on the second floor of the Hall of Justice would have gladdened the heart of Hildy Johnson. Cramped for space, reporters from the San Francisco dailies and the Oakland *Tribune* were jammed into two tiny rooms along with desks, telephones, a message blackboard, nude-women calendars, a water cooler, steel gym lockers, and a brass cuspidor. An adjoining marble-floored "john" had a single toilet and a wash basin. Then there was the firm leather couch, the most popular item of furniture in the press room. The names of people who were and people who would be prominent citizens and town characters who had stretched out with contentment or exhaustion on this couch to rest or recuperate would make an impressive list.

Huge sash windows looked out from the press room into a dirty, open lightwell which went straight up past the top floor where the city prison was. Reporters would open the window and shout up to call photographers back to the press room after they had taken their pictures of newsworthy prisoners. They would also holler up to the policemen stationed at the prison as jailers. It saved the trouble of picking up the phone. "Hey, Pat, you still holding a guy named Martin up there for robbery?" someone would yell up the lightwell. After a short interval for checking, the sergeant's clear voice would come ringing down, "Yeah, he's here. C'mon up!"

Throwing giant cannon firecrackers from Chinatown out into the lightwell landing just outside the press room windows, or placing them under the chairs of dozing "friends" was a common diversion on dull days on the "beat." The night- and early-morning-shift reporters sometimes did this at odd hours. A giant cracker exploding in the lightwell at 3 A.M. would wake up and terrify prisoners in the cells above, leaving them to wonder whether an attack, an escape, or an earthquake was underway.

The police beat took in the criminal courts on the second and third floors of the Hall, and informality was the theme. Early in the morning, reporters would lean their elbows on the benches of the judges in municipal court and tell His Honor which cases to call first from the calendar so that they could get the results in on time for their home-edition 11 A.M. deadlines. Most of the judges cooperated. The early-shift newsmen, who started coming in before dawn, would check the arrest reports downstairs, go directly up to the city prison, and check to see who had been booked in and who had been released on bail. Then they would tell, not ask, the booking sergeant to have a certain prisoner brought out from a cell so that they could question him or her. If they thought the office might want a photograph to run with the story, they would call their city editor and ask that a photographer be sent up to the prison. As a safeguard against an uncooperative or camera-shy prisoner, the camera would be set up so that the unsuspecting prisoner would be photographed stepping out of the cell or coming into the interview room. Then the prisoner, often bleary-eyed from being awakened before dawn, would be told that the picture already taken would not be flattering and that a posed photograph would present a better image, particularly prior to a court appearance before the judge. This play to prisoner's vanity was usually effective with women.

There were dull days at the Hall, also—no crime worth calling in, no good cases in either municipal or superior court. Then the reporters would get bored and start snapping at each other, weary of the periodic pinochle, rummy, or poker games for small—very small—stakes.

Every hour the police reporters took turns "calling the job." This consisted of telephoning all the district police stations, the emergency hospitals, the coroner, and the Coast Guard. The reporters came to know the sad story of every sergeant and station keeper, and were constantly squaring "beefs" for them downtown, setting up alibis for cops wandering off their beats, and generally setting things to rights while building up obligations for future exclusive stories. Reporters on the police beat often managed to "scoop" an exclusive

story by phoning in a tip to the city desk on a telephone away from the press room, having a staff reporter from the main office sent out to cover the story, and then playing dumb about how the office got the tip.

Among the second-floor City Hall beat reporters were some who had their shining moments and made memorable contributions to some "colorful newspapermen I have known" files. A good example was Fritz Goodwin at the infamous Monday afternoon "Helzapoppin" meeting of the Board of Supervisors. The extravaganza was named for the zany Olson and Johnson comedy stage show. The incident took place during the Thirties, when Goodwin was the City Hall reporter for the *Examiner*. Dick Chase was there for the *News*, and described it to me with obvious pleasure.

"Fritz was a funny little guy. He was the ghostwriter later for the Hopalong Cassidy newspaper column by William Boyd, the cowboy movie star.

"He gathered up some old alarm clocks; he had us and some friends bring them in. There were great big drapes there in the supervisors' chambers that hung down from the ceiling over the big window. They're still there, with long cords to open and shut them. He got these old clocks and tied them some way with the cords so that they were way up in the folds of the drapes, and he set all of them for a certain time of the day.

"Then he got the gavel that the chairman of the board used on the podium and an ink pad and he rubbed ink all over the handle of the gavel. The chairman was Jesse Colman, a distinguished guy who was the best supervisor the City had in the twenties and thirties. Colman had a habit, if something was bothering him or he was thinking of something, of rubbing his hand over his face.

"There were several temporary telephone booths out in the corridor for some special visiting press coverage and Goodwin went out and got the phone numbers. Colman had a phone on his podium desk in the Chamber, but it was hardly ever used. Fritz had that number already.

"Everything went off almost perfectly. Goodwin had planned it for weeks.

"The meeting had just started when the clocks went off, one right after the other. They were all going by the time the last one started.

"Colman called over the sergeant at arms, Tiv Creling, a little guy who used to handle fighters, and told him to see what he could do about the noises that were coming from over there.

"Some laughter and chatter had broken out in the chamber and Colman picked up the gavel and pounded for order. Then he did the expected slow burn and rubbed his now ink-stained hand over his face, which became smeared and streaked.

"Just then the telephone on his desk started ringing and the male voice on the phone started to bawl out dignified Jesse and call him every dirty name imaginable. Then the phones started ringing in the booths outside. There was a hell of a lot of noise going on. At that point, on a signal from Goodwin in the press box, one of the guys in the audience, started to get up and make a speech.

"He was an oddball whom everybody around City Hall called John Q. Public because he was there every Monday at the supervisors' meeting and he attended committee meetings regularly. But he never said anything. Just before the meeting that day, Fritz had taken him aside and told him, 'You should say something about these things once in a while. Now today at the meeting of the board, everyone is going to get stirred up and someone who really knows the situation around here could get up and make a little talk and calm them all down.'

"Well, when the situation was at the riot point, sure enough, Fritz signals this guy who gets up to make his speech. And he had a big, loud voice. Jesse was pounding away with the gavel, just about out of his mind, when he finally looked over at the press box and saw that all of us were laughing. Well, we were all friends. Jesse and some of the other supervisors used to play poker with us in the press room. So he finally shook his head, restored order, and the meeting went on."

Hilmar R. Bournmueller, usually known as "Borny" and sometimes as "The Baron," was a legend among San Francisco news photographers. A *Chronicle* photographer for some thirty years, he claimed to be descended from German nobility. Always smoking a smelly pipe or a drooping cigarette in the best traditions of Hollywood typecasting, Borny was the central character of many stories.

Probably the most famous story dealt with a visit to the City by King Albert of Belgium and his Queen. The royal guests were at a reception at the Palace Hotel's Palm Court, and Borny's instructions from the city desk were to get a picture of the Queen. With the King and Queen sedately seated at a table in the midst of more than six hundred San Francisco society women, the irreverent photographer crossed the elegant scene, walked up to the Queen's table, and casually focused his camera lens at her.

Then he suddenly lowered the camera and called sharply over to the table, "Queen, stand up!" While guests in hearing distance gasped, the startled Queen of the Belgians rose meekly. King Albert, equally dumbfounded, stood up with her. Borny topped everything by croaking with a trace of exasperation: "Sit down, King, I don't want you, the Queen is all I'm after." The King sat down with an expression of disbelief and Borny nonchalantly snapped the Queen, ambling away before open-mouthed Secret Service men could react. King Albert reportedly said later, "I got a big laugh out of that."

It was also Borny who was mixing cement in the bathtub of the house he was building in the Parkside district when the city desk urgently called him to cover a major story. He left on the run. It was a long day and night. When he returned, he had a bathtub full of hard concrete which had to be removed eventually—with great difficulty. The office agreed to pay him for a new tub.

The sports writers were a dazzling and eye-catching crowd themselves, featuring a belligerent, short-fused sports editor who challenged other writers to fist fights. He was Tom Laird of the *Daily News*. A big, handsome darkhaired guy, he was a good street fighter and crafty. Laird worked hard and was devoted to three sports—boxing, baseball, and horse racing. He wrote well although he had never finished high school. Six days a week he filled the *News* pages with columns and columns of prose and opinions, including a pungent column of personal views called "Looking 'Em Over." Other writers always added the phrase, out of Laird's hearing, "and walking away in disgust."

Laird not only lacked a sense of humor, but he defended his favorite athletes and teams with enthusiasm and venom, and occasionally with his fists. They included boxers Jack Dempsey and Stanley Ketchell, the St. Mary's College "Galloping Gaels" football team, Santa Clara College football coach "Buck" Shaw, as well as third baseman Willie Kamm, manager Joe McCarthy, and the immortal Joe Di Maggio from the baseball world.

Among the sports writers and columnists from opposition papers that Laird had fist fights with were

FRONT PAGE DAYS

Ringside at a San Francisco boxing match in 1947 are (left to right) Sports Editor Harry B. Smith of the Chronicle, *George Payne, San Jose newspaper publisher and member of the State Athletic Commission, and* Daily News *Sports Editor Tom Laird.*

Courtesy of the San Francisco Examiner

Pat Frayne of the *Call and Post* and Prescott Sullivan of the *Examiner*. Laird is remembered also for wildly chasing after little Roy Cummings of the *Bulletin* at a sports writers' party on the fifteenth floor of the Clift Hotel, jumping over tables in pursuit. But it was the fight with Sullivan that is remembered as a classic yarn.

Sullivan, who was approximately the same heavyweight size as the *Daily News* editor, had written a sarcastic column about a testimonial dinner for Laird that was to be given at the Bal Tabarin nightclub in North Beach. Never an admirer of Laird, Sullivan said that the dinner was overpriced at $7.50 a ticket. He added that he could not see how Laird had become a public benefactor anyway.

"I knew there would be repercussions," Sullivan remembers. "You couldn't write about Laird that way without getting in an argument or fight. I didn't give a damn. I thought I could beat him. I still do."

Sullivan's expectations came true; he knew his opponent.

"I was sitting in Siggie Rosener's Sports Club at 72 Ellis Street one afternoon. I'm just about ready to start my vacation. I was going to leave the next day. About two o'clock in the afternoon, Laird walked in. He said, 'We're going to have this thing out now. You stay here and I'll be back.' "

Sullivan waited—and waited—for three hours.

"Every hour there I had maybe five drinks. After three hours, I had given up on him, and was ready to leave."

Laird finally arrived. "By that time, I was half stoned," Sullivan remembers wryly. "But wait until you hear the rest of the story. He was cute."

Laird said crisply to Rosener, "Siggie, I want you to drive us. Let's go."

Laird and Sullivan climbed into Rosener's car. With Siggie driving, they headed west out toward Golden Gate Park. When they reached the Panhandle strip of park, the mellowed Sullivan suggested, "This is a good spot, what's the matter with this?" Laird snapped, "No, keep going." Entering the main park, they soon reached the Old Stadium area near 36th Avenue. Sullivan, still a little woozy, but semi-alert, again said, "Hey, what's the matter with this?" Again Laird answered, this time impatiently, "No, keep going."

Soon they approached the Beach Chalet and soccer field area at the end of the park and across from the ocean beach. Laird told Rosener to stop the car and the gladiators climbed out, Sullivan a little unsteadily but ready for the big battle. The sun was just starting to sink in the west, as they said in some novels of that day.

"I wasn't aware of what he was doing," Sullivan reminisced. "I was wondering what his motive was in coming all the way out to the beach. I didn't realize until it was too late what his scheme was.

"He had waited for a day they were going to have a clear day with a brilliant sunset. He had timed it and stalled, so that by the time we got there the sun would be at its lowest—right on the horizon. It was a twenty-minute drive at least out there.

"Even when we squared off, he said 'wait a minute' and stalled three or four minutes until the sun was just right. Then he said 'alright,' took a stance with his back to the ocean, and I'm looking right into the goddamn sun. And boom! I couldn't see anything. He hit me right on the kisser. He had a clear shot. He hit pretty hard too. I went down. With the first punch, I was destroyed. I got up and, boom, I went down again. I must have been down three times. I was a mess, cut and bleeding, and dirty.

"Rosener drove us back downtown and I went back to the office, cleaned up a little and wrote a story on it for the paper. I didn't want to be scooped on it. Then I went on vacation."

GOOD LIFE IN HARD TIMES

Then there was Alex McCausland, an *Examiner* sports writer in the late Thirties who had a phobia about crossing big bridges. McCausland absolutely refused to cross either the new Bay or Golden Gate bridges. And ferryboat service was undependable for fast transit back to the office when a story had to be written by deadline time.

Assigned to cover football, baseball, or basketball games in Oakland or Berkeley, McCausland would leave the office and find a place where he could listen to a radio broadcast of the game. Then he would return to the office and write his story. Eventually, the sports editor told him that someone had remarked that he never saw McCausland in the press box across the Bay. "Well, that's true," Alex answered, "I like to sit down in the crowd and absorb the spirit and color of the game." McCausland never did change his coverage system, or his story, until he finally left the *Examiner* for other fields.

The sports pages of those years were also livened up by a group of talented cartoonists. They were following in the wake of the group of caricaturists who had made San Francisco a veritable cartoonists' cradle. Before 1920, there had been "Believe-It-Or-Not" Bob Ripley, who came down from Santa Rosa to join Rube Goldberg on the *Bulletin* staff, first as a sports writer. Also "Tad" Dorgan on the *Call and Post*, Bob Edgren on the *Chronicle*, and Hype Igoe on the *Examiner* had all gone east to New York and national fame. Other artists laboring on the dailies in those days had also emigrated to Manhattan, using the comic page boom to establish themselves. They included "Bud" Fisher who did Mutt and Jeff; Russ Westover who created office secretary Tillie The Toiler, modeled after his wife; Jimmy Swinnerton whose strip, "Jimmy," was a fixture for several decades, and "Tack" Knight who went from the Oakland *Tribune* to the Chicago *Tribune*.

In the 1920s and 1930s, besides Chet Smith and Al Vermeer on the *Daily News*, Jack Lustig and Wiley Smith on the *Examiner*, Howard Brodie on the *Chronicle*, and J. C. Argens on the *Bulletin* and *Daily News*, there was the inimitable Jimmy Hatlo. Hatlo made a reputation for himself with his "Swineskin Gulch" football cartoons featuring the Bay Area college football teams. The drawings appeared on Saturday in the *Call Bulletin* before the games and then on the following Monday. Tension and near-catastrophic adventures were created on Saturdays. Stanford's "Big Red

Machine," the Cal Bear's "Golden Weenie" vehicle, the U.S.C. Trojan in his horse-pulled chariot, and various animals such as Santa Clara's Bronco were always on the verge of an impending crash or collision with each other or the forces of nature. The result of Saturday's game, to match the score, would appear in Hatlo's Monday drawing.

Hatlo was later to become syndicated and nationally known with his "They'll Do It every Time" panel drawing feature, but he had his rough days also, as Marshall Maslin, former *Call Bulletin* editorial writer, recalled. "Jimmy was working as an advertising solicitor at the *Call Bulletin*, handling automobile accounts, and he used to turn in sketches which occasionally were used," Maslin said. "He was a quiet guy and in those early years he was not doing much more for entertainment than renting a room at the Palace Hotel with a bunch of fellows from the advertising department every Friday afternoon to play poker. Jimmy got into the hole finally for $3,000 and for years he was paying it off at $50 a week."

Throughout the Twenties and Thirties, many of the chief boozing and eating spas of the hard-drinking newspaper crowd were located in the areas around Third and Market and Fifth and Mission streets. These were focal points for the plants of the five—later four—major daily newspapers.

Many of these sip-and-chomp emporiums opened up after the 1906 fire, which had wiped out the older favorite saloons. Their "action" and business volume had been cut back drastically through the Twenties and up to 1933 by the prohibition on the sale of alcoholic beverages—even wine—passed after World War I. During this span of dry years, newsstaffers—and everyone else—patronized illegal "speakeasy" bars which operated in backrooms and alleys all over town. The most popular ones were in the North Beach and downtown Tenderloin districts. The exception was Izzy Gomez's.

In his dilapidated loft up at 848 Pacific Avenue, the legendary Izzy dispensed drinks under the shadow of a black fedora hat with a turned-down brim; no one had ever seen him take that hat off. His unique saloon

This was cartoonist Jimmy Hatlo's explanation of how his famous feature "They'll Do It Every Time" originated in 1929. This drawing was not published, but was circulated among the Call Bulletin *staff.*

Courtesy of Marsh Maslin

was at the top of a bare, narrow, creaky, and dirty wooden stairway, and here Izzy held court. By the time you were halfway up the stairs, you could often see him—dark, rotund, and imposing—sitting on his favorite high stool behind the bar. Izzy usually had a cigarette dangling from his mouth and sometimes the ashes fell into the drinks he poured, but no one seemed to mind. You didn't go to Izzy's for food, although he did serve steaks. He'd prepare one if you insisted, or if you were a friend and he thought you needed it to sober up or just couldn't afford to eat otherwise.

During Prohibition, triangular Hotel d'Oloron, looking out on two short blind alleys just off of Columbus Avenue below Broadway, was particularly famous among patrons from the press for the ingenuity of its owner. Each time federal agents raided the hotel and its bootleg bar they would routinely ask the courts to shut down the premises at the hotel address. The owner would then call in a carpenter, have a new front doorway cut out to one of the alleys, and register a new operating address. The hotel and its clandestine bar eventually wound up with a string of front doors and became one of the classic tales of the North Beach regulars.

The Third and Market cluster of press favorites included such spas as Breen's, widely known as a "real newspaperman's hangout," the Kentucky Barrel House on Third Street, and, after the repeal of Prohibition, Jay Hurley's and Jerry and Johnny's, both near the *Examiner*. A block down Jessie Street, across from the *Call* on New Montgomery, was the House of Shields for the more discriminating drinkers. And around the corner on Market was the dark-wooded Hoffman Grill. Next door to the Hoffman, at 617 Market, "Monk" Young had his speakeasy. In 1927 he had a great chef named "Bimbo" Guintoli who became his partner when he moved around the corner to Second Street. After being raided and closed for violating the liquor laws, Young and Guintoli moved in 1931 to larger quarters further down Market at Fremont Street. This was the famous 365 Club which featured in its bar the "Girl in the Fishbowl," a live mermaid seemingly swimming around nude in a revolving hexagonal glass tank with the help of a projection system. Giuntoli bought Young out in 1936.

Izzy Gomez in his black fedora hat with its turned-down brim. (About 1938.)

Courtesy of Seymour Snaer

In Newman's College Inn, at Market and Powell, Charley Newman himself greeted customers as they came in and insisted they have one of his famous enchiladas "on the house." Another news-staff bar on Market Street was the Waldorf, known for its free ham sandwiches made on small hot biscuits.

The Fifth and Mission hub for thirsty newspaper employees and printers, the latter wearing square box hats made from folded newspapers, included the tiny Hanno's on the corner, the unofficial *Chronicle* social club. A block away on Mission and Fourth, was Gallagher's saloon, where many of the *Bulletin*, and later the *Daily News*, employees cashed their pay checks and shared the generous portions of booze that went into Gallagher's drinks.

There always seemed to be a "Shanty" Malone's saloon where newsmen and football players congregated. During Prohibition days, Shanty moved every time he was raided, and his customers followed him. In Shanty's Eddy Street place on a Saturday night after a game, you could run into a good part of a college football team lined up in formation on the floor to demonstrate the winning touchdown-scoring play earlier that day.

The *San Francisco Examiner* dominated the San Francisco population's thinking and was the City's most influential newspaper throughout the Twenties and Thirties. Reporters and photographers from the "Ex" were often given preferential treatment, and the *Examiner's* political endorsement of a candidate often decided an election. The other papers could not make that boast.

The *Daily News* was the low man on the San Francisco newspaper totem pole in the Twenties. Discounting the brief appearances of the *Journal* and young Vanderbilt's tabloid, the *News* ranked behind the other four dailies in circulation and influence. However, the *News* presents an interesting case history on the life and death of a big-city newspaper. A comparative latecomer in San Francisco newspaper history, it was founded in 1903 in a shack at 408 Fourth Street with money loaned by Edward Wyllis Scripps, founder of the Scripps-Howard newspaper chain and United Press International news service. It was still struggling for life when it moved in 1906, after the earthquake and fire, from a temporary location at 646 Natoma Street to a two-story concrete building at 340 Ninth Street, between Folsom and Harrison.

The *News* soon became the favorite paper of the

Harvey Wing of the News *holds some of the supplies for a Hall of Justice press room party in 1944. The happy reveler under the calendar is Sally Stanford, once the City's best known "madam," who found happiness as Mayor of Sausalito.*

Courtesy of Frank O'Mea

City's labor union members; its principal circulation base developed in the Irish-Catholic dominated Mission and South-of-Market districts. The majority of its retail advertisers, such as Lachman's and Rosenthal's stores, were in the busy shopping strip of the Inner Mission.

The *News* building on Ninth Street was designed neither for efficiency nor speed. A staff photographer rushing into the building to make the next edition had to be in good physical condition. After climbing the flight of stairs from Ninth Street, he had to make four trips back and forth from the photo lab in the rear of the building and the city editor's desk in the front before his photo was ready for use. On the way he had to run in figure-eight patterns through the printers in the busy composing room and the aproned workmen in the fume-laden stereotype room.

National and international news came in by Morse code signals to a group of veteran telegraph operators seated just outside the editorial room. Many of the operators bent red Prince Albert pipe tobacco tins around the receiving buzzers so they could hear the code signals better.

In 1918, the *News* increased its circulation in an odd manner. It raised its price from a penny to two cents. This matched a one-cent price increase to three cents by the other two local afternoon dailies, the *Call*

The San Francisco City Hall press gang with Mayor Angelo Rossi in his office. That's Eddie Murphy, the Daily News *photographer, resting on the floor. (Mid-Thirties.)*

Courtesy of Eddie Murphy

and Post and the *Bulletin.* The *Examiner* and *Chronicle* remained steady at a nickel. With the new two-cent price, the *News* was able to push successfully a "two papers for a nickel" gimmick in its street sales. This technique was especially effective at the Ferry Building, where the afternoon dailies registered their largest street sales every weekday. Commuters had plenty of time to read on the ferryboat and train trip home. Those who regularly raced to make a certain boat departure and didn't want to risk delay by waiting for two cents change for their nickels were often inclined to grab the *News* along with one of the three-cent papers.

"Dutch," a well known *News* vendor at the Ferry Building, allegedly sold as many *Calls* and *Bulletins* in this way for his fellow hustlers there as they did on their own.

In 1929 when the *Bulletin* was bought by Hearst and merged with the *Call and Post* over on Jessie Street, the *News* left its patchwork labyrinth on Ninth Street and moved up to the former *Bulletin* space on Mission Street near Fourth. The move signaled the beginning of the policy change that former staff members claim eventually caused the newspaper to fold. "We started to play up to the north side of Market Street," one former staffer explained. "The working stiffs no longer had a paper representing them, and they eventually lost their loyalty to the paper."

However the *News*, which had dropped "Daily" from its name, did have some energetic circulation

GOOD LIFE IN HARD TIMES

Photographers Clem Albers of the Call Bulletin *and Eddie Murphy of the* Daily News, *and reporters George Place and Dick Chase, wait for police to come out from investigating a robbery of a gambling operation on Euclid Avenue near California Street in San Francisco. The latest models in hats and caps were standard wear in 1930.*

Courtesy of Eddie Murphy

spurts before it expired. There was the Atherton graft investigation story in 1935, for example.

The natty *News* police reporter Harvey Wing, who introduced spats to the press room at the Hall of Justice, belonged to the sedate Union League Club, now the Press Club, on Post Street downtown and often played in a late afternoon pinochle game with several of the members. One of them, Sid Herzog, remarked casually one day as he picked up his cards, that the U.S. Collector of Internal Revenue in San Francisco, John Lewis, had made an amusing remark while speaking to a Rotary Club luncheon across the Bay in San Rafael earlier that same day. It seemed that a San Francisco police captain had come into Lewis's office unexpectedly and said he wanted to declare and pay the penalties on $100,000 he had received as his cut of illegal graft payments from houses of prostitution and horse-race bookmaking parlors in the city that year.

Wing hurried back to the *News* office and told Editor Wilbur (Bill) Burkhardt about Herzog's remark. Burkhardt had Wing call Lewis to confirm it. The blunt federal official told Wing heatedly that it was true and added, "What's more, I can prove it!"

The *News* broke the story the next day and kept on top of it. The story helped circulation to zoom up some 20,000, topping 100,000 during the next two years. The City, the police department, and the traditional power structure were rocked by a sensational graft investigation headed by ex-FBI agent Edward Atherton, who had been hired by the Grand Jury. As a result, thirteen police officials and department members were dismissed from the force. The potent House of McDonough bail-bond business, described by Atherton as the "fountainhead of corruption," was gutted of its power and influence. Wire-tapped phone conversations, madams, gamblers, and criminal types were paraded across the front pages. The four dailies had a field day, and street sales went up for all of them.

At that time, the *News* was under the strong guiding hand of Burkhardt, who had been sent to San Francisco from Norfolk, Virginia, by the Scripps-Howard chain in 1923. He beefed up the staff with several newsmen who had worked for him in other cities, including B. W. (Benny) Horne from Detroit as political editor. Horne was a natural for a leading role in *The Front Page.* He always wore a slouch hat pushed down flat on his head, had a thick German accent, and called everybody, including Mayor Angelo Rossi, "Toots." Also answering calls from Burkhardt were Art Caylor, a brilliant political columnist from Portland, Oregon, top newsman Dick Chase from Los Angeles, and editorial writer George West. The hard-driving but analytical editor strengthened the paper's role as champion of the underdog, campaigner for the "little guy" against the vested interests, and the favorite paper of the growing labor unions and their members. Under Burkhardt's management the *News* at one time led all the dailies in paid city circulation.

It was the *News* that battled tenaciously to have the two major bridges built across San Francisco Bay, east to Oakland and north to Sausalito. The Golden Gate and Bay Bridges were opposed bitterly by the Southern Pacific, which had a tremendous investment in and a lucrative traffic linked with its fleet of passenger and automobile ferryboats. The ferries carried travelers directly to the company's railroad terminals where steam and electric train lines fanned out into both long-distance and commuter rail systems.

The *News* was also up front in the successful drive in 1931 to pressure San Francisco into purchasing the Hetch Hetchy water and power system and the accompanying land parcels which stretched out toward the

The Chronicle *city room in about 1938. The fellow at far right in the eyeshade is Johnny Bruce, the city editor. The young reporter on the telephone in the second row of desks is Stan Delaplane, the later travel writer.*

Courtesy of the San Francisco Chronicle

City all the way from the high country above Yosemite Valley. However, the victory gained against the opposition of the Pacific Gas & Electric Company and other utility interests was only a partial one. PG&E succeeded in stopping the acquisition of feeder lines just short of the City, specifically at the town of Newark in the East Bay. Thus the company could still charge for bringing the power directly into homes in the City.

Through an old friendship with George Creel, President Franklin D. Roosevelt's close advisor, Burkhardt also was highly instrumental in obtaining federal approval for funds to construct Treasure Island as the site for the 1939 Golden Gate Exposition and World's Fair.

Former *News* staff members said that the loss of the Weinstein Department Stores advertising revenue contributed significantly to the demise of the *News*.

The Weinstein chain carried bargain merchandise, and their approach to advertising was anything but low key. The Weinstein advertising directors liked to use a lot of black ink in their ads to make them vivid and attention-drawing, if not aesthetically pleasing. One afternoon, a top Scripps-Howard chain official from New York was touring the *News* plant when he noticed a Weinstein advertisement being prepared for the paper. It was the usual layout—a blaring, eye-dazzling bombardment of black ink in thick letters—and a far cry from the normal type of full-page department store ads. Picking up the ad, the man from headquarters held it out at arm's length, frowned with an incredulous expression, and said, "What in the world is this?" Told that it was the *News's* top advertising-revenue producer and one of the most widely read pages in the paper, he said imperiously, "Take it out. Right now!" When the Weinstein merchandising and advertising chiefs were finally and hesitantly told that they would have to change the style of their ads, the result was predictable. The ads were switched to other dailies. The loss in revenue, but more importantly, the loss in readership from thousands of shoppers who had looked to Wein-

GOOD LIFE IN HARD TIMES

Mike de Young in 1924 in his new office at the Chronicle's *Fifth and Mission building. The elaborate furnishings were moved from his former office at the de Young Building, Third and Kearny Streets.*

Courtesy of the San Francisco Chronicle

stein ads for their daily bargains, was probably the first slip downward for the *News*. With Burkhardt's death in 1940, it was only a matter of time before the paper hit the bottom of the slide.

Although Roy Howard of the Scripps-Howard chain always said he would never leave San Francisco, he eventually sold the *News* to Hearst's competing *Call Bulletin* afternoon daily for $500,000 in 1958. San Francisco was then left with only one afternoon daily for the first time since 1850.

The rough, tough work of San Francisco journalism in that colorful era of 1920 to 1940 was dominated by other men besides Burkhardt at the *News*. The *Chronicle*, the City's traditional Republican paper, was guided by publisher M. H. (Mike) de Young until his death in 1925, aided by a strong managing editor, John P. Young. De Young had established the *Chron-*

icle with his brother Charles back in 1865. After his brother was shot and killed as a result of a bitter press campaign carried on by the *Chronicle*, Mike de Young ruled the paper as a benign and respected patron.

De Young was a short, dynamic man who shuffled around the editorial rooms with a unique gait. He always represented the San Francisco social and economic establishment in San Francisco journalism. A staunch Republican, he was active in local politics and particularly interested in the Board of Supervisors. He organized a luncheon "Cabinet Table" at the Palace Hotel to which he would invite people who were prominent and influential in the City's life. He attended the Cabinet luncheon practically every day. The peppery de Young never hesitated in using his influence and the paper. When the Opera House construction was being completed, he asked for two boxes to be permanently at the disposition of the *Chronicle*. Told that only one would be available, he reputedly told the Opera House hierarchy that if he didn't get two, the *Chronicle* would never mention the Opera House in its columns. A quick realignment of the boxes produced an extra one for the *Chronicle*.

De Young had the City's first skyscraper built in 1888, the ten-story *Chronicle* clock-tower building at Market and Kearny. He lived to build the present Chronicle Building, at Fifth and Mission Streets, moving the paper to the new location in 1924. When de Young died, he left the paper to his four daughters as joint owners. His son-in-law, George T. Cameron, became publisher.

In 1923, de Young hired a young Stanford University graduate who had been the *Chronicle's* campus correspondent before joining the American Expeditionary Force which went to Siberia in 1918. Earle T. Behrens had been wounded, returned to San Francisco's Letterman Hospital for recovery, and had then gone to work in 1921 for the experimental *San Francisco Journal* as political editor. De Young asked him to come over to the *Chronicle* on the same job. Young Behrens reported in and stayed for fifty-one years, a record for political editors anywhere. The name "Squire" Behrens became known and respected by every politician in the country, including all the occupants of the White House.

But the editors who probably left the deepest impression on the City's newspaper history and the members of the newspaper staffs of those years were Fremont Older, Edmund D. Coblentz, Edgar T. (Scoop) Gleeson, and William C. (Bill) Wren. All four were Hearst executives, although Older had already cut out a niche for himself as a crusading and fearless editor before Hearst succeeded in luring him over to the *Call and Post* shortly before 1920. Three of them had covered the 1906 San Francisco fire and earthquake. Wren had come along later.

From the day he became managing editor of the evening *Bulletin* way back in 1895, Fremont Older was the crusading stormy petrel of the City's newspaper world and a national figure. In 1935, when he died at seventy-nine from a heart attack, quietly driving his automobile over to the side of the road near Sacramento when he felt the attack coming on, he was still active as the editor of the *Call Bulletin*.

Older had been a fighting reform editor. He followed the lead of earlier muckrakers like his friend Lincoln Steffens, and preceded the Watergate journalistic bloodhounds. In 1918, he became convinced that radical labor organizer Tom Mooney was innocent of the 1916 Preparedness Day parade bombing on Market Street which killed ten persons and seriously wounded more than forty. Mooney and Warren Billings, another

Fremont Older, the crusader editor, with one of his five-cent cigars.

organizer, had been convicted of the bombing and Mooney was sentenced to death. When his bosses at the *Bulletin* would not go along with his campaign to clear Mooney, Older received a message from Hearst: "Come to the *Call.* Bring the Mooney Case with you." He did, at the then astronomical salary of $20,000 a year, and stayed with Hearst until his death. Older eventually succeeded in convincing California Governor Culbert Olson to commute Mooney's sentence to life imprisonment. Mooney and Billings were eventually pardoned, but only after Older died.

In 1920, Older at sixty-four was still a controversial, hell-raising editor. "A great physical hunk of man with a brain to match," is former *Examiner* managing editor René Cazanave's thumbnail description. He was tall—six feet two—and heavy, an imposing figure with his seedy walrus moustache. Friends claim he looked the part of an editor. Older had a habit of constantly rubbing a hand across his forehead as he talked. When called by Hearst, he moved from his small, shabby, and littered office at the old *Bulletin* on Market Street opposite Grant Avenue, to a rehabilitated and refurnished one at the *Call and Post*. The noisy exploding exhausts of the circulation trucks below on Jessie Street as they pulled out to deliver the pink-covered *Call and Post* to the City's neighborhoods were audible evidence of the paper's vibrant life.

However, the move didn't change Older's habits. Soon the new office, like the old, became coated daily with cigar ashes, proof sheets, newspapers, and assorted debris. At the end of the day, he always pushed all unimportant mail that had accumulated on his desk off onto the floor. The new mahogony desk soon acquired a free-style pattern of old burns and discarded and foul-smelling stale butts from the five-cent White Owl cigars that Older smoked every day to a variety of lengths.

Older surrounded himself with a varied assortment of staff members, some of them a bit strange in the world of journalism. There was "Doc" Mundell who served as the editor's "private eye" for about ten years. Mundell wandered around the City picking up tips and rumors on such things as politics, municipal operations, and vice and crime. Older would assign reporters to dig out the facts, or lack of them, on Mundell's tips. Mundell never wrote a line of copy all the years he was with Older.

John Black, on the other hand, proved to be a talented writer. Black was a convicted robber and burglar who had spent most of his adult life in prisons. He came to Older's attention when the editor was visiting the county jail in San Bruno to check on conditions. Noticing that Black seemed to be in a depressed mood behind the bars of his cell, Older stopped to ask him why he was in jail. Unexpectedly, Black merely said, "I'm guilty as hell." Older was impressed by Black's candor, made a check with jail authorities, and arranged for Black to come to work for him at the *Call and Post* on his impending release.

Black was given a job in the library and, at Older's encouragement, wrote a book called *You Can't Win*, an autobiography of his life in crime. Black was frequently invited to stay at Older's country home down the peninsula in Saratoga while he was working on the book. The book was published in 1926 and was highly acclaimed. Older considered the discovery of Black to be one of his outstanding good deeds.

The aggressive Older made enemies, of course.

There was the time that he innocently strolled into the elegant Happy Valley Room in the Palace Hotel and an irate former district attorney Charles M. Fickert, a burly former football player, suddenly veered from the bar and smashed him to the floor with a punch. The crusading editor, then nearly seventy, had to be carried out to a room in the hotel. Older had printed a sensational report in the *Call and Post* exposing the district attorney as being linked with intrigue against accused bomber Tom Mooney.

The arrangements for publication of that particular story demonstrate the verve and flair resulting from the competition for news during those years. The *Call and Post* office was under guard all that morning, and no one was permitted to leave it. The doors to the street-level room where the presses roared were watched carefully for any strange faces. Shortly after noon, the "Final Home Edition" came tumbling out and was trucked out into the streets of the City. Fickert had read the paper and was steaming angrily at the bar, downing whiskeys, when Older appeared to trigger the DA's physical explosion.

However, Older couldn't carry grudges. He was once characterized as being "like a tiger that turns and licks the wound of his victims." Years later, when Fickert was in dire straits, it was Older he went to and who helped him.

Older was constantly in danger of losing his life because of his root-out-the-rascals policy. Once a gunman managed to enter his office on Jessie Street, pointing an ugly-looking .38 revolver at him. Older talked and talked and talked. An hour later, when nervous staffers finally edged in, he and his recent threatener were in chairs, smoking cigars, and exchanging experiences.

Older always dressed in loose-fitting clothes. His tailor was Joe Poheim, who had been a police commissioner. Older would call Poheim and say, "Joe, this is Older. Make me up a suit. No, it doesn't matter what the material is." And Poheim, Gene Block recalled, "would unload some cloth he had been trying to get rid of." Older never tried on the suit until it was delivered.

In 1929, when Older became editor-in-chief of the newly merged *Call Bulletin*, he was beginning to slow down, but only his old friends and staff members were aware of this. He still kept his defiant independence and retained his loyalty to his staff. In the early Thirties, when *Call Bulletin* executives had their full salaries restored after only six months of Depression

Eugene B. (Gene) Block is given the inevitable "farewell party" on his retirement from the Call Bulletin *in 1939 after more than thirty years with the Hearst papers in San Francisco.*

Courtesy of the San Francisco Examiner

pay cuts, Older refused to accept his until his reporters and other lower-echelon staff members were given similar treatment. They never were while he was alive, and Older stood by his position.

Older made a reputation for his ability to pick fiction serials to boost circulation. He launched the first continued serial featured in a daily newspaper. He would buy serials submitted by outside writers after trying them out on the switchboard operators at the paper and the waitresses at the waffle shop next door to the *Call and Post* on Jessie Street. He rated these as

average readers. One of his great discoveries was a red-headed writer named Eleanor Meherin who turned out boy-girl romances exclusively for the *Call and Post*. The most famous one was a serial called "Chickie"; it proved to be one of the greatest circulation boosters in U.S. journalism history.

"I remember one day," Gene Block recalled, "in one of the installments, Eleanor had the boy die very suddenly just before the wedding. We were swamped with telegrams from readers saying that if we didn't give the boy a decent burial, they were going to cancel their subscriptions."

The serials became a *Call and Post* institution. They were even overlapped so that readers would always have an ongoing interest in what happened to the different, but not-too-different, characters in the romantic episodes. Later, radio appeared with its soap

GOOD LIFE IN HARD TIMES

operas to doom this sure-fire circulation booster. Followers only had to listen to relieve the drudgery of everyday chores; they didn't have to take time out to read.

Edmund D. Coblentz was another force whose influence in the City was felt throughout the flamboyant era of the Twenties and Thirties. Like Older, "Cobbie" was a Hearst man. He had come up to Berkeley as a teenager from Santa Maria in Southern California to enter the University of California with a scholarship. He wanted to be a journalist right from the start. While he was over on the Berkeley campus registering, he learned there was a menial job open at the *Examiner* in San Francisco. He immediately went back across the Bay to the City. He applied for the job, got it, and never returned to attend a class at the campus. Like Older, he covered the fire and earthquake in 1906. Unlike Older, Cobbie left San Francisco for a span of years, called east by Hearst to rejuvenate the ailing *New York Journal American*. He returned after Older's death in 1935 to head up the *Call Bulletin*.

Although more the executive type than Older, who tended to get closer personally with his reporters, Coblentz is still considered by those who worked with, or against, him on the newspaper front as one of the great publishers and editors.

"Take a look at the paper under Cobbie," Jimmy McFadden, who was an office boy under the editor, said. "The paper thrived under him." McFadden remembers Coblentz as a kindly man who "took as much interest in an office boy as he would in a star reporter." McFadden recalls, "Everytime I did something for him, he had a tip for me. He used to call me Clancy; he never could remember my name. But he really had style and class."

"The remarkable thing about 'Cobbie' was his contacts around town," Gene Block said. "If it was a slow day, he would say, 'For Christ sake, can't you guys pick up some news? Guess I'll have to go out.'

"One day he'd come back with some story of some new medical research for the University of California's Hooper Institute. Another day he'd come back with a story of some new corporation formed. Another day a new shipping line. He had his angles all over and he was respected all over."

Another staff member called Coblentz "the most colorful editor of all; he was really the last word." Meticulous and immaculate in dress, Cobbie always used cologne and carried a cane. He often sported a white or red carnation in his buttonhole and, in later years, Homburg hats and gray spats. Cobbie even had a stylish green eyeshade, the standard insignia in those days for editors, copyreaders, and linotype operators. Instead of the run-of-the-mill round shade, however, Cobbie had one with square corners.

He was quiet but tremendously whimsical, with a great flair for telling stories. He was also fiercely loyal to his friends. When Herbert Fleishhacker of the pioneer and influential San Francisco family was found guilty in a court case and long-time friends started to avoid him, Cobbie made a point of being seen with him constantly in public.

Edgar T. (Scoop) Gleeson, possibly the most respected city editor of the 1920-1940 era among newspapermen themselves, started out as a "combination reporter." He carried his own Kodak and took his own pictures of the story he was covering. He joined the *Daily News* in 1904, when he was only twenty. His salary then was one dollar a week. Two years later he made a name for himself with an exclusive eye-witness account of the havoc, death, and devastation of the earthquake and fire. Gleeson's break came because the *Daily News* was the only San Francisco newspaper that managed to publish on April 18, the day of the quake. The edition was printed at a nearby job-printing shop which was relatively undamaged. Part of that day, young Gleeson, dressed in the Easter suit and Panama hat he had slipped on after being jolted out of bed in the morning, rowed back and forth along the waterfront in a boat on the Bay.

Young Gleeson's zeal resulted in Older, then managing editor of the *Bulletin*, hiring him in 1906 and making him financial editor. When Older moved from the *Bulletin* to the *Call and Post* in 1918 he took Gleeson with him. For the next two decades, Gleeson filled a wide spectrum of key jobs on the paper brilliantly. As sports editor he was an intimate friend of such heroes of the so-called Golden Era of sports as heavyweight champion Jack Dempsey and lightweight kingpin Benny Leonard, Helen Wills and Helen Jacobs, the bitter rivals for queen of the tennis world, and baseball immortal Ty Cobb, the "Georgia Peach." Later, he was city editor and managing editor with the *Call and Post* and the *Call Bulletin*.

Gleeson is remembered as a hard taskmaster right up until each final edition of the paper was "put to bed." He was always after the "Big Story." Reporters

William C. (Bill) Wren, Examiner *city editor, when he allegedly "ran the town" in the Thirties.*

Courtesy of the San Francisco Examiner

were repeatedly told "I want that story. Don't come back without it." Gleeson's knowledge of the City and of the people who lived in it is remembered with awe and fascination by those who worked under him when he was city editor.

"You'd call in from a fire or a crime scene, explaining things, and he'd give you the name of somebody who lived two houses away and could tell you what you wanted to know," one of his former reporters said.

Tall, slender, and with an aquiline nose, Gleeson was a snappy dresser and a renowned story teller once he had slipped on his hat and left the city room.

William C. (Bill) Wren, sometimes known as "The Iron Duke," was the controversial city editor of the *Examiner* when it reputedly "ran the town." The mayor's office, the district attorney's office, and the police department, from the commissioner and chief on down, listened when Wren sent messages or telephoned. He was heard calling one mayor at home early one morning and yelling, "If you don't tell me about it, you sonuvabitch, I'll blast you all over town."

Allegedly, an *Examiner* reporter only had to say to certain high city officials "Bill Wren wants," and desire would become command. One remark attributed to the short, cigar-chomping Wren was, "Every city editor has two or three supervisors on hand whom he owns." Symbolic of Wren's power was the frequency with which the Police Commission cars often filled the parking spaces in front of the *Examiner* at Third and Market Streets.

Born in Boston and orphaned in infancy, Wren followed a veritable Horatio Alger novel course from poverty to fame and fortune. He ran away to New York when he was only thirteen, sold newspapers on the street and lived in a newsboys' lodging house. He wandered around the country and finally rode a freight train to the west coast and Seattle where he worked as a copyboy and cub reporter. He first arrived in San Francisco in 1908 when he was seventeen, "penniless, in torn pants, with an over-sized turtleneck sweater hiding the fact that he owned no shirt," according to a later *Examiner* story.

He went to work for the *Examiner*, and spent thirty-seven of the next forty-six years with the paper. During his last twenty years there he was the paper's domineering, hard-driving managing editor. He kept a framed sign behind his desk which read, "Tell me nothing in confidence."

Early in his *Examiner* days, Wren decided he needed more education and enrolled at the University of California in Berkeley. He ground through two years of frenzied commuting on ferryboats and trains, attending classes in the daytime and working on the copy desk at night before his health broke. He went east for a few years, enlisted in the Army and fought with a machine gun company in France during World War I, before returning to the *Examiner* in 1919.

Wren's overwhelming passion was betting on horse races. His attachment to sports in general was reflected in the space and attention given to sports in the *Examiner*, including horse racing. Wren spent consid-

GOOD LIFE IN HARD TIMES

Scott Newhall, Chronicle *photographer (far right), being assaulted by a construction foreman while attempting to take photographs on a cave-in at Fleishhacker Zoo in San Francisco in 1936. Newhall later became executive editor of the* Chronicle.

Courtesy of Eddie Murphy

erable time at the Tanforan and Bay Meadows tracks down the peninsula in San Mateo County, with an *Examiner* cameraman driving him down to the tracks and back. The cameraman would take a few pictures of the races as justification for the chauffeuring assignment, but, with rare exceptions such as a major handicap race, the photos were never used.

One cameraman recalled trips down to the track with Wren: "He sat in the front seat alongside me all the way down and back and never said a word. Except once when I had to stop suddenly and my brakes grabbed. It threw him against the windshield and squashed his cigar all over his face. All he did was to turn to me and say, 'You ought to get those brakes fixed.' It was the only time he said anything to me."

Examiner staff members said that the occasional articles that appeared in the *Examiner* sports pages under the byline of "Fair Play," charging that certain races had been "fixed," were written by Wren after he had a bad day at the betting windows.

In the City, Wren patronized a variety of bookmakers and allegedly had arrangements with them to be paid off at the track odds, instead of the lesser odds

normally given to off-track bettors. One was Paul "Bouquet" Cohn, who operated a chain of cigar stores and owned the Bonanza Club bar on Montgomery Street in the financial district. Once Cohn reportedly made the mistake of refusing to pay Wren off at track odds on a bet. Subsequently, Cohn's headquarters office above the bar was raided by police and a state undercover agent. Cohn was convicted on a felony bookmaking charge that was vigorously pursued by the district attorney's office. Cohn received a surprisingly stiff sentence of a year in San Quentin from the San Francisco judge.

Wren was described by one former reporter who was with the *Examiner* for more than thirty years as "a successful city editor, but a sonuvabitch. He had bad habits, he was always by himself, he was secretive, but he was a damn good man when he was sitting there at the city desk. He could make up his mind in a minute what he wanted to do. There was no hesitation. I believe he's the one who first thought of covering an election by sending men out to the precincts to get a glimmer of how the race would go. He called a meeting, told us all how we were going to do it, and everybody who could be spared was sent out.

"He was a strict disciplinarian who would cut you off at the shoelaces if you did anything wrong. Brusque with reporters, he was respected for his ability as a city editor. You had to produce and he kept everyone on his toes. On the *Examiner*, you always had to be alert for that exclusive story."

On the other papers, alertness was not the guiding principle. The city editors needed other qualities, including an ability to catch up quickly with *Examiner* exclusives. "I'd pick up the *Examiner* every day and just shudder," said Dick Chase, who served time on the city desk at the *News*.

Gene Block recalls vividly one strategy duel he had with Wren in the early 1920s. Block was sitting on the *Call and Post* desk then and, across Jessie Street, Wren was the *Examiner* city editor.

"There was an elephant out at Fleishhacker Zoo that was condemned to be shot because he had killed a zoo keeper," Block said. "It was a good story. There was a hell of a lot of conferring between ballistics experts and animal anatomy specialists to determine the type of ammunition that would kill the elephant the quickest. They were afraid that if they just wounded him, he might stampede and injure someone.

"The *Examiner* was close to Herbert Fleishhacker, the president of the Park and Recreation Commission, who had the say on the execution time. He set the hour at three in the afternoon, which was too late for us to use it. We argued and we pleaded but Fleishhacker was in the *Examiner's* pocket.

"Then I had an idea. It was screwy, but I thought it might work. It was then about twelve o'clock and the execution time was only three hours away. I called up Al Mooser, an attorney who used to hang around the police court. We had publicized him in the past as a champion of saving dogs from being done away with.

" 'Al,' I said, 'how much would you like to get your name on the front page of every paper in America?' He said, "How?'

"I said, 'You're famous now for saving dogs. How would you like to save an elephant?' He said, 'How?'

"So I said, 'They are going to execute that elephant at three o'clock today. That elephant belongs to the public. As a taxpayer I have a stake in that elephant. I want an injunction to stop it.'

"Mooser caught on right away. He said, 'I'll draw up the petition for the judge and you get a judge to sign it.' I called up one judge and he said, 'Don't ask me to do it, I have to go up for re-election in a couple of months and I can't risk antagonizing the *Examiner*. Ask some guy who has just been re-elected.' I finally got another judge to sign the petition for the injunction to enjoin the authorities from carrying out the execution.

"At half-past two, the execution site out at the zoo was crowded with press and the movie newsreel cameras. The *Examiner* reporter and photographer are up front and ready. Then up comes the process server and serves the injunction, knocking the whole thing out. Everybody went home.

"Well, the next day, the injunction was dissolved in court, of course, but we appealed to the appelate court. That used up another week before that appeal was denied and by that time a couple of big local stories had developed and nobody gave a damn about the elephant anymore. Incidentally, when it was finally shot, it was at 11 o'clock in the morning—on our time!"

A former *Examiner* reporter said, "Wren was not only a pugnacious-looking guy, but he wanted to investigate everything, sometimes to use the information for his own benefit. He used to call reporters into his office from the beats and ask them, 'What's doing?' He wanted to know if you were going to be of any trouble to his friends. He really knew what was going on everywhere. He'd try to trap you. I'd never tell him anything. He was a Nixon in a way. He'd tell you to leave so-and-so alone."

Another reporter, from a rival paper, described Wren as a "kindly man." The *Examiner* editor "was not an egomaniac," this newsman said. "Wren knew the news and how to develop a story. He knew how to get it and how to play it. He made the *Examiner* the power that it was under him. He exercised his power on behalf of the *Examiner*, the paper, not for himself or for Hearst. The *Examiner* was really the 'Monarch of the Dailies' under him. He was personally a simple man with simple tastes."

When Bill Wren died in March, 1956, in his twentieth year as the paper's managing editor, his obituary story in the *Examiner* was one to gladden the heart of anyone who had ever truly loved the underpaid, but fascinating, newspaper business. "Even in the hospital with the end near," the story read, "Mr. Wren was concerned with *The Examiner* and the plans he had carefully laid for the news coverage of the Democratic and Republican conventions. Virtually his last thought before lapsing into the coma from which he never emerged was of that job ahead, his physician said."

Bill Wren, the editor who would have fit right into *The Front Page* scenario, died, you might say, with his copy pencil in hand and his green eyeshade—instead of boots—on.

2

Big Brother and
The Blue Monday Jamboree

The first radio in our family was a crystal set that my Uncle Ivan gave me for my birthday. It consisted of a one-foot-long piece of stained board on which was mounted a crude black cardboard condenser with a numbered wood tuning dial, and a tiny piece of quartz crystal under an inverted transparent glass shield. A movable "cat's whisker" wire was inside the glass touching the crystal. The only other part to our radio was an earphone headset with cord-covered wires running to metal clips on the board.

You whirled the dial which turned the condenser and music came into your ears. Sometimes, if you tuned in late at night and moved the wire about for a while, you could get KFI way down in Los Angeles, some five hundred miles away. There was a lot of static on all the stations and you tried to move the "whisker" to a spot on the crystal where the reception was clearest. It was my set, but my mother or dad would occasionally slip on the earphones and listen to the new wonder.

Later, my father bought our first speaker set—an Atwater Kent. The receiver was in a gray metal case with rounded top corners. It dropped into the open top of a simple metal stand, and became quite warm to the touch after it was on for a while. It had a lighted dial window, a knob for tuning in the stations, and another one for the volume adjustment. The speaker was a separate square box which sat on top of the receiver. I became particularly fond of this set because it was placed in my room against the wall and within reach of my unfolded wall bed. When the bed was up, the radio was in the "dining room." I used to slide the big dining room table back into position every morning.

When you wanted entertainment at home in the Twenties and Thirties, you listened to the radio. If you wanted to see a movie, you had to go to a theater. Certain radio programs had the same kind of following

that some TV programs have today. Families gathered around their sets in the living room to listen instead of watch.

However, before radio reached its highest level of popularity, it had traveled a long, rough road. Not until the Thirties did radio entertainment really hit its stride in the Bay Area. Radio had started out as a novelty, a gimmick, a promotional oddity to be used for a while until the inevitable day arrived when its uniqueness wore off. Much of the early radio activity took place in the Bay Area.

A few San Franciscans are still around who can recall a lecture sponsored by merchant Prentis Cobb Hale, Sr., at Native Sons Hall in the City shortly after the 1906 earthquake and fire.

The speaker was a brilliant twenty-year-old named Francis McCarthy, who talked about something new called "radio." Using a telephone instrument on the stage, young McCarthy talked to a receiving earphone in the back of the hall. Spectators queued up to take turns listening to McCarthy say over and over again, "Hello, hello, this is the wire that's talking."

In 1909, Dr. Charles David Herrold, a scientist and inventor who ran an engineering vocational school in San Jose, fifty miles south of San Francisco, started to send out experimental voice broadcasts on a little fifteen-watt arc transmitter. Herrold's device has been called the world's first broadcasting station, although it had no call letters. Instead Herrold opened his broadcast with the message, "This is San Jose calling" followed by the name of the school, the Herrold College of Engineering. To get out his signal, Herrold strung eleven thousand feet of wire between two seven-story office buildings and used water-cooled microphones.

Herrold's "hobby" had a practical angle. It served as a publicity gimmick advertising his school. It was

BIG BROTHER AND THE BLUE MONDAY JAMBOREE

The NBC Firestone Group of orchestra and singers under the direction of conductor Max Dolin was a headliner on KPO.

Courtesy of Station KNBR

meant to attract a select audience of teenage amateurs interested in the new field of wireless communication, and who presumably were devising receivers. They were the likeliest prospects for enrolling in his school.

The early broadcasts were simple, but they set precedents which are still in use today. With his assistant Ray Newby, Herrold read newspaper articles over the air, and added his own comments in a style resembling that of our modern news commentators. He also put on an informal talk show, though he had no feedback by phone or relayed voices from the listeners. Mrs. Herrold is credited with being the first woman

disc jockey. She also launched the first giveaway show in broadcasting. She sent out to lucky listeners free phonograph records donated by a San Jose music store.

Using an antenna at Mare Island on the Bay in 1913, Herrold broadcast a signal more than 950 miles to the army transport *Sherman* at sea, establishing a world's record for long-distance radio transmission. Two years later, the station elaborated on young Francis McCarthy's earlier demonstration at Native Sons Hall in San Francisco by broadcasting music directly to the Panama-Pacific Exposition in San Francisco. Just as at McCarthy's demonstration, visitors lined up to listen over earphones.

That same year, 1915, Herrold hired two high school boys to sing and play the ukelele on live entertainment broadcasts from his station. They were Al and Cal Pearce, eventually to become well-known radio personalities on KFRC's Blue Monday Jamboree

Al Pearce (standing at left) and the Happy-Go-Lucky Hour crew that went on from KFRC to NBC and national network exposure. Edna Fischer is at the piano. Monroe Upton wears the tophat and monacle as Lord Bilgewater, Harry (Haywire Mac) McClintock holds his guitar, and the young fellow with the classy white-top oxfords down front is Tommy Harris, now the proprietor of Tommy's Joynt in San Francisco. (About 1931.)

Courtesy of Tommy Harris

and Happy-Go-Lucky Hour. Later, "Al Pearce and His Gang" was to be heard on the NBC network.

The Federal Radio Act of 1922 required any "voice transmitter" to have a license and call letters. Herrold applied and was granted a license and the call letters KQW to start regular broadcasts.

By 1922, new inventions and developments in radio transmission had made a popular, rather than specialized, audience feasible. These included an amplifying system devised by Dr. Lee de Forrest in his Palo Alto laboratory which made the use of loudspeakers practical. These improvements increased the number of listeners, and there was a flood of applications and approvals in the next few years for new stations. In 1922, KPO and the San Francisco *Examiner's* KUO, claiming to be the first newspaper broadcasting station in California, went on the air in San Francisco, and KLX started broadcasting in Oakland. KGO, claiming to have the "world's largest radio transmitter," started broadcasts in Oakland in 1924.

Some people involved in the new field of radio realized that it was not just a temporary promotional tool or hobby that would soon lose its appeal. One of these was Joe Martineau, a former Navy man. In 1921, he had approached Vice President Reuben Brooks Hale of the Hale Brothers department store in San Francisco, and proposed that together they build a fifty-watt radio transmitter on the roof of the store at Fifth and Market Streets. Martineau had managed to gather enough equipment and parts together for the project.

Martineau had chosen the right target. Hale's brother Prentis was the man who had sponsored young Francis McCarthy's "show" fifteen years before. Justifying their investment as a public service even if radio turned out to be a temporary fad, the Hales agreed to finance Martineau's radio station. It was built for $2,400, and the newly franchised KPO made its first broadcast from studios on the sixth floor of the store in 1922.

A long glass window permitted the public to watch the cast and crew broadcast the KPO programs. All equipment and personnel, and even the program monitor were in a single room. Outside the viewing window, several rows of chairs were placed for visitors. A speaker carried the program sound out to them. Although the Hales had been sincerely interested in the development of radio for some years, the commercial value of attracting a live audience was not lost on them. The remainder of the sixth floor of the store was used for the display and sale of the increasing number of radio sets being turned out by manufacturers.

At first, KPO only broadcast for one hour a day, in the morning between eleven and noon. The station shared its 360 meter wave length broadcasting channel with eleven other stations that had mushroomed up in the Bay Area. Some of these stations were little more than amateur, back-room operations. KPO was the only station using all live talent—announcers, actors, singers, and musicians. The other stations used phonograph records exclusively. The Hales paid large fees for quality entertainment at a time when sponsors were scarce. They imported Reinald Werrenrath from New York in 1923 to sing on a special Southern Pacific Railroad broadcast, paying him $2,500 for the single performance. John Charles Thomas had been contacted first, KPO musical director Cy Trobbe recalled, "but Thomas said that the fee they offered him was what he usually paid his agent."

Hale Brothers was not alone in linking showy demonstrations with sales. In 1924, the City's major retail music outlet since 1870, Sherman Clay & Company at Sutter and Kearny Streets, installed a studio in its ten-story building for another newly licensed radio station, KFRC. The music firm, whose branch stores were rapidly appearing throughout the

Singer Reinald Werrenrath was imported from New York in 1923 for a single appearance on KPO.

Courtesy of Station KNBR

Bay Area, became the retail jobber for several brands of radios. Soon the radio department was occupying more and more space, infringing on the store's phonograph, piano, sheet music, recordings, and musical instrument sections as the sale of sets increased.

Nineteen twenty-five was an eventful year in the history of commercial radio. Dr. Herrold down in San Jose boosted KQW's power to 500 watts and sold the station to the First Baptist Church, which began to broadcast religious programs. The station's call letters were now held to be an acronym for "King's Quickening Word." Also in 1925, KPO participated in its first national hook-up. It was one of fifty stations broadcasting the inauguration of President Coolidge. And the

San Francisco Chronicle finally caught up with the *Examiner*, and its station KUO in the Hearst Building at Third and Market Streets by becoming a partner in KPO with Hale Brothers. A new 1000-watt transmitter was erected on the Fifth and Market store roof, a block from the *Chronicle*.

The stations now had their own frequency channels. KPO began to broadcast for more hours, presenting a greater variety of programs. The station now took part in several national hookup weekly programs. One featured the original "Happiness Boys," Billy Jones and Ernie Hare, a singing duo with a piano accompaniment played by Jones. Their introduction to each program went, "How do you do, everybody, how do you do." I remember them best when they were sponsored by a men's socks company with the catchy hello and goodbye jingle, "We're the Interwoven pair, Jones and Hare."

"Scotty" Morton, a *Chronicle* columnist, read the Sunday comics to children listeners, and "Big Brother" told them stories in a popular six-day-a-week program timed for just before families usually sat down for dinner. And KPO took part in another innovative happening, the first linking of radio with the movies. The station broadcast the voices of Norma Shearer and Lew Cody, romantic silent-screen idols of the day, to a receiver on the stage of the Loews Warfield Theater as the beginning of a movie they starred in, *Slave of Fashion*, was flashed on the screen.

Later in 1925, KPO marked up two more "firsts" in Bay Area radio history, both on August 4. It transmitted the first picture to be sent from a radio station, using an invention of a man named Francis Jenkins. A picture of Andy Gump, one of the *Chronicle*'s comic strip characters, was sent and received on two of Jenkins's machines. George T. Cameron, the *Chronicle* publisher, signed the picture with a message saying: "Radio's latest wonder—pictures through the air— what new marvels will this science bring forth?" The answer, of course, to name but two of the marvels, was commercial television and broadcasts from the surface of the moon.

On the same day, KPO broadcast a play-by-play description of the opening game of baseball's World Series between the Washington Senators and the Pittsburgh Pirates. KPO was one of twenty stations across the country to participate; all were affiliated with newspapers that were members of the Associated Press news wire service. And on November 21 of that year,

KPO carried the California-Stanford Big Game football classic from Memorial Stadium in Berkeley. The *Chronicle* described the broadcast as "the most elaborate example of remote control broadcasting ever attempted in the West."

Things moved along rapidly after that. Fred J. Hart, who had operated KQW in San Jose for a year, turned it into a true commercial station when he sold Sperry Flour Company a five-day-a-week, fifteen-minute cooking program. It eventually, in 1949, became the CBS network station in San Francisco, KCBS. In San Francisco, KPO began to broadcast grand opera from the Civic Auditorium stage. KTAB, sponsored by and named for the Tenth Avenue Baptist Church in Oakland, began broadcasting in 1925. Ten years later it became KSFO in San Francisco.

In 1927, the National Broadcasting Company formed a thirty-five-station national broadcast service. NBC embraced an already established Pacific Coast network which included San Francisco's KPO and KGO in Oakland. The new national network was inaugurated on Washington's Birthday with an address by President Coolidge from the nation's capital. One of the first nationwide commercial shows broadcast by the network was the Dodge Victory Hour. Appearing on the opening program were Will Rogers, Al Jolson, Paul Whiteman and his band, and Fred and Dorothy Stone. The fact that the voices on the air originated thousands of miles away was still a novelty to the listening public. From coast to coast they echoed the sentiment, "Will wonders never cease?"

National radio brought fabulous entertainers, until then only heard on phonograph records, or perhaps in the brand-new talking pictures, "live" into people's homes. These included Russ Columbo, Rudy Vallee, the Boswell Sisters, and Xavier Cugat and his orchestra. Many entertainers from local programs now went on to national fame. Among those who began their careers in Bay Area stations were Meredith Willson, Don McNeill, Vera Vague, Art Linkletter, Alvino Rey, and Harold Peary.

In 1928, for the first time, a national political convention was broadcast live to the entire country when the Republican meeting in Kansas City was carried on NBC. The 1924 conventions of both the Democrats and Republicans had been heard in sections of the East, but this was the first time that the hoopla of a national convention had been heard by the entire nation as it occurred. Later that year, Herbert Hoover

BIG BROTHER AND THE BLUE MONDAY JAMBOREE

In 1932, Herbert Hoover came home to Palo Alto to deliver his final presidential campaign speech by radio from the basement of his home. This is the crowd that waited to greet him at the station.

Courtesy of the San Francisco Public Library

delivered his final campaign speech in his successful run for the Presidency against Al Smith, the brown-derby Democrat from the sidewalks of New York. Hoover spoke to the nation from the basement of his Palo Alto home. The latest type of portable speech-input equipment had been installed and microphones were set up in his library. Later, when the election results were announced, additional microphones placed in front of the house picked up the blaring band music and enthusiastic demonstration by Stanford students and Hoover's Palo Alto friends and neighbors.

Radio's golden days lasted all through the Thirties and into the early Forties. In the Bay Area, as well as throughout the country, political campaigns and politicians depended on radio to carry their messages. When Franklin D. Roosevelt wanted to speak to his "fellow Americans" about such things as the Great Depression or the "New Deal," he used radio. And no one used it to greater effect than FDR.

Boxing fans listened to heavyweight championship fights "direct from ringside." Play-by-play accounts of baseball's World Series could be heard all over the Bay Area from speakers set up outside stores. The *Examiner* sponsored a broadcast outside of its building at Third and Market Streets, setting up a giant scoreboard so that the crowd in front could follow the action visually to some degree.

Lots of the popular humor of the day came from radio programs and the comics. Singers and bands depended on radio for fame. Stage appearances and even movie contracts resulted from radio stardom. The country's largest corporations sponsored hour-long programs on the national networks and paid what were considered excessive salaries then to lure the great names of Broadway and Hollywood for appearances on the air.

As radio became more popular, it was just a question of time before car radios were developed. This eventuality stirred up some concern from auto safety authorities. By 1930, Massachusetts and New Hampshire had passed laws prohibiting "motor radio" sets operating within their states. New Jersey was considering a similar ban, San Francisco's *Broadcasting Weekly* reported, because the sets were considered to be "antagonistic to the principles of road safety." The magazine explained it was believed that "anything that takes the driver's mind off the road is a menace."

The radio boom also created radio columns in the newspapers. The *Chronicle* needed a new one in 1936 and brought down a twenty-year-old kid from Sacramento who had been writing for the *Sacramento Union*. A short time later he suggested a daily column on San Francisco life and personalities to skeptical *Chronicle* editor Paul Smith. He finally convinced Smith to let him try, and he never went back to Sacramento. Instead he stayed to top even the most devoted native son in boosting San Francisco and become the City's highest paid daily writer. His name was Herb Caen.

Even at the height of its popularity, when the program topped the Neilsen ratings, Archie Bunker and "All in the Family" never dominated the air waves the way Amos 'n Andy did in the very late Twenties and early Thirties. The activities of the Fresh Air Taxi Company in Harlem fascinated millions of listeners across the country. Families gathered punctually at seven o'clock every night except Sunday to follow the latest adventures and mishaps of the pair and their friends and enemies. George Stevens, the Kingfish of the Mystic Knights of the Sea lodge, and Madam Queen, Brother Crawford, Henry Van Porter, Sapphire Stevens, Shorty the barber, and Lightnin' became as well known as any movie star. "I'se regusted," "Buzz me, Miss Blue," "Ow wah! Ow wah!" and "Check and double-check" were popular expressions around the country. Some movie theaters and stores piped in the fifteen-minute program so customers would not stay away during the broadcast.

Freeman Gosden played the industrious and serious-minded Amos, and Charles Cornell played Andy, the blustery, would-be entrepreneur who always had romance problems. On May Day in 1929, the two stars came to San Francisco during a cross-country personal-appearance tour. They were officially welcomed by Mayor Rolph, who wore a white suit, and had a primrose in his lapel. The comedy team did a vaudeville act in blackface at the Pantages Theater at Market and Hyde Streets. It was based on an incident in the Fresh Air Taxi Company office.

In the early days of radio, one of San Francisco's hit attractions was a sweet-voiced tenor named Maurice Gunsky. A printer, he had successfully auditioned for Jean Crow, KPO program director; she was impressed with his clear diction and put him on the air. Gunsky became a fixture on KPO programs and made recordings for Columbia Records. Soon he was the toast of San Francisco, singing love songs and kindling romantic dreams and visions among female listeners and fans. His delivery of "Lay My Head Beneath a Rose" was said to have dampened many a handkerchief with tears.

Gunsky was urged to go on the stage. He finally agreed to make some personal appearances at various theaters around the Bay Area. The publicity was sent out. Now all the women who had paused in the midst of their chores to sit entranced and be carried away to paradise by Maurice's romantic whisperings would be able to see him in person.

He appeared in Oakland at the Grand Lake Theater, in Morgan Hill at the Granada Theater, in Gilroy at the Strand Theater and, of course, in San Francisco. "Paul Ash signed him to appear at the Granada Theater for a week with the stage show," musician Cy Trobbe, then at KPO, recalled. "The story was that he was being paid $1,000 for the one week."

The opening performances in each city and town were mobbed by eager women and their husbands or sweethearts. All the openings were disasters. Gunsky, the singing idol of the air lanes, turned out to be short, dumpy, baldheaded, and no beauty. Someone pointed out that Gunsky's past publicity photographs always showed him with his hat on. "I pleaded with him to put on a top hat and stand back leaning against the piano," said Dan McLean, then manager at the Grand Lake Theater in Oakland, "but he wouldn't listen. He just stood out there baldheaded, fat, in a blue-serge suit." Gunsky's popularity plummeted after word got around, and he became just another tenor.

Mystery serials were extremely popular radio fare. The violence on such programs was generally

BIG BROTHER AND THE BLUE MONDAY JAMBOREE

Maurice Gunsky was the sensation of San Francisco radio as a romantic-sounding tenor on Station KPO.

confined to shouting or crying voices expressing terror, surprise, or protest, and the sounds of falling bodies, crashing vehicles, crinkling metal, and splintering glass. When we listed to detectives Sam Spade or Pat Novak prowling around San Francisco's waterfront, we used to turn the lights out in the room so that we could feel closer to them in their risky meanderings. Later, the "Inner Sanctum" program was especially suited to the darkened-room setting because it was always introduced by the eerie creaking of a rusty-hinged door being opened slowly, slowly.

In 1919 Cyrus Trobbe was a young violinist, newly arrived in San Francisco from Brooklyn. In 1924 he was leading an eight-piece salon orchestra at the Palace Hotel's Palm Court when Radio Station KPO was forming its first staff musical group. Jean Crow doubled as the station's program director and piano player for the group. She signed up a cello player

named George von Hagel, but needed a violinist. She offered Trobbe the job. He accepted, and was to become a fixture on the City's radio scene for almost twenty years.

Soon Trobbe was also doing a remote control broadcast from the hotel's Palm Court from 3:30 to 5:30, customary teatime hours, every afternoon except Sunday. The program, called "Tea at the Palace," was a listener-request hour. A telephone was placed on a stand near Trobbe so he could take the calls directly. Some unusual calls did get through, but with the informality and elasticity prevalent in broadcasting in those days they were easy to deal with.

One call came from a breathless nightclub owner who said he had a problem which Trobbe, as an old friend, might be able to solve. He pleaded that it was an emergency. He was in a telephone booth at a motel to which he had finally succeeded in luring a lovely young lady. She was in a room at the motel but he was not having any success in carrying out his lustful objective. "He explained that she was cold to him and nothing seemed to be working," Trobbe recalled. "There was a radio in the room, though, and he asked me if I could play something that would warm her up if he tuned in to our program, 'Tea at the Palace.'

"I told him to go back to the room. In a few minutes I had the fellows play 'Clair de Lune,' the romantic and soothing Debussy melody. An hour later, he called me again. 'Thank you very much, Cy,' he said happily, 'it worked wonders.'

"The thought did occur to me then, but just for a passing moment," Trobbe recalled with a grin, "that this might be a lucrative little side field for extra income, sort of an early-day Muzak for lovers, but it was just a stray thought."

On another afternoon at the Palm Court while the program was on the air, Trobbe received another unorthodox request. Joe Walker, a musician friend, telephoned and explained that he was at home practicing, but was having trouble tuning up his bass viol. Would Trobbe have his men play a few "A" notes over the air so that he could tune his instrument?

"I just can't stand at the mike and have 'A' notes played over and over again," Trobbe explained patiently to Walker. "But I'll play a tune entirely in the key of 'A.' " He did!

Announcers had to improvise in the early days of broadcasting, as former staff members will relate with warm pleasure. It was all rather informal then. A vocalist would call over to an announcer suddenly just before starting a song: "Just go on the air a minute, will you, while I find my accompanist? She was just here a few minutes ago." The announcer would scurry to the microphone and, without rehearsal, put out a commercial sales pitch for a lube job at a service station, a new cleanser powder, or a permanent wave special. One announcer always kept a copy of a newspaper in his pocket. When anything went wrong with the program, he would whip out the paper and cut in with a "news flash," reading some item out of the columns.

Probably no local radio program ever gained the popularity and following that the "Blue Monday Jamboree," on San Francisco station KFRC, attained during its lifespan in the 1920s and 1930s. The names of the Jamboree "gang" still stir up melancholy memories and reminiscent smiles among long-time Bay Area residents. Local listeners tuned in on Monday nights from eight to ten as religiously as they did for many years to hear Amos 'n Andy.

Edna Fischer, who joined the Jamboree in 1926 as the program pianist, expressed the typical views of most program entertainers and performers of those early days. "I'm not saying that now isn't better than then, but there isn't really the naturalness and the freedom to be yourself like there was. I have the memories of being able to play what I wanted to play. You really had to be very good. You had to know what you were doing because you didn't get that second chance. Everything was live talent, no matter what it was. There were no recordings made and no tapes. If it was a great performance, it was gone. If it was bad, then everybody heard it.

"In those days on the Jamboree, Harrison Holliway, bless him, would say to me at five minutes to eight, 'What do you want to play tonight, Edna?' And I'd say, 'I don't know. What should I play?' We never had a rehearsal, unless just before the show went on I'd run through a song with Bob Olsen that he was going to sing, or something like that. And most of the people appearing on the Jamboree were just starting out. I was one of the few professionals. Bob Olsen had been a S&W coffee salesman.

"If I'd like a song, I'd say while we were on the air, completely on the spur of the moment, 'You know, that's beautiful, I think I'll play that again.' It didn't matter.

"A funny example of how we used to improvise

and how loose we were in doing the programs is the incident we had with Harrison Holliway's father during one program.

"His father was Cap Holliway, who had been a police reporter on the old *Call and Post*. He was a little guy, about as tall as I am. He was retired and he used to hang around the studio and wait for Harrison. But everybody loved him. Sometimes he would sit outside the studio and go to sleep. One time he came into the studio where the red velvet davenport was, lay down there, and started snoring his head off. So while our program was on the air, we put a microphone in front of him—I remember holding it under his nose—and said over the live mike to the public, 'You'll get a prize if you can write in what this is.' You really could do anything in those days.

"Then the networks came along and you had to get off at the exact right second. It became entirely professional and Big Business. Before, if we ran over a little bit, it didn't matter.

"I left the Jamboree and KFRC in 1932 and went over to NBC at 111 Sutter Street as a staff pianist to fill in when the network broke down, or didn't connect with the station. If there was a storm in Omaha, they'd have to reroute the whole thing. They'd holler, 'Standby,' and I'd run down that hall and get on the air. I'd have to 'fill up' the west coast network until they got the thing together."

The Jamboree's original musical director was Frank Moss, and the master of ceremonies was Harrison Holliway, the station manager. Al Pearce played the roles of Eb of the Eb and Zeb comedy team, and also was the idiotic Elmer Blurt in a laugh routine. Harry "Haywire Mac" McClintock sang ballads in his deep, rasping voice and played his guitar. Bill Wright changed voices frequently to become Professor Hamburg, Reginald Cheerily, Steamboat Bill, Zeb, and Santa Claus at Christmas time. Monroe Upton was Simpy Fitts and Lord Bilgewater, Eugene Hawes was Pedro Gonzales, and Ed Holden was Frank Watanabe who kept saying "oh, so" in response to almost anything. The male singers included tenors Robert Olsen and Norman Neilsen, baritone Charles Bulotti, and the popular young vocalist Tommy Harris. Soprano Juanita Tennyson seemed to draw the biggest hand from the studio audience among the female singers. In addition to playing piano accompaniment, Edna Fischer "did everything but pack lunch." A

BIG BROTHER AND THE BLUE MONDAY JAMBOREE

Benny Walker, one of the Bay Area's top radio stars as a program master of ceremonies, appeared on the NBC Woman's Magazine of the Air *with violinist Josef Hornik conducting the orchestra.*

Courtesy of Station KNBR

weekly Doakes and Doakes domestic comedy skit was put on by the husband and wife team of Hardy and Betty Gibson.

When he developed the "Happy-Go-Lucky Hour," an afternoon show intended to increase the upward surge of KFRC's share of listeners, Holliway used pretty much the same troupe of entertainers. Under Al Pearce, the "Happy-Go-Lucky Hour" went on five days a week from two to three o'clock in the afternoon. Included in the regular cast was Elmer Blurt, done by Pearce himself, the timid door-to-door salesman who knocked boldly on doors with a staccato rhythm, but who said audibly to himself, "Nobody home, I hope, I

hope." Tizzie Lish appeared too, really Bill Comstock using a high falsetto voice, to gush "Hello, folksies" and describe crazy recipes, first waiting patiently while everyone had time to get a pencil and write them down.

The KFRC staff of the Thirties contained some names which were to become nationally prominent in the entertainment industry. The young director of the Seattle Symphony Orchestra was hired as musical director in 1932. After he left KFRC in 1936 to join NBC, he went on to write such smash musical shows as *The Music Man* and *The Unsinkable Molly Brown*. His name was Meredith Willson. Two young staff announcers were also to be heard from later. One was Pat Weaver, later president of NBC for several years. The other was Mark Goodson, whose wife helped out the family budget by selling pastrami sandwiches at a concession stand at the 1939 World's Fair at Treasure Island in San Francisco Bay. Goodson-Toddman Productions later became a multimillion dollar giant of TV productions.

In 1928, Station KYA came on the air from the Clift Hotel; two years later it moved to the Warfield Theater building basement. At about the time it moved, the station broadcast for a year or so the man who was possibly its biggest star. He was Charley Hamp, and women listeners idolized him. He played the piano and sang in a low voice and spoke slowly and silkily to his listening audience. "He killed every other program on the air at the time," said George Taylor, then at KYA with his "Sunshine Hour" program.

Hamp was a flashy dresser with thick gray hair. He was sponsored by Dr. Straaska's Toothpaste, a Los Angeles company. His commercial message, "If you want your teeth to shine like pearls, buy Dr. Straaska's Toothpaste," was heard everywhere and heeded. "He sold that stuff by the ton," Taylor recalled.

Hamp appeared at the Pantages Theater for a week, and the attendance was phenomenal. Standing-room-only crowds filled the theater for every performance. Unlike Gunsky, Hamp's personal appearances turned out to be an asset and increased his radio audience. Hamp returned to Los Angeles while still riding high in popularity at KYA.

In 1934, KYA was purchased by William Randolph Hearst and tied into the promotion program of the Hearst newspapers in the Bay Area as "The Voice of the *Examiner*." One unsettling incident occurred at the gala opening program under the new sponsorship which was probably as good an example as any of the things that could happen in radio in those years. The all-star show featured stage and screen actor Leo Carillo. The announcer was the popular Ernie Smith, and the eminent Cy Trobbe was conducting the large orchestra. When the magic moment came to go on the air, Trobbe raised his baton in his usual elegant manner. When the signal came, he swept his arm down grandly and the instruments broke out in musical response.

However, the result was not the usual one. Some wag, or drunk, had distributed sheet music orchestrations for two different selections on the music stands. Half the musicians started to play one piece and half played the other one. Trobbe dropped his arms and looked horrified. As the grating, discordant rumble of sounds came to a trailing off half like a train rolling its last few feet on arrival, Trobbe grimly and furiously snapped his baton into several pieces, threw them

down and stomped out of the studio and out of the building.

Remote control broadcasts of band music from hotel and dance spots became a staple in late-hour programming, and in 1932 you could have heard a wide variety of Big Band music styles. Anson Weeks played at the Mark Hopkins Peacock Court. The Griff Williams-Jimmy Walsh band played "Mama's Gone Goodbye" for dancers at Tait's-at-the-Beach. Vocalists Muzzy Marcelino and the Debutantes performed with Ted Fiorita at the Embassy Room of the St. Francis Hotel.

Nineteen thirty-two was also the year that NBC purchased KPO from Hale Brothers and the *Chronicle* for $600,000. The national network moved the station to new studios at the top of the twenty-two story building at 111 Sutter Street. NBC also staged the first ship-to-shore commercial broadcast in 1933. It sent Hugh Barrett Dobbs, the popular "Captain Dobbsie," and the entire "crew" of his "Ship of Joy" show to Honolulu on the Matson Line's *Malolo*, and transmitted a show from mid-Pacific.

One of radio's great all-time serials, "One Man's Family," was introduced in 1932 over KPO and NBC stations in Los Angeles and Seattle. Writer Carleton Morse created the Barbour family and their trials and joys in their Seacliff district home in San Francisco, and many a Bay Area youngster would come to feel that he or she had grown up with Jack and the other Barbour children. And many parents would have the sensation of having grown old with Henry and Fanny Barbour. The characters' voices began to age unmistakably over the years as they reiterated the family's trials. "One Man's Family" was the longest-running serial drama in U.S. radio history, not ending until 1959. It was also the first serial originating out of San Francisco for the entire NBC network.

Also on KPO then was young Harold Peary, formerly Perez, of San Leandro. Later he became a national favorite as The Great Gildersleeve. Peary entered radio in 1929 on the Associated Spotlight program in character roles that included Tony Spagliarini, George Washington, U.S. Lee, and the Laugh-

Bernice Berwin (left) played Hazel, Minetta Ellen was Mother Barbour, and Kathleen Wilson was Claudia on the long-running One Man's Family, *the first NBC network serial to originate in San Francisco.*

BIG BROTHER AND THE BLUE MONDAY JAMBOREE

ing Villain. In the latter role he developed the leery crescendo laugh that was to become his trademark.

Sports quickly assumed a prominent role in the blooming commercial radio field. Probably the dominant figure in Bay Area sports broadcasting—from its real beginnings in the late Twenties and throughout the Thirties—was Ernie Smith, a former star swimmer and water-polo player. Smith could paint a word picture over a microphone that sometimes made the event more exciting for his listeners than for the spectators actually watching it. I can recall hearing him broadcast a fight from Dreamland Rink that had him apparently almost breathless from excitement and certainly had his listening audience on the edge of their chairs at home. It came over the air as a savage Pier Six brawl in which punches were being thrown constantly and the fighters didn't stop to clinch at all. The next day, the newspaper fight writers described the same bout as one of the dullest, most boring exhibitions ever staged; one the referee had constantly threatened to halt for lack of action.

Many years later, Smith explained that the reason for his vivid descriptions was that Jack James, the *Examiner* sports editor, had negotiated with fight promoter Benny Ford to broadcast the boxing bouts from Dreamland. The one stipulation to the agreement demanded by Ford was, Smith said, that "every fight would be a great battle."

With Smith at the mike, the fights were great battles, but the announcer had an embarassing moment on his second broadcast, describing a fight between two middleweights. "Recalling instructions from James, I had a gory first round, a fast second, and a wild third," Smith said, "until Referee Toby Irwin walked to the center of the ring, raised both hands above his head, and declared, 'No fight,' because neither protagonist would fight."

Smith broadcast the baseball games of the San Francisco Seals from the "Old Rec" field during the mid-Twenties. He had no spotters, statisticians, producers, or director. He was strictly on his own at the scene of the action. No Smith, no broadcast.

Smith carried his own broadcast amplifier to send out his descriptions over the air. He set up his announcing booth by removing a carbon microphone from the amplifier box, plugging in KYA, connecting PG&E power, turning on the microphone, and then

BIG BROTHER AND THE BLUE MONDAY JAMBOREE

going down to the office of Seals co-owner Charley Graham to call the station. He would get engineer Fred Eilers at the station and synchronize his watch with that of Eilers. "At 1:45 p.m. I would make my salutation into the mike, with a quiet prayer that I was on the air," Smith said.

Smith was the third San Francisco baseball announcer. The first one lasted only two days. The second was Jack Keough, who was hired away by KGO. Smith always praised Keough as "one of the greatest" local announcers.

Keough, unjustly according to Smith, is commonly identified as the protagonist and victim in an incident which has become a legend in the radio industry. The usual anecdote was Keough, in the role of Big Brother on a popular KPO children's program, blurting out, when he thought the microphone was dead at the end of a broadcast, "I guess that will hold the little bastards for tonight." Keough allegedly was fired and black-balled from radio as a result.

Smith argues that the incident was actually a staged skit presented at the 1926 Low Jinks show of the prestigious Bohemian Club. "The gag was pinned on Keough," Smith claimed. On the other hand, George Taylor, the former KYA star, said that Keough told him that the story is true and he was the announcer. It's a good story anyway.

Smith was a busy man when radio began to blossom. People were making the purchase of a radio their number one target. In a similar way, TV sets were to become more of a necessity than a luxury several decades later. Performers in the industry who proved successful were bound to be in demand and to become involved in pilot projects. For example, Smith did the first Pacific Coast broadcast of a basketball game, describing the Stanford-California series from Kezar Pavilion when that San Francisco arena was dedicated. This series was the first to be played by the two major Bay Area colleges off campus. Smith's announcing "booth" was a makeshift platform perched in the rafters.

Smith once broadcast the Stanford-California football Big Game from a telephone booth on top of the Memorial Stadium press box in Berkeley because his transmission equipment had failed. In 1929, he broadcast the opening of the luxurious Fox Theater in San Francisco with a microphone mounted on a broomstick, interviewing Gary Cooper, Lupe Velez, and other Hollywood stars attending the opening.

Those early broadcasts called on the innovative

Jack Keough was a popular Bay Area sports announcer and later "Big Brother" on KPO's children's hour program.

Courtesy of Station KNBR

genius of radio engineers. A small turnout could sometimes be anticipated for certain games or events. When this occurred, sound-effects records with the calls of hot dog vendors, the shouts of fans calling the names of players expected to be in action, and general crowd noise were made ready. These would be blended into the sportscast at the studio to make an exciting show for the listeners.

It was comedy, music, and song, however, that really dominated the home-entertainment life of an average family household in the Twenties and Thirties. The top radio shows featured laughter and punch lines. Never heard were swear words or sophisticated humor that might cause irate parents to write in and complain that the program was shocking and undermining the morals of their children or teenagers.

The list of programs heard in San Francisco and the Bay Area was long, and sprinkled in amongst the local radio personalities were Broadway and Hollywood stars in network shows, mostly from New York and Hollywood. There was "The Jack Pearl Show," for

The cast of the National Broadcasting Company radio program, Back to Good Times, *sponsored by the Bank of America out of the San Francisco NBC studios at 111 Sutter Street. Standing left to right in this 1932 photograph are Nathan Stewart, baritone; Harry Stanton, basso; Myron Niesley, tenor and Ben Klassen, tenor. Sitting are Eva Gruninger, contralto; Emil Polak, musical director; Barbara Blanchard, soprano, and Everett Foster, baritone.*

instance, with Baron Munchhausen, who always squelched his partner's doubts that his ridiculous, exaggerated stories were true with "Vas you dere, Sharlie?" There was "The Fred Allen Show," often eulogized as the funniest and cleverest comedy show ever heard on the air. Allen's cast of outrageous and unforgettable characters included Senator Beauregard Claghorn, Mrs. Pansy Nussbaum, Titus Moody, and One Long Pan, the famous Oriental detective. My favorite was Senator Claghorn from the Deep South, whose booming cliché-stuffed phrases and bad attempts at humor ended with an explanatory "That's a joke, son." I classified many a politician I have seen or listened to since then as "Senator Claghorn returns."

"The Fibber McGee and Molly Show" was another program that was a must. The McGees lived at 79 Wistful Vista and their friends included Throckmorton P. Gildersleeve, who was San Leandro's Hal Peary entering the national network scene from KPO. Eddie Cantor, the Broadway and movie comic and singer, had his own show and featured a dialogue every week with "The Mad Russian," Dave Rubinoff, who always opened with "How *do* you do."

"The Ed Wynn Show," with Wynn as The Perfect Fool, was another favorite. Wynn, with his silly high-pitched laugh and giggle, was one of Broadway's most imaginative and popular comedians. He was also the father of Keenan Wynn, who came along later as a movie and TV actor. The elder Wynn was probably known best on the air as The Texaco Fire Chief. The program would open with an explosion of sirens and clanging bells. Wynn was featured in Texaco gasoline advertisements and signboards wearing a fire chief helmet.

The Baby Snooks Show, starring the aging but still funny comedienne Fanny Brice, was the top-rated radio show for some time. Snooks's brother, Robespierre, and Daddy Higgins, her frustrated father, were her chief foils. Publicity for the show featured Fanny, who had appeared on Broadway with W. C. Fields in the Ziegfield Follies before World War I, in a short little girl's dress and hair bow, licking a huge sucker.

Faithful listeners to "The Aldrich Family" waited for the program's opening shouts of "Henry! Henry Aldrich!" and the answering "Coming Mother."

Band leaders became national figures when they headed their own shows. There was Ben Bernie, The Old Maestro, with his low-keyed "yowsah, yowsah, yowsah" soothing listeners between numbers. He signed off each program with "au revoir, pleasant dreams." Kay Kyser's College of Musical Knowledge had for its theme song "Thinking of You." And Rudy Vallee and his Connecticut Yankees starred in The Fleischman Hour, where Rudy crooned "My Time Is Your Time" and "I'm Just a Vagabond Lover." We used to give imitations of Rudy by pulling down the outer edges of our eyebrows into a Basset Hound look and saying, "Heigh-ho, everybody," Vallee's standard audience greeting.

"Dr. I.Q., The Mental Banker," was probably the most popular quiz show. Playing from a different city each week, the good doctor would station aides with supplies of silver dollars and microphones at different locations in the audience. "I have a lady in the balcony," an aide would call out when his turn came. "I have ten silver dollars for that lady in the balcony if she can tell the name of George Washington's birthplace," the doctor would say. If the lady answered correctly, the listener could hear the silver dollars clinking into the lady's hands. If she could not, you would hear, "Oh, I'm sorry," the correct answer, and "But give that lady a box of Mars candy bars anyway." The highlight conclusion of the program was a biographical sketch quiz with clues paying up to seventy-five dollars for the correct identification, the amount growing less as the clues progressed.

Mysteries were popular too. There was "The Fat Man," with its cold, flat-voiced introduction: "He's

stepping on the scales, now, weight [long pause while the scale needle apparently was settling on the right marking], three sixty. Who? [pause] The Fat Man!"

Long before he went to Los Angeles and became Sergeant Friday on "Dragnet," Jack Webb worked the San Francisco waterfront as a private eye on radio in "Johnny Modero, Pier 23," and "Pat Novak for Hire." When the fog horns blew mournfully and the waves slapped up against the wooden pilings as Johnny or Pat wandered along the Embarcadero at night, San Franciscans didn't need a picture tube to put themselves there. The "mental picture" effect was perhaps more riveting than a TV image. Sam Spade was also around then, dictating reports at the end of the program to his jaded secretary, Effie.

Other names and sounds and programs pop out of memories. The "Edgar Bergen and Charley McCarthy Show" was proof of the effectiveness of radio in conveying mental pictures. How else can you explain the geat success of a ventriloquist and his dummy whom you couldn't see? "Major Bowes and His Original Amateur Hour" was a Sunday show my father never missed; he participated by predicting which ambitious singers or musicians would be stopped short by the ominous gong signaling that their talents were in other fields. And the heckling of comedian Phil Baker by Beetle and Bottle, invisible not only to the audience but to Baker as well, drew high ratings.

Following World War II television came along to take over and dominate the home-entertainment stage. Still, radio managed not only to survive, but to prosper. More stations than ever before offered entertainment and cultural and informational programs while competing effectively for allocations from advertising budgets. The new supply of FM broadcast channels contributed heavily to this growth.

Admittedly, TV stars and personalities have, in general, replaced radio performers and artists in popularity and glamour, but there are those who believe that the radio stars of yesterday could experience more personal satisfaction in their careers. "Radio created vivid impressions of its personalities on the listening audiences," Edna Fischer explained. "People took you into their hearts through their minds in those days. They had to listen and though they couldn't see anything, they would make mental pictures that stay alive today because they never saw any change. You remain to them like Goldilocks, you never get old. It's a wonderful thing."

3

Fifty Cents with Wine

San Francisco is still known as one of the great restaurant cities of the world, but it was even better years ago, and much cheaper, as seasoned San Francisco trenchermen and gourmets will fondly recall. There have always been restaurants all across the City for those who wanted to eat well but not pay too well. Some were landmark spots in the history of San Francisco good eating.

North Beach as an eating paradise—at workers' prices—had its finest hours in the Twenties and Thirties. Restaurants were everywhere—on Columbus Avenue, upper Grant Avenue, outer Powell and Mason, Broadway, off North Point and Bay, and on almost every sidestreet between Chinatown and Fisherman's Wharf. Some nestled up on Pacific Avenue above the heart of Chinatown.

Many North Beach restaurants started as saloon speakeasies before Prohibition was repealed in 1933. The Italian wife of the owner would cook for her family, and they would gather in a back room to eat their meals. The aroma of garlic and onions and rich spices would drift out to the old, pre-Prohibition bar where Italian bachelor workmen who lived in the neighborhood had stopped in for sneak drinks at the end of the day. The workmen would ask if they could eat dinner with the family in the back as "boarders." Soon a regular table or two would be set every night and dinners served for fifty or seventy-five cents. The next logical step was to open as a public restaurant. Some of these family-type restaurants are still serving meals today, though not necessarily at bargain prices.

Some of these small restaurants were opened by couples fresh from Italy during Prohibition. To satisfy the Italian customers who were accustomed to drinking wine with their meals, the owners would often make their own in the basements of the restaurants or their homes. The illegal wine was always served at tables in coffee cups to avoid suspicion from strangers who might wander in. "Bootleg" whiskey by the shot was also available to trusted friends and customers.

Even after the Volstead Act dry law was repealed and wine could be served from bottles bearing federal tax stamps, the basement production continued as an economic boost to what were often marginal profit operations.

"The law allowed any family to produce two hundred gallons of wine a year for its own use, but not for sale," one North Beach operator of a family restaurant explained. "My dad used to buy about the same amount—two hundred gallons—of wine in bottles which had tax stamps on them and he'd keep them here at the restaurant for sale. But, Christ, he'd make fifteen to twenty barrels at home in his basement, and each barrel held fifty gallons. Then he'd use this wine to refill the bottles at the restaurant. They took better care of the barrels in those days than they did their wives. That was the secret of good wine.

"Eventually one of my dad's 'paisanos' turned him in to the feds and that was the end of that deal. That was too bad because he produced a better grade of wine. It was a different type. You put your hand in his wine and it would come out red. The other type, like what they have now, you could put your hand in all you want and it comes out like it was in water."

One of the family restaurants still around is Natalena "Ma" Mechetti's Gold Spike at 527 Columbus Avenue, near Green, now operated by her son, Paul. The Gold Spike originally started as a candy store with unmolested small-time gambling activity going on in a side room. Some food was served in a small back room, and bootleg whiskey by the shot was available to friends and neighbors. After Prohibition was repealed, the candy store became a full-time restaurant and bar operation. During the Thirties, after repeal, one of the

In 1939, the Gold Spike was going strong as a restaurant and bar when some of its customers joined in the City's celebration of the opening of the Golden Gate International Exposition on Treasure Island.

Courtesy of Paul Mechetti

specials of the house was seven Coffee Royals lined up on the bar for a dollar. This was a popular draw for the laborers who would drop by in groups for a drink after work.

"Dinner was fifty cents," Paul Mechetti said. "with lots of French bread, which cost six cents a loaf then. Pasta like spaghetti was ten cents a pound. Dried beans for the minestrone soup were five cents a pound. Guys who worked at the cement plant and lived around here used to come a lot."

A few blocks away from the Gold Spike, on the corner of Grant Avenue and Vallejo, was the Benedetti family's New Pisa. The menu listed on the board of card slots on the back wall, still read about the same in April 1977, when the restaurant moved to Green Street, as it did in 1930 when it was first put up.

The Benedetti brothers, Gino and Ezio, were actually from Torre Del Lago, a town near Pisa in Italy. In 1921, they bought the original New Pisa, at 623 Vallejo Street, from another Italian from the famed leaning-tower city in the Tuscany area. But the Benedettis were forced to move a half block to the Grant Avenue corner when the property was bought for the new Rossi Market site. The original clientele were principally Italian employees of the wholesale fruit and vegetable firms in the nearby produce market area off the waterfront. They usually paid their board bill by the month, averaging about twenty dollars.

In 1930, with Gino's oldest boy, Dante, learning the business, the Benedettis served a twenty-five cent lunch and thirty-five cent dinner. The lunch included soup; spaghetti, ravioli, or macaroni; a choice of entrees; coffee, and home-made cookies. The entrees were the typical Italian ones: tripe with sausage and beans, meat balls, stuffed zucchini, kidney or lung stew, and veal sauté or scallopini. The dinner, ten cents more, included salad and a platter of antipasto—salami, olives, celery stalks, raw carrots, and green peppers. There were two specials on the regular menu that raised the dinner tab. Rib steak or chicken cost fifty cents.

New Pisa restaurant in 1921 with the Benedetti brothers, Gino and Ezio behind the bar. Germana and Dante are perched on the bar. This was 623 Vallejo Street.

Courtesy of Dante Benedetti

When Prohibition ended, a small bottle of red wine was added to lunch and dinner, but the prices remained the same. In about 1936 lunch and dinner went up to forty and sixty cents, and in 1939 to seventy-five and ninety.

Today Dante Benedetti, Gino's oldest son, has some very definite thoughts about the traditional family restaurants of North Beach. Now in his late fifties, he still puts in some time daily behind the bar of the New Pisa, and also supervises the buying and preparation of food, tasks his father and mother, Eugenia, used to do. Two sisters still work in the restaurant with him.

"We've always been a family operation," Benedetti says. "Ninety per cent of the restaurants in the Beach were family places. That's how they got along. But all these places are going down the drain. You don't have enough family help left and you have to abide by the same rules and legislation as the large places. If it wasn't for my sisters I might as well close up. Look, I'm paying the bartender forty-seven dollars a day and some shifts the bar only takes in eighty dollars.

"I owe my life to my sisters, I never could operate the place without them. If I make money, I give some to them. If there isn't any, I don't. I've never given them a salary.

"I don't know who the hell is going to take over from me. But I'm more concerned about the human part of all this. These kinds of restaurants were a part of the good things in life. I've had a dozen offers over the years to go into things where I could have made more money, good money, some of them in the last year or two. But I've stayed here because I hate to see places like this go. And we're losing them. Why are we moving that fast so that we start to lose these kinds of places? I can't see losing the good things in life."

Ernie's, now blue-ribboned with awards and ultra-expensive, was in business in those days, too. Called Il Trovatore Cafe until 1937, it was in the same location on the Montgomery Street hill below Pacific Avenue and the old Barbary Coast block. The old-fashioned and ornate mahogany bar, with the carved back bar arch capping a spread of stained glass, mirrors, and columns, is still there today. Also there is the original ancient metal cash register on the back bar counter among the bottles and glasses. On top of the register was a sign reading "Special Lunch 30¢."

In the old days, Ernie's had no parking attendant, no foyer with crystal chandelier, no thick carpets or costly period furnishings, and no separate cocktail lounge with soft, subdued lighting. The outside façade was plain, and the interior was clean and run-of-the-mill. The stereotype red-and-white check tablecloths were the main concession to planned color and decoration.

Ernie Carlesso's partner, Ambrogio "Joe" Gotti, worked the daytime hours and Ernie the evening shift behind the bar. If you came into the restaurant in 1934, you might have seen a thirteen-year-old bus boy picking up dishes from the tables, or filling water glasses. That would have been Vic Gotti. With brother Roland, he was to develop Ernie's into one of the world's outstanding success stories. Ernie Carlesso died in 1945 and the Gottis have operated Ernie's as a single-family enterprise since then.

The bulk of the patronage at Ernie's in those early years was made up of cops, firemen, city officials, politicians, middle-class San Francisco families, and students from the all-male Bay Area Catholic colleges of St. Mary's, Santa Clara, and the University of San Francisco. A complete dinner with hors d'oeuvres, soup, salad, spaghetti or ravioli, choice of entrees from a wide selection on the menu including filet

FIFTY CENTS WITH WINE

This is the original Ernie's in 1934 when it was still Il Trovatore Cafe. Ernie Carlesso (left) and his partner, Joe Crevero, are behind the bar. This same year, a waiter working for them bought Crevero's share of the business. The sons of this waiter, Vic and Roland Gotti, have made Ernie's world famous.

Courtesy of Vic and Roland Gotti

mignon, vegetables, potatoes, dessert, coffee, and a small bottle of the house red or white wine, was fifty cents. On Saturday and Sunday nights, the dinner price zoomed up to sixty cents. Cocktails were twenty-five cents and a glass of tap beer ten cents.

At Lucca's, on the corner of Powell and Francisco, the food was delicious, and the quantity served per meal was famous. All you can eat for fifty cents, they advertised. And as kids we could really eat—two or three entrees at a sitting after preparing for dinner by fasting all day.

Lucca's, although it didn't open until 1930 and was a comparative newcomer in North Beach, is often cited warmly by dyed-in-the-wool "old San Franciscans" as an outstanding example of "the way it used to be." However, Lucca's was an exceptional operation, and probably no economy-priced restaurant in the city ever equaled it.

Pierino Gavello, a handsome, curly-headed Piedmontese from Turin in northern Italy, opened Lucca's

at the height of the Great Depression. The new restaurant was promptly inundated with crowds of diners who responded not only to Gavello's "All You Can Eat for Fifty Cents" advertisements, but also to the little extra touches that he added to basically tasty food.

Gavello was no stranger just off the boat from the Old Country. At the time he opened Lucca's on Francisco Street near Powell he was a partner in two night club restaurants in North Beach, the Lido on Columbus Avenue and the Apollo on Union Street where he had started out as a waiter. He sold his interest in the clubs approximately six months after opening Lucca's.

Crowds immediately deluged the new restaurant at the lunch hours and filled it at night. A special policeman was hired to control the traffic and keep order in the long lines that stretched down on Francisco Street to Powell, and around the corner. Customers were still lined up at the end of the eleven-to-two lunch hours. For a time, the front double doors had to be locked to keep people out so that the kitchen workers would have an opportunity to wash the dishes and set the tables for dinner. As soon as he could, Gavello bought the building next door and enlarged Lucca's to accommodate the crowds.

Just inside the entrance off Francisco Street were lines of children's high chairs to indicate to diners, and

Long lines of waiting diners stretched down Francisco Street to Powell from Lucca's entrance in the mid-Thirties.

Courtesy of Elmer Gavello

anyone peeking in, that family trade and kids were welcomed. "They are my customers of the future," Pierino always said.

About a year after the opening, Gavello had to hire another special policeman to stand guard on the Powell Street side of the restaurant after some stink bombs were thrown through the transom windows on that side. Although nobody was apprehended, some speculated that rival North Beach restaurant owners had been involved, since several Italian restaurants had recently closed, allegedly forced out of business by Lucca's low prices and ample menu. "Their customers started to ask, 'Don't you have spumoni? Why don't you serve petits fours like Lucca's?' " son Elmer Gavello said.

Lucca's had a long and varied menu, served large amounts of good food, and provided an atmospheric Italian setting for fifty cents. All the plates Gavello used at Lucca's were Florentine Majolica crockery imported from Italy. The meal was something that gluttonous Henry VIII would have appreciated, even though he could have afforded to pay more.

A typical meal at Lucca's is worth recording for posterity's sake. Its likes will not be seen again, at least not for fifty cents. It began with five platters of antipasto selections. Elmer Gavello recalled that the pearl onions for the antipasto were delivered to his father's restaurant in fifty-gallon wooden barrels. They were lowered to the basement storage room with ropes through a sidewalk elevating platform. "Every once in a while, one of the barrels would get away from the men, and what a mess it made when it hit the bottom!" Gavello recalled. Serving as a base on which the diner arranged the antipasto assortment was an individual green salad. And crowded onto the table along with the antipasto was a platter of fresh, crisp sour French bread, baked in Lucca's own bakery across the street from the restaurant on Francisco.

The soup followed the salad course. It was usually fresh minestrone in a traditional huge, deep bowl, with a ladle for serving. Pasta followed—usually a platter of spaghetti and ravioli, half-and-half, served piping hot from the oven where Gavello insisted that all platters be placed before being served to the tables (all plates were either heated or cooled to fit the order). The pasta was superb; if you wanted more, the waiter would bring another platter-full.

Repeat orders were valid for anything on the menu, with one limitation. You couldn't repeat the same entree unless you had eaten through the entire list first, an imposing obstacle. However, you could order as many different entrees as you could manage. The major dilemma facing big eaters was deciding where to concentrate the attack. You could easily run out of internal storage capacity too early in the meal. "Doggie bags" were unknown in those days, and taking uneaten food home was strictly a sneak operation.

"We had some trouble with women who would come in with large purses and slip food into them," Elmer Gavello reminisced, "even including olives. They must of had their purses lined with plastic. When they started to slip entrees into them, the waiter would tell them, 'You have to eat it here.' "

There was a fine selection of entrees. Usually listed were roast beef, roast squab, roast chicken, sweetbreads, steak, turkey, baked ham, veal birds, and roast duck. These were accompanied by potatoes or yams and fresh vegetables. Elmer Gavello would accompany his father down to the old produce market below Sansome Street every morning except Sunday at five A.M. to select fruit and vegetables for the day.

With every entree came a dish of fried cream, not considered a dessert item then. The desserts were something special, and among Lucca's most celebrated attractions. They featured petits fours from the restaurant's own bakery. Included were chocolate eclairs, Napoleons, cream puffs, chocolate cake with jelly layers, and colored sugar-coated bonbons. These were served all together on a tray; the ones you didn't eat you could take home with you—and we always did. The waiter placed them in special long cardboard boxes.

Each diner also received a dish of Italian spumoni ice cream that was eighteen per cent butterfat. Nobody even thought of cholesterol in those days. To parties of six or more, special molds of spumoni in the shape of a swan, cow, rabbit, or pig were served. Lucca's claimed to be the first restaurant in San Francisco to include spumoni and petits fours in the regular price of a dinner.

Regular customers knew they could get an extra treat not listed on the menu by asking the waiter. It was frozen orange. The top of an unpeeled orange was cut off, and the pulp removed and used to make an orange sherbet which was then stuffed into the orange peel shell, frozen and served.

Wine was served in a long-necked and straw-encased flask with a spout; in the glass was an indentation pocket for ice, capped with a straw stopper. Pints of wine were twenty-five cents, quarts were fifty. Shortly after Lucca's opened, Gavello added special crockery wine flasks, shaped into figures such as horses and doves. You could take the flasks home, and many now stand on the shelves of former Lucca's patrons.

In the late Thirties, Gavello opened a Lucca's in Los Angeles, applying the same formulas that had succeeded in North Beach. He continued to personally supervise the booming Lucca's on Powell and Francisco until 1939, when he opened the Monaco theater-restaurant on Pacific Avenue in the old Barbary Coast area. He expanded again by launching the Riviera restaurant on Union Street, across Washington Square park from Saint Peter and Paul's Church. Gavello was a good business operator. Taxicab drivers knew they could get a free meal back in the kitchen of Lucca's by bringing hungry tourists to the restaurant.

When son Elmer informed Pierino that he preferred real estate and investments to the restaurant business, the elder Gavello started to dispose of his successful establishments. Lucca's was closed in 1952 while it was still profitable. Pierino Gavello died in 1975.

The New Tivoli restaurant on upper Grant Avenue, following Lucca's example, also had take-home petits fours boxed for their customers. The special attraction here was a bocci ball court in a rear building under a glass roof. Benches were provided for spectators and students of the Italian version of lawn bowling, usually played on a narrow dirt court.

Contributing to the fame of North Beach were the counter restaurants on Broadway off Columbus Avenue—not just the well-known Joe Vanessi's, but also New Joe's and Louis's, where the hamburger sandwiches on French bread and the spinach, scrambled egg, and hamburger "specials" were rated highly at reasonable prices.

Bunched up in the same immediate area were the Fior d'Italia, Larry's, and La Pantera around the corner on Grant Avenue below Benedetti's New Pisa. Across the street from New Joe's on Broadway was Rena Gaggero's Blue Moon Cafe bar, with a couple of tables against the side wall. Rena sometimes served people she knew with food tourists would never know about unless a knowledgeable San Francisco friend of hers brought them in at the right time.

Further up Broadway near Powell and the Nuestra Señora de Guadalupe Church was the City's main Spanish-speaking neighborhood of those years where the Basque restaurants were. My family frequently went to the Abaurrea family's Hotel Español, on the alley corner of Broadway and Cordelia, after Prohibi-

GOOD LIFE IN HARD TIMES

tion was repealed and it was opened to the public. Like the Jose Lugea family's Hotel de España further up the block, the Español's customers had been limited to the sheepherder boarders who lodged there on brief visits to the City. Even after the Hotel Español began to serve outsiders, for several years there was no sign to indicate that the restaurant was open to the public.

The Abaurreas charged forty cents for dinner, which included salad, soup, and petit entree such as rice and clams or meatballs and red beans; the main dish, usually roast lamb, roast veal, or fried chicken, and an apple and cheese, plus coffee. A glass of red or white wine was included with the dinner. Mixed drinks were fifteen cents at the bar. As in most restaurants in North Beach whose bars were supposedly mothballed and inactive during the Prohibition years, Repeal cut down profits for the Hotel Español owners. "When we got legal, we couldn't pour the good stuff," recalled Martin Abaurrea, Jr., who was fourteen when he started working for his father at the restaurant. "We used to buy 100 percent proof Harper's, Grandad, and Hoteling bourbon from the drug store for 'medicinal' purposes at $6.75 a pint. We'd pour it for friends and customers we knew for fifty cents a shot. At the new prices of fifteen cents a drink, there was no way we could afford to use the 100 proof stuff, even if we could get it."

In 1935, Angela Abaurrea was shocked when her husband, Martin, told her he was going to raise his dinner price to fifty cents. "You're crazy, you're going to lose all the customers," Martin, Jr., remembers his mother saying.

Some restaurants established during those years did not last too long. One memorable downtown example of here-today-gone-tomorrow was the Merry-Go-Round Cafe, a rare experiment which still evokes fond memories for those who like to eat a lot, if not too fussily. In 1931 lunch there was fifty cents, dinner seventy-five cents. Given the restaurant's policy on salads and desserts, we just knew the place couldn't last.

The Merry-Go-Round opened at 171 O'Farrell Street, near Powell, a few doors from the old Orpheum Theatre, after a barrage of newspaper publicity. A long, U-shaped counter supported a slow-moving conveyor belt. The belt was capped by a tunnel with little curved glass doors on the outer side that could be lifted up. A counter and row of stools faced these doors on one side of the restaurant and a series of wooden booths snuggled up to them on the other side. Riding on the belt was a constant display of plates filled mainly with salads and desserts.

You could eat as many of the salads and desserts from the conveyor belt as you wanted—and had room for—without paying extra. You just watched the passing parade of food while you were working on one dish, made your selection mentally, and when you saw it approaching you again in the transparent tunnel of goodies, you lifted the nearest glass door open and deftly snatched it off the belt as it came by.

There were luscious pies and cakes of all kinds, topped and filled with real whipped cream and fruits. If you wanted any of the desserts à la mode, no problem. All you had to do was ask the waitress inside the U to put a scoop of ice cream on top of the whipped cream. No extra charge, of course.

The rest of the meal, including the entree and drink, were served to you. As youngsters, however, we were not too interested in the more conventional parts of the meal. We used to go downtown after not eating all day, go into the Merry-Go-Round before we went to the movies, and concentrate on the desserts. Plate after plate would be emptied and piled alongside of us on the counter while replacements were placed on the belt as it passed through the shielded pantry-kitchen area in the back of the restaurant. Ah, the elastic stomachs of youth!

But our enthusiasm was not unusual and, needless to say, the Merry-Go-Round changed its policy after only a short time, placing a limit on the number of selections you could take off the belt. With the removal of the glutton appeal, plus the fact that the novelty of the conveyor belt operation soon wore off, the Merry-Go-Round soon closed up. It remains a memorable, if not significant, chapter in the City's restaurant history.

On Powell near the cable-car turntable at Market Street, was without a doubt the most dignified cafeteria the City has ever enjoyed. Clinton's Cafeteria featured dinner music played by a string orchestra from six to eight. The huge basement restaurant had marble floors dotted with potted palms, tubbed ferns, and leafy plants. Customers descended a wide, steep stairway with shiny brass handrails into a noisy but properly decorous atmosphere, where even the clatter of dishes on metal trays seemed to be muffled in propriety and politeness.

Across the Powell Street cable car tracks from Clinton's was the elegant Pig 'n' Whistle chain's candy, ice cream, and pastry emporium, catering heavily to shoppers-luncheon and after-the-theater soda

FIFTY CENTS WITH WINE

In 1922, Julius Castle was under construction on Telegraph Hill and there wasn't much else around, not even Coit Tower.

Courtesy of Julius Castle

and coffee cake trade. It carried Easter baskets and assorted holiday candy items for children, sweethearts, mothers, and assorted relatives.

On the site of the present BART station entrance at Market and Eddy Streets, Leighton's, another popular basement cafeteria, but smaller than Clinton's and without music, did a good business with reasonable prices and high quality food. A block down at Fourth and Market below street level, The States Hof Brau restaurant advertised an orchestra and dancing every evening. A frescoed ceiling featuring golden oranges and lacy foliage provided an ornate touch to the States. In the mid-Thirties, the Hof Brau moved to Eddy and Market, replacing Leighton's.

Out at the Ocean Beach, Whitney Brothers had taken over the four run-down concession and amusement blocks just south of Seal Rocks in 1929 and installed some commendable and economical eating spots that were to become well established in the City's list of recommended food places. Topsy's Roost, below Sutro Heights, featured a half of a southern fried chicken plus hot corn pones and honey for fifty cents.

You could buy your meal at a dispensing counter; standing there you could see the huge glass tank of cooking oil into which the chickens were dropped. Or you could go inside for dinner and dancing at night.

Designed to resemble a huge barn, Topsy's could seat more than a thousand diners. Its highlight was a slide which shot you and your companion down from the balcony level where the tables were into the area of the dining room dance floor. Drawings of roosters covered the walls and painted chicken tracks ran across table tops. You ate your chicken with your fingers—no knives and forks were provided—and a playground bucket filled with water was brought to your table so you could wash your hands after you finished.

The Hot House, in the next block, featured enchiladas sprinkled with grated raw onions and cheese that probably have never been duplicated for taste and value. The It Stand specialty was hamburgers cooked without grease and electrically grilled hot dogs. The Pie Shop was a sidewalk bakery behind huge glass windows where you could watch the tasty, fresh fruit-packed pies being prepared and baked. You could buy a slice of pie and eat it on the spot or take a whole pie home.

Then there was Julius Castle up on Telegraph Hill, below the site of Coit Tower. The Castle is still in operation today. In the old days, it had a turntable for automobiles because there was no room to turn around at the dead end of Montgomery Street above the Embarcadero.

Julius was no fifty-cents-with-wine restaurant, even when it opened in the early Twenties. A complete dinner was $1.25, and a de luxe version was two dollars. Among the entree choices on the latter were filet of sole with sauce Julius or tenderloin steak with zucchini Florentine. The house Riesling wine was sixty cents extra for a pint, or a dollar for a large bottle. Lunch, with such entrees as lamb chops, was seventy-five cents—quite expensive at the time.

Elmer Gavello of Lucca's recalled "sole owner and manager" Julius Roz, who built the restaurant in 1922. "I'll never forget him driving down Union Street in North Beach in a Chrysler Imperial convertible. I can see him as if it just happened now. He had a big, camel-hair polo coat on and wore a hat. He always had the convertible's top down and two beautiful Collie dogs in the rumble seat which had its own windshield and side windows to keep the wind off the dogs. God, what a magnificent sight!"

Coffee Dan's was a unique club restaurant that drew tourists, entertainment-world figures, the sporting element, and the late-night crowd. In the O'Farrell Street basement near the northeast corner of Powell, where George Mardikian's Omar Khayyam's restaurant is now, Johnny Davis ran one of those places that could never be duplicated. You can still hear the cable cars as you come up the stairway from Omar Khayyam's to the street, but gone are the "wharf plank" table tops which you pounded with little wooden hammers in place of applause for the entertainers on the tiny bandstand. Almost all the stars who played in San Francisco on the vaudeville bills in the stage shows, plays, and musicals, and in the big night clubs seemed to find their way to Coffee Dan's after the last show. One of them was Al Jolson. In fact, the basement club setting was used as the background scene for one of Jolson's singing appearances in the classic early talking picture, *The Jazz Singer*, based on Jolson's life.

The action didn't get under way at Coffee Dan's until after 9 P.M. Frank Shaw was master of ceremonies and Les Poe was at the piano. Shaw would greet bald-headed customers coming in with the line, "Here comes the president of Herbicide," the trade name for a liquid claiming to restore hair.

The house special, which almost everybody ordered, was ham and eggs; it cost seventy-five cents.

There was no cover charge, no one cared how long you stayed, and you were sure to see some impromptu performances by some star or other appearing in one of the shows or at a club around town who dropped in during the evening or early morning. There was a slide going down along one wall of the stairway, but the "regulars" sneered at it as being a gimmick meant only for tourists or drunks.

Way out on Geary Street near Eighteenth Avenue in the Richmond District was the Koffee Kup restaurant, the favorite after-theater and late-hour snackery for San Franciscans who knew their way around town. From a huge vertical sign in the shape of a coffee percolator with a cup and saucer perched on top flowed a constant spiral of steam which puffed up and drifted out high above Geary. The Kup seated about 120 diners and snackers and was open twenty-four hours a day. The prices were right, the food was excellent, and the patronage came from every level of the City's makeup—from society after-theater party groups to high school kids and their dates stopping in after a gymnasium or church dance.

In 1936 the Kup was purchased by Will King, San Francisco's favorite burlesque and vaudeville comedian since shortly after the 1906 quake and fire. The wiry-haired stage comic exuded good cheer and hearty fellowship as he personally greeted the couples and groups that flocked into the Kup. Sandwiches and fine bakery goods were featured, but the Kup had its specials too, such as "Frog-on-the-Log," a filet mignon steak and baked potato for eighty-five cents. The Kup finally closed in 1954.

Schroeder's on Front Street was a favorite for German food, as it is today. Originally it was at 111 Front, one block closer to Market and across the street. Even then it had the crusted authenticity that only age can give. I only ate there with my father when my Uncle Moe was in town from New York. Both the bar and the huge, dark, wood-panelled restaurant were for men only. The sauerbraten with potato pancakes was seventy-five cents. An order of weiner schnitzel was ninety cents, and thick, fat Swiss sausages with red cabbage cost sixty cents. Light or dark beer in a pewter stein was ten cents.

In 1931, the elegant Bal Tabarin supper club was opened on Columbus Avenue in North Beach by partners Frank Martinelli and Tom Gerunovich, the latter, formerly of Pierino Gavello's Apollo Club. The plush club seated six hundred diners and was open seven nights a week. Despite the Depression, it was a

FIFTY CENTS WITH WINE

Schroeder's at its original 111 Front Street location in 1935.
Courtesy of Max Kniesche, Jr.

smashing success, and no wonder. For $1.50 you could get a complete dinner with a choice of roast chicken or a club steak, dance to the music of Gerunovich's sixteen-piece "Famous Brunswick Recording Band," and see a floor show at 10:30 or 12:30 complete with a dancing line of eight dazzling chorus girls and three or four acts of entertainment in the "Parisian Follies." And there was no cover charge.

If you didn't want dinner, the $1.50 minimum per person could be used for three "drinks." The beverages were limited to White Rock soda or Canada Club ginger ale, since the country was still dry and Prohibition was to remain in force for two more years. The fifty-cent drinks came with a bowl of ice. While no liquor was served, you could bring your own "bootleg" supply in a flask and pour it into your glass with no problem. After Prohibition ended in 1933, both cocktails and beer were served at the "Bal" for thirty-five cents.

If you felt flush with coin and were hungry, you could order the deluxe dinner for $2.50. This consisted of crab legs on ice or a shrimp cocktail, soup, frog legs Provençal, a thick, tender filet mignon with vegetables and potatoes au gratin, an ice cream cup, and coffee.

The Bal Tabarin had competition a block away on Columbus Avenue from the Lido. However, the Lido was really a poor man's version of the Bal. It gave you more food, with a vast spread of hors d'oeuvres, but it had a little less of other things. It only seated four hundred in its main floor and basement rooms and the regular band, of Val Valenti's, only had eight musicians. However, on Thursday and Saturday afternoons the Lido had two orchestras, one on each floor, for the highly popular matinee dances. The attendance on these days was no barometer of the business volume, however. Big spenders were scarce. Young newspaper reporters, with little change in their pockets and none in their bank accounts, rated it a great spot to drink up and find company economically.

"We'd go down to the Lido," one of them remembers, "with gin in a hip flask. It had a big singles trade and the girls would be sitting at tables. You'd go around and sweeten up their soft drinks from your flask —there was absolutely no alcohol sold—and then you'd dance them around. All it cost you was twelve cents a pint. That's what it figured out to make your gin. Everybody made their own gin. You'd buy alcohol made out of potatoes for two dollars a gallon from a bootlegger. It would be in a tin. Then you'd add a gallon and a half of distilled water and put in the juniper berries, or whatever else you added, and you would have two and a half gallons of gin. After you danced for a while you'd go out to a White Log Cabin and have a hamburger for five cents and they were just as good as any today. We usually went to the one on the corner of Bush and Grant Avenue."

There are still vestiges of the old North Beach fifty-cents-with-wine restaurants. Places with the same informal, close-knit feeling of familiarity that was so common forty and fifty years ago still exist. Today's plush restaurants and sky-high revolving bars have not completely erased the easy, old-shoe feeling of the family-owned Italian restaurant. Daughters, cousins, sons-in-law, and other members of a single family working together seem to create a welcome-to-our-house atmosphere that is difficult, if not impossible to duplicate by non-family restaurateurs. In the most authentic little restaurants still in North Beach, there is no officious maitre d', no waiting list for a table on which your name is written, no subtle or not-so-subtle attempt to steer you to the bar for drinks, no dress requirements causing open shirt-collars or sweaters to draw frowns from waiters or fellow diners. You wait around in an easy fashion as you would in a friend's house.

The drinks there are reasonably priced and honestly made with full portions of whiskey, or brandy, or gin, or whatever your pleasure is. The food ranges from good to excellent. Any restaurant that serves poor food cannot compete in North Beach for long. Though family pride would shut such a restaurant down before it went under anyway.

4

When the Seals Played Baseball

Recreation Park was a rickety baseball stadium a few blocks off Market Street, at Valencia and Fifteenth Streets. During the 1920s, when I remember it as a kid and a fan, it was a focal point for much of the City's sports action. It was the home of the San Francisco Seals of the professional Pacific Coast League from 1907 until 1930, except for a few months in 1914. That year and for five years beginning with the 1926 season, the San Francisco Missions team in the same league also called Recreation Park home.

In 1930, the old baseball park was abandoned; both teams moved to the newly constructed Seals Stadium, a more modern plant close by, at Sixteenth and Bryant Streets. Many San Franciscans stubbornly claim that baseball has never been the same in the City since that move. It is a matter of record that during their Recreation Park era the Seals spawned an enthusiasm and following among several generations of baseball followers that weathered even defeat. For example, in 1926 the Seals finished last in the league standings, but still outdrew every other team and was first in attendance for the season.

The park may have been built from warped lumber and hazardous chicken wire, and its structures may have creaked when the wind came up, but it had an intimacy and warmth that was lost when the Seals and Missions moved out at the end of the 1930 season. The wild-eyed loyalty and spirit of the City's baseball fans seemed to fit snugly into this small enclosure as they never did in the windy expanses of Seals Stadium, or in the Candlestick Park bowl, built later for the imported-from-Manhattan Giants of the National League.

Recreation Park was justly called a "crackerbox" by the baseball writers. Built in 1907, a year after the earthquake and fire had burned down its predecessor at Eighth and Harrison Streets, it was already considered inadequate for a top minor league team by 1913. In response, J. Cal Ewing, then president of the Seals, built a new stadium, which he modestly named Ewing Field, after himself. It occupied the site of the former vegetable gardens on Masonic Avenue, below the high sand hill on the west called Lone Mountain and across the street from Calvary Cemetery. The Seals only stayed there for half of the 1914 season, though, because research on the site had not been thorough enough. Embarassingly, it was discovered that the new field was in the direct path of the rolling fog. As a game progressed, the field would become wet, the fans would grow cold and miserable, the players would grumble, and fly balls and outfielders would disappear from view for suspenseful intervals. Balls came down out of the gray blanket to fall for hits before outfielders or infielders could get under them in time.

Midseason, the Seals moved back to Recreation Park in the Inner Mission, where the sun shone in keeping with the ancient cliché applied to the district, "Best weather in town." They shared use of the field that year with the San Francisco Missions, the former Sacramento team which had moved down to the City. It only stayed one season, moving on again to Salt Lake in 1915. For the next sixteen years, the Valencia Street park filled with avid baseball fans, colorful ball players, and varied characters on and off the field. The aura of a traditional old-time baseball park conjured up visions of crusty baseball greats like John McGraw and of kids peeking through knotholes in the fence. Grandstand tickets at "Old Rec Park," as it was called, were $1.25 for adults and twenty-five cents for kids. Bleacher tickets were fifty cents, and ten cents for kids. On Friday afternoon, kids were admitted free to the bleachers; and the absence rate was predictably high in San Francisco schools that afternoon.

If the last out of a game the Seals won was caught by a Seal outfielder, the kids would pour out of the

WHEN THE SEALS PLAYED BASEBALL

Opening day at Recreation Park in 1923. Mayor James (Sunny Jim) Rolph, Jr., his baseball pants tucked into his boots, is about to pitch the first ball to start the season. To Rolph's left is Alfred "Buster" Putnam, the Seals mascot and son of G. Alfred Putnam, one of the Seals owners. Next is Chief of Police Daniel F. O'Brien who served as Rolph's catcher for the ceremony. Far left is Jack (Dots) Miller, manager of the Seals. To the right of Rolph is Dr. Charles Henry (Doc) Strub, president of the Seals and another owner. Far right is Bill Essick, manager of the Vernon Tigers team.

Courtesy of William Weiss

bleachers, climb on to the top of the inner left field wall, hang by their arms, and drop down into the outfield. They would surround the outfielder who caught the fly ball and he would throw it into the air for a wild scramble for the cherished souvenir.

The Seals had been owned since 1917 by three partners who came to be known as the Valencia Street Vanderbilts. They were Dr. Charles H. Strub, a former dentist who later became head of the lush Santa Anita Race Track in Southern California; George Alfred Putnam, a rotund former Sacramento sports writer and promotional genius; and Charles H. Graham, a former major league catcher who served as the Seals field manager for three years.

The nickname Vanderbilt came into use after a series of players developed by the Seals at Recreation Park and sold to the major leagues became outstanding stars of the game. These included Vernon (Lefty) Gomez of the New York Yankees, Paul Waner of the Pittsburgh Pirates, and Earl Averill of the Cleveland Indians. Later, after the move to Seals Stadium, the

Seals' owners were to sell many other players, including, in 1935, a young outfielder from a crab-fishing family in North Beach named Joe Di Maggio.

Strub, the most astute businessman of the partnership, had brought some of the trappings of good salesmanship into Recreation Park by installing a private dining room under the stands near third base in which to entertain scouts from the major league teams. Rudolph, the chef, presided over the culinary treats and the pouring of beverages that were meant to put the scouts in an expansive and kindly mood for talking about money. Between 1921 and 1929, the Valencia moguls peddled a total of $475,000 in players to Big League clubs from Recreation Park alone.

The sale that focused the attention of the baseball world on the Seals was the record-setting sale in 1922 of a young third baseman named Willie Kamm to the Chicago White Sox for the then jaw-dropping amount of $100,000 cash, plus several players. Kamm had been a favorite of Charley Graham, and the young native son was given $5,000 of the sale price. This

Members of the 1922 pennant-winning San Francisco Seals team line up in front of the Booze Cage at Recreation Park. Left to right are: (Back row) Doug McWeeney, pitcher; Ernie Alten, pitcher; Pete Compton, outfielder; Bob Geary, pitcher; Sam Agnew, catcher; unidentified player; Charley See, outfielder; Alvin Crowder, pitcher; Pat Shea, pitcher. (Third row) Jack (Dots) Miller, manager; Denny Carroll, trainer; Andy Vargas, catcher. (Second row) Archie Yelle, catcher; George Stanton, pitcher; Bert Ellison, first baseman; Willie Kamm, third baseman; Jimmy O'Connell, infielder; Pete Kilduff, second baseman; Jim Scott, pitcher; "Chili" Tejeda, mascot. (First row) Tom Walsh, utility infielder; Gene Valla, outfielder; Oliver (Twist) Mitchell, pitcher; Fred Coumbe, pitcher.

Courtesy of Willie Kamm

procedure was followed later in other sales. Gus Suhr, for example, received $1,000 out of the $45,000 that Pittsburgh paid to the Seals triumvirate in 1929.

The "Booze Cage" at Recreation Park was something special. It was a closed-off section of about eight rows of elevated church-pew-type benches at ground level with the playing field. The cage was under the grandstand and ran from just in back of third base, around the back of home plate, to just beyond first base. Only a chicken-wire screen, with a fragile wood and screen door near home plate, separated the spectators from the field and the players. Real baseball nuts were fascinated by the proximity of the baselines, only about fifteen feet from the Booze Cage. The fans in the cage could, and did, trade insults with the players,

shout words of praise or encouragement up close, and even throw or squirt beverages at players waiting just outside the screen for their turns at bat.

"You walked some ninety feet from the dugout to bat, along the side of the Booze Cage," reminisced Gus Suhr, the old Pittsburgh Pirates slugger who played with his hometown Seals club in the mid-Twenties. "If you were going bad, they'd ride you. 'Where were you last night, Suhr, drinking up?' they'd yell. 'Suhr, you're a bum.' "

Willie Kamm, who went to the Chicago White Sox from the Seals, remembers hearing stories about "a big left-handed pitcher named Harry Ables. Some guy was on him all the time, and finally Ables said he'd come in and get him. There was a little swinging wooden door

WHEN THE SEALS PLAYED BASEBALL

into the Booze Cage back of home plate, so Ables went in, but he didn't get out for a while. They ganged up on him when he went in to challenge this guy.

"Then there was this manager, Bill Leard, in the semi-pro Winter League at the park. Some guy was on him, razzing him, and Leard looked in. You couldn't see in too well because it got kind of dark in there, so Leard tells the guy, 'Come up here, I want to see you, c'mon, c'mon, you're a wise guy.' So the guy, with half a heat on, I guess, stuck his nose up against the wire and Leard spit tobacco juice right in his face.

"When somebody said you were a lousy hitter or a bum, you could hear them as you walked by. Not now. You could holler your brains out, and nobody would hear you."

The name of the Booze Cage originated in pre-Prohibition days, before 1919, when the seventy-five cents admission ticket to the cage included either a shot of whiskey, two bottles of beer, or a ham and cheese sandwich, considered to represent fifteen cents in trade. A part of the ticket was redeemed for the shot, beers or sandwich from a vendor who came around balancing a tray. Or you could redeem your trade portion of the ticket at the long, enclosed bar on the Fifteenth Street side of the park, outside the Booze Cage. After Prohibition came in, a soft drink was substituted for the beer or whiskey, to which fans added bootleg whiskey and gin from their own pocket flasks and other portable containers.

The Booze Cage attracted a noisy, hard-drinking, tough-talking crowd, with teamsters and other "working stiffs" heavily represented. Women never sat in the Booze Cage unless they were impervious to bad language, suggestive remarks, and the cramped and sometimes cold and dank conditions.

The upper unreserved grandstand seats above first base had the gambling section. About one hundred bettors would congregate in a solid group to make wagers on the game action. Bets were made on anything from the final score to whether the next pitch would be a ball or a strike. The betting was done openly; the amounts offered and accepted were sometimes shouted out loudly. The bets were often high, and a considerable amount of money changed hands, but never in the stands. The cash was collected later. Though gambling was illegal, police never disturbed the action. It was accepted as part of the San Francisco baseball tradition at Recreation Park.

A brief flap of scandal arose about 1920 when two

Seal pitchers were accused of being involved with gamblers in the stands in betting coups influenced by their performance on the field. Some of the alleged "monkey business" included signals to the pitchers by gamblers waving white handkerchiefs from the grandstand betting section. The pitchers were released by Charley Graham and were "blackballed" from organized baseball.

Some of the regular bettors in the stand were well-known San Francisco gamblers. Prominent was Joe Bernstein, the "Silver Fox of Turk Street," whose big cigar and loud voice earned him the additional title of "Pop-off." Another famous gambler was "Tomato Face" Harry Cook.

Foul balls caught in the stands by fans had to be returned to the playing field. Around 1920, the two uniformed special policemen stationed near the bleachers were Hugh Smith and a fellow named Spelman. In those days there was also a right-field bleachers along the foul line. Later the grandstand was extended all the way to the right-field fence. When a ball was hit into one of the bleacher sections, Smith or Spelman would rush toward the place where the ball would come down. Some Seal fans claimed that Smith and Spelman could judge fly balls better than some of the Seal outfielders, unfortunately.

Fans would often try to pass the ball down their seat row, or to the rows below, before the special policeman arrived. With luck, the ball could be a hundred feet away before Smith or Spelman reached the landing spot. Sometimes several kids would have a signal system set up for foul balls that landed near them in the bleachers. One would hurry below while the others sought to get the ball and drop it down between the open plank seats. Occasionally a fan would attempt to put the ball in his pocket. If he was caught, he could be taken into custody. The crowd would boo the policemen walking him out from the stands. Usually, he would be turned loose outside the park.

Foul balls hit outside the park, either popped back over the grandstand roof or arched over the left- or right-field stands out to Valencia or Fourteenth Streets, were another matter. Clusters of kids, many of them wearing their baseball gloves, always hung around outside during the games waiting for a chance to grab a ball coming out of the park.

However, the Seals had a system designed for maximum efficiency in recovering the baseballs. As soon as it could be determined that a foul was going to land outside the park, a Seal employee inside pushed a button. It activated a buzzer out at the main entrance to the park at Fifteenth and Valencia. One buzz meant the ball was going to land on the Valencia Street side and two buzzes indicated that it was headed toward Fifteenth Street. A ball "hawk" employed by the park and stationed at the entrance would then take off at a run in the right direction. If he arrived in time, he could recover the ball himself, or claim it from the kid who had chased it down and was willing to surrender it in exchange for free admission to the game. If he arrived a little late, the chances were that the kid was off and running with the ball.

In those informal days, kids with gloves were often allowed onto the field during pre-game batting practice to "shag" fly balls. Nobody thought then of insurance risks from possible injuries, and no parents would even think of suing anyone if their pride and joy was conked on the head by a ball. One of the youngsters who scampered around to field the balls was Alice Marble, later to become the world's best woman tennis player. And sitting up behind the scoreboard, inserting the correct numbers, was a young fellow named Ira Blue, later one of radio's best-known Bay Area sports announcers.

Recreation Park seated about 16,500 around three sides of the small field. Twenty or so rows of bleacher seats lined the front of the left-field fence. The distance for a home run into the seats was rather short, 311 feet from the batter's boxes. However, the back wall of the bleachers was low, and the strong west wind that usually blew in from the Pacific Ocean puffed back many fly balls that seemed destined to go out of the park or into the seats. There were about forty rows of additional bleacher seats along the left-field foul line down in the far corner, divided from the grandstand by a chicken-wire barrier.

In deep center field, the most distant corner of the park, was the clubhouse. It was a ramshackle, wooden cottage with a peaked roof, and two floors for the players' dressing rooms and lockers. A flagpole near the clubhouse displayed an American flag, and usually a Pacific Coast League championship pennant flapped there too in the slight breezes that occasionally came up. In the decade of the Twenties, the Seals won five championship pennants.

The Seals used the upstairs rooms in the clubhouse and the visiting team dressed downstairs. There were only two showers upstairs and two downstairs, so the players had to line up and wait for turns to wash off after the games. "With twenty-five ball players waiting, the trick was to get in and get out while the water was hot," former Seal Gus Suhr said.

The only time a player didn't have to wait in line for a shower was when a pitcher was yanked out of the game and sent to the clubhouse early. But an immediate shower wasn't much compensation. The walk from the pitcher's mound to the clubhouse was a long, mortifying 325 feet, almost 110 yards. The dejected hurler would be subjected to boos, catcalls, and whistles, and occasionally was the target for a cushion hurled desperately by some irate fan. Spectators indulging in this practice were taking a chance since they could be arrested and jailed for it by one of the policemen stationed at the game. Nevertheless, a lot of cushion tossing took place, especially after the game. Retired cop Charley Foster remembers that at one time it was considered such a menace that twenty-five men from the Mission police station were detailed to the ball park on undercover duty in "plain clothes" to make arrests on malicious mischief or battery charges.

The scarcity of showers in the player dressing rooms resulted in at least one unusual event at Recreation Park. The main character involved was Herb Hunter, a Seal outfielder. Hunter was a fancy dresser who always wore a white carnation. It went with his prematurely white hair. Even when he was low in cash, he was always outfitted in a snappy suit and had the white carnation in a buttonhole. Although flamboyant in dress, Hunter never smoked or drank, and was considered by some of the players as a "sissy" type. He was also a good ball player with a tremendous throwing arm, speed on the bases and in the field, and a good hitter. Herbie's handicap, according to his teammates, was that he was not too bright.

Hunter was always the last player to leave the clubhouse after a game. He took his time about dressing. "His eyebrows had to be in place just so and he had to be so pretty," one ex-Seal player recalled. The Seal shortstop, little Jimmy Caveney, on the other hand, was the first one out of the clubhouse every day. "You could bet anything on it that Hunter would be the last one out and Caveney the first one," said Willie Kamm, the great third baseman who later played thirteen years in the major leagues. "Caveney would get into the clubhouse, and before I had my uniform off, he'd be coming out of the shower. He'd be dressed before anybody would get through with the shower."

WHEN THE SEALS PLAYED BASEBALL

Kamm remembers one particular incident at the ball park vividly. "This one day we're playing and it was the ninth inning. We're one run ahead and Herb is playing left field. So somebody hit the ball to left center and Herbie is running and he makes a great one-handed catch. He keeps on running to center field and right on up the stairs into the clubhouse.

"Well, we're standing there waiting because there's only one out. We don't know what to do. Charlie Graham was running the club at the time and he had to go out—and he was no spring chicken in those days—from the bench, run across the field, and climb the stairs to the upper clubhouse. Meanwhile, the crowd, and us, are wondering what the hell is going on.

"Well, here's Herbie taking a shower. Herbie had thought he made the last out with his catch. So Graham gives Hunter hell while he waits until Herbie quickly throws his uniform back on. Hunter finally gets back on the field and we get the side out.

"Charlie Graham was a very mild person, but he wasn't mild this time after the game. Herbie was sitting there in the clubhouse and Charlie is giving him hell. "Graham goes on and on to Herbie and Herbie's just sitting there. This went on for three or four minutes. So finally, Herbie looks up at Graham and says, 'My, Mr. Graham, aren't we having a wonderful year?' Graham was speechless and just turned around and walked away.

"Herbie explained to us later that as he's catching the ball, all he could think of was, 'This is one time I'm going to beat Caveney.' And that was why he ran to the clubhouse."

Caveney, who was sold to the Cincinnati Reds for $40,000 at the end of the 1921 season, caused a lot of aggravation to many perplexed San Francisco families who bought their sons new baseball gloves. A kid who wanted to be a shortstop had a natural tendency to attempt to imitate Caveney. This included cutting a gaping hole out of the center pocket of the mitt, exposing the bare palm. Caveney, with his ham-like hands, was a brilliant fielder, and he would scoop up hot grounders and stab scorching line drives with a sharp, smacking sound effect as the ball hit his bare palm. The parents didn't know that Caveney always asked the other Seal players for their old mitts and used them to make his unique cut-out models. "Ike" wouldn't think of buying a new glove.

Caveney was well-known as a man who liked his "schnapps." When he had a few "geezers" of liquid

The 1919 Seals infielders clown a bit before a game at Recreation Park. Left to right are Phil Koerner, first base; Willie Kamm, third base; Jimmy (Ike) Caveney, shortstop; and Roy Corhan, second base.

Courtesy of Willie Kamm

refreshment before a game, he would call over to Kamm, "Hey, Will, you take all the pop flys." Kamm would understand that Caveney would get too dizzy if he had to look up. So whenever a pop fly came down around the shortstop area, Kamm would move over from his third base position and take it. It wasn't until twenty years after he retired from baseball that Kamm, a native San Franciscan, learned with much chagrin that the Seals fans thought he had been "hotdogging," greedily taking plays away from Caveney.

Recreation Park was infamous around the league for its short right-field fence, only about 235 feet from home plate. To compensate for its vulnerability to home runs by left-handed batters, a towering wire screen had been erected on top of the wooden fence. The top of the screen was about fifty feet high and it ran almost all the way to the center-field clubhouse. A batter had to hit a ball up to heaven to clear the fence, and some did. What happened frequently was that long line drives and ordinary fly balls hit to right field would crash into the screen or fence. It turned home runs into singles or doubles and easy outs into run-scoring hits.

The all-time home run record for a single season by a Seal player was set by first baseman Gus Suhr with fifty-one in 1929, but he laughed about it after because most of the balls were hit over the short right-field fence. "I was a left-handed hitter and I could loft the ball pretty good over the high fence. The next year I was in Forbes Field in Pittsburgh and the balls were being caught instead of going for home runs."

Right fielders on all the clubs had to learn the idiosyncracies of the right-field fence at "Rec." There were soft spots in the screen from which the ball would drop straight down to the waiting outfielder. Occasionally, a hard-hit ball would become wedged in the screen and the smiling batter would circle the bases for a "cheap" home run while the right fielder waited fruitlessly for the ball to drop and the crowd roared. There were also rigid areas, on each side of the vertical wooden poles that supported the screen, from which hard-hit balls would ricochet back for some distance.

Beyond the right-field fence and grandstand, on the other side of the soaring screen, were some of the choicest viewing locations and seats, for which the Seals couldn't collect a dime—the roofs and back porches of a row of houses on Fourteenth Street, between Valencia and Guerrero. At the Valencia Street corner stood the Oregon Hotel and Kenealy's saloon, and in the middle of this block on Fourteenth Street was the Norwegian and Danish Methodist Episcopal Church. Residents and their visitors would set up chairs on the porches and roofs to watch the games. If you were fortunate enough to know one of the families living in these houses, you might be invited to come over for a Saturday or Sunday afternoon and join them on their sunny back porch or on the roof to watch the ball game. With homemade beer, or bootleg whiskey, available in the kitchen, plus sandwiches and potato salad, it made a delightful day at the ball game with no charge.

Ewing, the owner of the Seals when they moved to the Valencia Street park, had wanted to buy the strip of lots lining Fourteenth Street in the purchase of the new ball field site. He wanted this land even more when the church started complaining about the noise coming from the ball games and other sports events, such as boxing matches, that were staged at Recreation Park. The church was especially sensitive on Sunday mornings during the first game of the usual Sunday doubleheaders. The raucous crowd noises would carry into the church and upset the deliverance of the pastor's sermon. Also annoying was the wave of screaming voices and the thump of a baseball bouncing off the roof that sometimes followed the explanation of a Bible text. "Sometimes, a baseball would go into the church and break a window," according to Jim Leary, former vice president of the Baseball Managers Association,

who can remember the Seal teams all the way back to 1910, when he first sold peanuts and candy in the stands at Recreation Park. "I think the Seals allowed them to keep the ball," Leary said with a broad smile.

Eddie Mulligan, a scrappy third baseman for the Seals in the Twenties, remembers when the Seals' owners desperately paid for the addition of a second wooden wall to the back of the church in an early attempt at soundproofing. "It was not the solution," Mulligan said.

The complaints from the church were one of the reasons the Seals played their Sunday morning games with the Oaks over in the Emeryville stadium across the Bay. "Doc Strub tried to buy the church property," Leary, later a city worker in the Purchasing Department said, "but there was some covenant which prohibited the church from disposing of the property for any other use. If the church moved away, the property reverted to its original owner."

To hit a home run out of Recreation Park in deep center field, a batter had to smash the ball clear over the clubhouse and scoreboard in the far corner; the drive had to carry the ball more than four hundred feet. The first player to manage this herculean deed, according to witnesses and recorded accounts, was Harry Heilmann, later to become one of the greatest hitters in American League history. It came in 1915, when Heilmann was playing first base for the Seals as an optioned player from the Detroit Tigers. The blow is also credited with being the longest home run ever hit by anyone at Recreation Park.

Jim Leary was there that day. He was only fifteen then, hawking peanuts, scorecards, and candy bars at the ball park. "He cut the clubhouse in half," Leary said. "The ball went over the clubhouse, over the fence, over the houses and everything else. It landed on the front steps of the Building Trades Temple at Fourteenth and Guerrero. They saw it come over. It was the furthest anyone ever hit one."

Not so fabled in history, or traceable in recorded accounts, are three other home runs hit over the center field fences. Leary saw two of them. "Roy Corhan, the Seals infielder, hit one, but not as far," Leary said. "It was to the left of Heilmann's. Later on, Roy went into the insurance business and put a sign up there on the fence between the clubhouse and the bleachers where the ball he hit went over. His ad said, 'Yours For Life. Roy Corhan.'

"Then 'Cack' Henley hit one over there, but that

was an accident. He was the pitcher who threw that record twenty-four inning game for the Seals. It was the only home run he ever hit, I guess. He got a hold of one.

"The only other one I know of, and I didn't see it, was one hit by 'Schnoz' Lombardi, the Oakland catcher."

Al Erle, the respected ex-scout, did see it. "It was on a Sunday morning in the late Twenties when they were holding double-headers at Recreation Park, emptying the crowd out after the first game and then collecting a second admission in the afternoon. Lombardi's blow went over the fence back of the club-house, to the left," Erle said.

Heilmann's prodigious home run smash was even more amazing because it was hit during the era of the so-called "dead ball." Later, more resiliency was built into baseballs to keep up with the home-run demand and popularity brought on by Babe Ruth.

Leary has a difficult time convincing listeners that Corhan and Henley actually powered baseballs out of the park near the distant clubhouse. "Corhan had trouble hitting anything longer than a pop fly and his batting average equaled his weight," one former teammate said.

One explanation was given by ex-Seal Eddie Mulligan. "There was one spot just to the left of the club-house where there was no wind, sort of a dead spot." That fits in with Leary's placement of Corhan's drive.

"For anybody to hit one anywhere near the club-house was super-human," Willie Kamm commented.

One of those super-humans was frustrated. First baseman Gus Suhr witnessed the incident. "It was when Earl Averill was playing center field for us," Suhr said. "Someone whacked one out there. There was a little spiral of wooden steps, about three or four, there at the base of the clubhouse before you climbed up to our dressing room. Well, Averill ran up these couple of steps and caught the ball for an out. He just happened to judge it right."

The center-field clubhouse and the area around it made a fascinating display of prizes for a long ball hitter, sort of like a pinball machine with grass. There were all kinds of lures out there besides the possibility of joining Heilmann, Corhan, Henley, and Lombardi in posterity as the only players to hit a center-field home run out of the park. For instance, just to the right of the clubhouse, coming out from the right-center-field fence at an angle, was a wooden cut-out figure of

They called Gus Suhr a bum from the Booze Cage at Recreation Park.

Courtesy of Dick Dobbins

a bull, about fifteen feet high. It was an advertisement for Bull Durham tobacco, which came in little cloth sacks with an attached book of thin papers for roll-your-own cigarettes. Any batter who hit the bull sign with a fly ball was given fifty dollars by the tobacco company.

A short distance from the bull was an advertisement on the right-field fence for Tom Dillon's hat store on Market near Third Street. There was a drawing of the back of a man's head on the sign and it said, "Hit Me and Meet Me Face to Face." Batters who hit the sign could go down to meet Dillon and get a free hat.

Wade (Red) Killefer, the Missions manager, chased Christensen to the clubhouse after the outfielder dropped the ball.

Courtesy of Dick Dobbins

Finally, there was a gambler's chance, a long shot but still a possibility, to get an automatic home run by hitting a ball into a hole at the bottom of the clubhouse building. It was an opening of about a foot and a half square in the front of the building. Inside was the gas meter, left uncovered for the meter reader. According to the ground rules, a ball that rolled into the hole was a home run.

A truckload of local heroes and characters in the players line-ups—or just on the field—gained their fame at Recreation Park. "Pop" Hardy was the elderly, rotund, and bowlegged groundskeeper who kept a goat under the stands. He turned the goat loose to graze on the outfield grass during the week and thus help to keep the grass short. Before the games, he sold tickets at the bleachers window on Fifteenth Street. "Pop" had played baseball in the 1880s with the San Francisco Pioneers.

"Doc" Frost was a thin, mustached man in his fifties who served as the Seals' "ball boy," making sure the umpires always had enough baseballs available to keep the game going. He wore wild clown-like baseball uniforms which he bought himself. They usually consisted of different colored parts of various uniforms, but he had others too, including one in polka dots. He seldom wore the same uniform twice in a week. He reputedly was from a distinguished Boston family and well-fixed financially.

"Doc" put on an entertaining show at every game, catching pop foul balls which came off the protective screen in front of the grandstand. Allegedly he was paid twenty cents for each ball he caught one-handed, and fifteen cents for those he caught with two hands. The fans would yell "Go get it, Doc!" and cheer him when he made a one-handed catch with a flourish, thrusting the ball high over his head to show everyone he had it. When he missed one, he would sometimes take his cap off disgustedly and throw it to the ground.

Jack Condon, the chief usher, was known as "The Fourth Outfielder." His job, aided by a small staff of ushers, was to help the special park policemen recover balls hit into the grandstand, bleachers, or out into the street. He had a sign reading "Chief" on his baseball cap. His regular job was as a janitor at the Hall of Justice where he put in four hours work in the morning, and then returned after the game for night work.

Otto Makowski was a one-armed announcer who, solemnly and with a dramatic flair for grandeur of presentation, would stroll out to the pitcher's mound before each game was about to start. Holding a large megaphone in his one hand, he would slowly raise it to his lips, turn toward the left-field stands, and dramatically announce the "batteries for today's game," giving the names of the starting pitchers and catchers for each team. Then he would turn toward the right-field stands and repeat the announcement. Later, from the sidelines, he would announce each player and his position before the first time at bat. Makowski also made special announcements of coming events. Fans were especially fond of hearing Otto announce, "Thursdays, ladies will be omitted free."

Another memorable character was "Foghorn" Murphy. About 1911, he was employed by the Seals to ride a white horse up and down Market Street and verbally advertise the Seals games. Using a megaphone, Murphy would shout, "Baseball today," and announce the visiting team and the starting time at Recreation Park.

There were numerous oddballs and zany characters on the Seals and Missions teams. Some were particularly memorable, such as Walter "Seacap" Christensen, the center fielder for the Missions in the late Twenties. Sometimes called "Cuckoo" by the players, Christensen used to perform such antics as somersaults in the outfield while the game was in progress.

One of his favorite stunts was to do a quick headstand in the field before jumping up in time to catch a fly ball which had been hit exceptionally high. I'll always remember one game in which this trick didn't turn out too well. It was the last half of the ninth inning with the home team Seals at bat. The score was tied, there were two outs, a runner was on third base, and unless he scored, the game would go into extra innings. When the batter lofted an easy high fly to center field, an extra inning game appeared to be a certainty.

Seacap was in center, and he decided to give a little zing to the final moment by doing his headstand routine. The crowd laughed in appreciation as he did the upside-down-crowd pleaser, then stood up, set himself, and deftly caught the ball—almost. The ball popped out of his glove, the runner was already across the plate, and the game was suddenly over.

A screaming and cursing Wade (Red) Killefer, manager of the Missions, came charging out of the team dugout, wildly waving a bat over his head. He started running toward center field and Christensen, who was no longer smiling. Seacap, with a safe headstart, made it to the clubhouse before Killefer could reach him.

Perhaps San Francisco's all-time favorite baseball player and personality was Frank (Lefty) O'Doul, born in the City's meat-packing Butchertown district south of Market Street. He was first drafted by the New York Yankees from the Seals in 1918 as a rookie pitcher. Ten years later, after he had suffered arm trouble, he was drafted again from the Seals as an outfielder by the New York Giants. In 1929, while playing for the Philadelphia Phillies, he led the National League in hitting, batting a remarkable .398. He repeated in 1932, when he was with the Brooklyn Dodgers, this time with a mark of .368.

O'Doul's popularity as a player and manager with the Seals lasted over a span of more than thirty years. At Recreation Park it peaked in 1927 when "O'Doul

Frank "Lefty" O'Doul, native Butchertown product of San Francisco's sandlot baseball, was probably the most popular player in San Francisco history.

Courtesy of Dick Dobbins

Day" was held to honor him. Approximately 18,000 fans—8,000 of them kids admitted free—turned out for a double-header against the Missions. The South San Francisco Parlor of the Native Sons of the Golden West was prominent in organizing the event for their well-known member.

A highlight on O'Doul Day was the appearance of almost a dozen "Butchertown cowboys." Wearing red kerchiefs, chaps, and cowboy hats and riding horses, they circled the field in spirited dashes and gallops with O'Doul himself on horseback in the lead, waving to the delighted crowd of admirers. The "cowboys" were actually handlers who herded the cattle in and around the packing plants before the butchers took over.

GOOD LIFE IN HARD TIMES

O'Doul Day in 1927 at Recreation Park.

O'Doul, sometimes known as "The Man in the Green Suit," was exhilarated by the tribute. He pitched the game and came through in true fictional hero Frank Merriwell fashion. He threw a two-hit shutout in the afternoon game, and the Seals won 3 to 0. Before the game, thousands of youngsters had mobbed the field. O'Doul and the other players threw them miniature baseball bats and bags of peanuts, the latter donated by Gus Oliva, the wealthy "unofficial Mayor of North Beach." After the game O'Doul went up on top of the grandstand roof and threw dozens of baseballs over the top of the protective screen to the scrambling kids—and some adults—below on the field.

Between the morning and afternoon games, O'Doul was presented with a check for $2,000 by Harry Williams, president of the Pacific Coast League. The money had been raised through donations from fans, contributions having been limited to a maximum of one dollar.

The between-games show included cowboy stunts, a rope-throwing exhibition by "Knucker" Sullivan, the "champion of the world," and the singing of "When Irish Eyes Are Smiling" by R. T. Hunter, the commuter known as the "Caruso of the Ferries." The Columbia Park Boys Club staged a skit called "Kill the Umpire." Somebody borrowed Gus Oliva's straw hat

and held it up at the plate while a pitcher threw a fast ball right through the crown.

The nearest thing to the excitement of O'Doul Day that I can recall at Recreation Park was the day Babe Ruth and Lou Gehrig of the Yankees came to town after the World Series was over back east. They headed two all-star teams in an exhibition game before leaving for a Japan tour. The teams had eye-catching uniforms with the names "Busting Babes" and "Larruping Lous" prominently emblazoned across the chests. After the game, the two stars distributed little miniature bats on the field, walking and pushing their way through a swirling wave of kids who clutched at them, just trying to touch them, as well as get one of the toy bats.

In 1926, San Francisco banker Herbert Fleishhacker purchased the Pacific Coast League franchise of Vernon, a Los Angeles suburb, and transferred it to San Francisco so that the City could have continuous baseball. When the Seals were on the road traveling, the new team, the rejuvenated Missions, played as the home club at Recreation Park. The franchise cost Fleishhacker a reported $300,000.

Despite Fleishhacker's spending spree for players, as in 1914, the Missions did not catch on with San Francisco baseball followers. They were considered interlopers, and their gate receipts suffered accordingly. The biggest crowds they drew were when they played the Seals at home. The Missions stayed in San Francisco for 12 years, five at Recreation Park. When

WHEN THE SEALS PLAYED BASEBALL

the 1937 season ended at Seals Stadium with a lot of red ink on the club books, the owners finally threw in the towel. The League approved the transfer of the team franchise to Hollywood for the 1938 season.

The great rivalry in professional Bay Area baseball was between the Seals and the Oakland Oaks. Crowds were the thickest, noise the loudest, and feelings the most intense when these two clubs played a series of games. Thousands of fans would travel across the Bay by ferryboat to either Recreation Park or to the Oaks' park in Emeryville. When the Seals were the home team, they played their Thursday afternoon and Sunday morning games with the Oaks in Emeryville.

Although the Pacific Coast League was in the highest bracket of the many professional minor baseball leagues that existed in those years, the so-called Triple-A bracket, the Seal ballplayers going over to Oakland rode streetcars from their homes just like any ordinary worker. "I took the Hayes Street car down to the Ferry Building from my house," recalled Gus Suhr, whose father owned stables at Pierce and Eddy Streets. "I'd buy a Key Route ticket, the fare was twenty-one cents, and take the ferryboat to the Key Pier and the orange electric cars to 40th and San Pablo. Then I'd walk up to the Emeryville ball park, a few blocks away. We'd all go over individually, although sometimes four or five of us would happen to catch the same boat. Some of the fans would be on the boat and train too, and we'd talk with them sometimes on the way over. No, nobody would ask you for your autograph in those days.

"Even Bert Ellison, our manager, would ride over that way. It was a fast trip on the Key Route. Twelve minutes on the boat and then seven or eight minutes to 40th and San Pablo."

Riding the ferryboats to Oakland and back, long before Suhr played, was Jim Leary. "Kids got two bits to 'pack the turkey' for the players," Leary related. "Every ball player had to pack his own 'roll.' That was a brown twill bag that rolled up like a valet pack. Inside of it went his uniform, his glove, shoes, and his bat, which stuck out of the roll like the neck of a turkey. I used to pack Buck Weaver's 'turkey.' He was the Seals' third baseman. I'd go down and meet Buck at the Ferry Building and he'd buy me coffee and a doughnut on the boat on the way over. I'd get in the game free over in Emeryville. On the way back he'd buy me another doughnut and coffee, and I'd get into the afternoon game at Recreation Park free."

The players and the fans on both sides of the Bay took delight in the rivalry. There was the case of "Rowdy" Elliott, a belligerent Oakland catcher who was a favorite with the Oak fans but the target for constant abuse, and occasional thrown cushions, when he appeared at Recreation Park.

Eddie Hennessy, a veteran semi-pro baseball manager and avid Seal rooter, remembers with relish one game when the slow-footed Elliott was deliberately served up to the delighted San Francisco fans for derision.

"After 'Rowdy' received his usual warm welcome of boos as he stepped up to the plate to bat," Hennessy related, "he hit a ball on one bounce back to the Seal pitcher. Instead of routinely throwing to first base for the out, the pitcher threw the ball back to the catcher and the catcher relayed the ball to the first baseman, and they still got the lumbering 'Rowdy' by ten yards. The crowd roared and you almost could see 'Rowdy' turn as red as a tomato.

"Ball players were sure different in those days," Hennessy said. "They were always chatting with the fans. When they returned to Old Rec from Oakland for the Sunday afternoon game, the players would enter the park under the grandstand and pass the old right field bleachers on their way to the clubhouse in center field. The fans would ask the players who won the morning game and how it went. The players would stop and tell you who won, who pitched, who may have hit a homer, and everything else. Ball players had class in the old Pacific League.

"And I remember that it was nothing to see Doug McWeeney of the Seals pitch a doubleheader on a Sunday. Do you think they could ask a pitcher today to work a doubleheader? The player would want overtime, or would contact his agent to file suit."

The last game at Recreation Park was played in October, 1930, after the World Series ended. An all-star team of major leaguers lost to the Seals 17 to 7, in an exhibition game. Jack Kavanaugh, a young southpaw pitcher then in the Bay Area semi-pro leagues, pitched one inning for major league stars because the Philadelphia Athletics were interested in him as a prospect. Kavanaugh, later the Chief Probation Officer in San Francisco, remembers that one of the major leaguers managed to hit a home run over the center-field clubhouse, the last one in Recreation Park. Fittingly, it was Harry Heilmann, who had hit the first recorded home run fifteen years before.

5

Fillmore in the 1920s

Like New York, San Francisco had a lively Jewish section in the Twenties and Thirties. It flourished as a part of the Fillmore District for about forty years. Before the Jewish families living there moved out to more fashionable residential areas of the city or to the suburbs, shoppers poured into the busy food stores and markets on Fillmore and McAllister Streets on Saturday nights and Sundays. There they bought Kosher meats and chickens at the butcher and poultry counters. On Saturday nights stores opened after sundown when the twenty-four hour Jewish sabbath ended and stayed open until eleven o'clock.

This heavy concentration of Jewish families and businesses began to appear immediately after the 1906 earthquake and fire razed much of the South-of-Market area. Many of the Jews who had come to San Francisco before the turn of the century had settled in the houses that lined Minna, Natoma, Clementina, and other narrow streets "south of the slot." When their homes were demolished they moved up to McAllister and the Fillmore District.

For a short boom period after the 1906 catastrophe all but leveled Market Street and the main downtown business core, Fillmore Street even served as San Francisco's main business artery. However, by 1912 the large merchandising stores had returned to downtown locations, abandoning temporary sites on Fillmore as well as on Van Ness Avenue and Mission Street, also untouched by the fire.

Though the Fillmore, as it has always been known, was dominated to a large degree by the Jewish merchants and stores on McAllister Street and up Fillmore to Sutter, the district had a varied ethnic and cultural mix. The City's Japanese colony was concentrated in a few blocks on Post and Sutter Streets, east of Fillmore. A substantial number of the City's black families were clustered around Ellis and Scott Streets.

Italian, French, Irish, and Russian and other nationalities were also well represented.

In the decade I recall most vividly, the 1920s, sweeping metal arches studded with white electric light bulbs reached up from the four corners of each intersection on Fillmore between Fulton and Sacramento Streets. The arches curved high over each of the fourteen intersections like the illuminated ribs of a huge umbrella. From the elevated center points where the four branches met, large and ornate globes of opaque glass hung down on chains, and smaller globes of light sat on top.

At one time, additional night lighting along Fillmore came from gas street lamps mounted on short iron poles. These were lit up at dusk by a city lamplighter carrying an ignition stick who walked a regular route like a mailman.

The arches had been erected in 1907, shortly after the fire, by the newly organized Fillmore Street Improvement Association. This merchants' group was praised for "making Fillmore the most brilliantly illuminated street in America" and adding "glamour and distinction" to its business district. The original cost of the arches was paid by an extra three-dollar-per front-foot assessment on property along Fillmore Street. By 1913, the Association had 225 members and proudly boasted that the electric arches had cost more than $18,000 to build and $2,000 a year to maintain. The arches remained in working order until 1943 when, their lights extinguished by World War II dimout restrictions, they were torn down to provide scrap metal for war-industry use.

The variety in the types of businesses and activities in the area was dazzling. Food, of course, was a chief commodity. In the 1920s, the Fillmore had several heavily patronized food markets, with an emphasis on Kosher meats, fish, and delicatessen

At Fillmore and Geary Streets during the nighttime Diamond Jubilee Parade in 1925 honoring California's seventy-fifth birthday.

Courtesy of the Matt Boxer Collection

items. The store windows displayed tempting bakery goods, fresh candies, smoked meats, chickens roasting on spits, and choice fruits and vegetables. A block off Fillmore, on Steiner Street, the Sanchez family had a small tamale and tortilla factory and store.

But food wasn't the only concern. In fact, if you had overindulged you could weigh yourself free at three different drug stores. Caesar Attell, one of the three fighting Attell brothers of past boxing glory (the others were Abe and Monte) had a jewelry and watch repair shop on Fillmore near Turk Street. The Bank of Italy had two branches on Fillmore, one near McAllister and the other on the corner of Post. Also on Fillmore were music stores, hat stores, and a Woolworth five and ten, with its dark, oiled wood floors and open display counters polished to a shiny luster.

There was also variety in the entertainment available. The upstairs New Fillmore Billiard Parlor near O'Farrell attracted hustlers and hangers-on. And the second-floor Majestic Hall ballroom on the corner of Geary drew dance lovers from all corners of the City. No less than four United Cigar stores occupied Fillmore corners—and all had "21" dice games up front in view. Zimet's Toys fascinated the kids; it was a narrow walk-in store lined with magazines, tricycles, dolls and doll buggies, and games. At Son's Sporting Goods, where we bought our baseball mitts, we could pick up free books from the manufacturers on how to play baseball like the current greats.

Of course, there were clothes stores in almost every block on Fillmore. And in those days before medical and dental buildings, doctors and dentists occupied "one-flight-up" offices, over the ground-floor stores. The former headquarters and social rooms of the San Francisco Labor Lyceum Association were in a basement at 1740 O'Farrell Street. The old Workmen's Circle and Socialist Party activities centered here.

Crowds would gather on the street at certain times of the year. Radios were not commonplace in homes yet and groups formed around loudspeakers in front of stores to listen to broadcasts of World Series baseball games or round-by-round broadcasts of championship prize fights.

In 1927, "Lindy" flew into San Francisco's Mills Field and was paraded up Market Street to City Hall for an official welcome by Mayor Rolph. Here Lindbergh waves at the crowds on Market and "Sunny Jim" checks out the voters at the curb.

Courtesy of San Francisco Department of Public Works

During the Jewish High Holidays, Rosh Hashanah and Yom Kippur, other crowds could be found throughout the day in front of the district's three synagogues on Geary, Webster, and Golden Gate Avenue. Many people merely came outside periodically for some fresh air and a break from praying at the services inside. A good percentage, however, stayed outside all day. Some couldn't afford membership in the congregations. Others were nonbelievers who nevertheless felt a need to identify themselves as Jews on the special days and "be counted."

If you could have taken a walk around the district with me in 1927, you would have gained a pretty good sense of the old-time Fillmore District as it was. A few details will serve to put the year in perspective. Nine-

teen twenty-seven was the year that "Sunny Jim" Rolph, Jr., was elected to his fifth term as San Francisco's mayor, defeating Supervisor James E. Power by a vote of approximately 90,000 to 59,000. Rolph was a florid and sartorially elegant Hollywood prototype of a big-city mayor. This was also the year of the "Long Count" in Chicago's Soldier's Field—Jack Dempsey lost the world heavyweight championship after forgetting to go to a neutral corner quickly enough following his seventh-round knockdown of Gene Tunney. In June, Captain Charles A. Lindbergh made the first solo flight across the Atlantic in his single-engine plane, *the Spirit of St. Louis.* In September, Lindy flew the tiny plane into San Francisco's Mills Field municipal airport, below San Bruno on the Bay shore, and was paraded up Market Street to City Hall for an official welcome by Mayor Rolph.

If we had started our walk down around McAllister and then headed up Fillmore toward Sutter, making some detours on the side streets, we would have covered the heart of the Fillmore District's commercial and cultural life as I knew it. Some of the places I would have pointed out are described in the following pages and identified on the map, page 81.

1. Dave's Barber Shop. 1215 McAllister Street. Dave was Barney Apfel's father. Barney was my best friend and a classmate at the Golden Gate grammar school, a few blocks away. The Apfels lived in the upper flat two doors away from the shop. Every Sunday night I would go over there to meet Barney, his father, mother, and sisters Bertha and Fannie, and we would all go to the old Orpheum Theater downtown on O'Farrell Street, across from the present Macy's. The family had reservations every Sunday night for a string of twenty-five cent seats in the first row of the center section way up in the second and highest balcony, where high-power binoculars were commonly used to watch the vaudeville acts below.

One time a movie was made around the corner from the Apfels' flat on Fillmore. This was long before San Francisco became a favorite location for movie and TV productions. It was the silent film *Greed*, based on Frank Norris's novel *McTeague*. The film-crew members shooed back from camera range the crowds that had gathered to watch stars Gibson Garland, Jean Hersholt, and Zasu Pitts, and director Erich von Stroheim.

2. Cat & Fiddle. 1015 Fillmore Street. This candy store sported a small, classic marble-topped soda fountain with a brass foot rail and about six stools. It also had a few wooden booths in the back. Morris and Pauline Schneider were the owners. Morris wore a white apron and coat and had reddish, bushy hair that stuck out straight on both sides. When we lived around the corner on McAllister, my mother used to give me fifteen cents every day to get a malted milk here after school in an attempt to fatten up a very skinny kid. Milk shakes were only ten cents, and so were fresh-made roast beef sandwiches. The malted milks and shakes were delicious—rich, creamy, cool but not so cold that you felt a pain over your eyes. I didn't get fatter despite the hundreds of malted milks I drank over a period of several years.

Morris made candy in the back of the store and kids would come in and ask to help him. He would let us crank the taffy machine and sometimes dip the ice cream bars in chocolate. Every Christmas season, Morris put a huge red-and-white-striped candy cane in the front window. You were invited to guess its weight, step into the store, and fill out an entry slip.

The closest guess won the cane. Morris changed the weight of the cane every year.

3. Royal Ice Cream Company. 1155 McAllister Street. The Royal had the best selection of "home-made" ice cream in the district—not just the popular maple nut and pistachio to go with the regular vanilla, strawberry, and chocolate, but exotic flavors for those days such as tutti-frutti and rocky road. Banana splits at twenty cents were a treat given by parents to their children on special occasions such as a school promotion. The numerous peanut and popcorn wagons that circulated around the City used to stop here in the morning to load up their stock of ice cream supplies, and in the evening to unload. You would often see five or six little horse-drawn popcorn wagons lined up along the curb in front. There was the time that little Joe Gordon, riding a new bike borrowed from a neighbor, lost control and ran into one of the wagons. The frightened horse started kicking wildly and Joe came out of it with a broken leg.

4. Langendorf's Bakery. 1160 McAllister Street. Langendorf's was considered to be the Number One Jewish bakery in the neighborhood. During the High Holidays, from Rosh Hashanah to Yom Kippur, the windows of the retail store would have on display jumbo-sized "challah" (egg twist) breads. Some were filled with raisins and candied fruit pieces, and the braided top crusts were sprinkled with colored candy beads or poppy seeds.

Bernard Langendorf came to America from Vienna when he was sixteen. He moved his small bakery west from Chicago to San Francisco in 1895, establishing Langendorf's Vienna Bakery on Folsom Street, south of Market. His rye bread was reportedly made from an old Viennese formula. After the 1906 earthquake and fire destroyed his small bakery, Bernard re-opened at 878 McAllister, near Laguna. In 1915, with $400,000 raised from ten prominent San Franciscans, he built a new, expanded plant at 1160 McAllister. The emphasis was on wholesaling. By the early Twenties, a fleet of delivery wagons with two-horse teams rented from a nearby stable, together with several battery-operated White trucks, were covering the City. Neighboring merchants and former employees remember Bernard boarding the No. 5 McAllister streetcar and carrying a paper bag full of bakery cash on his way to the bank.

5. Ukraine Bakery. 1125 McAllister Street. One of the many excellent bakeries in the Fillmore District,

One of Langendorf's new White delivery trucks (early 1920s).

Courtesy of Herman Guehring

the Ukraine was famous for its bagels, pumpernickel bread, and apple strudel. Later it moved across the street and down to the corner of Webster, where it remained for many years.

6. **Waxman's Bakery.** 1080 McAllister Street. As Avis is to Hertz, so was Waxman's to Langendorf's. Among many Yiddish-speaking critics of bakery goods, Waxman's was considered to have the finest rye bread in town. The founder, Louis Waxman, formerly worked for Langendorf's.

7. **Heineman & Stern.** 1040 McAllister Street. This was a sausage and meat-products factory with a retail counter. You walked into the white-tile-front store to a wooden floor covered with clean sawdust. Featured were displays of Kosher-style hot dogs, salamis, and balonies. The factory, established in 1877 on Larkin Street, moved to this location after the 1906

earthquake and fire. It remained here until 1971 when the business was sold and moved across the Bay to San Lorenzo.

8. **Jefferson Market.** 1002 Buchanan Street. The Jefferson, owned by I. Goldstein, was one of the four principal fresh-chicken headquarters for San Francisco's Jewish community. The others were Sosnick's, Diller's, and Shenson's. The market also had a Kosher meat counter, but the place bulged with screeching chickens. A cloud of feathers constantly filled the air. Cages of noisy chickens were piled up on the sidewalk outside, leaving only narrow aisles for passing pedestrians and entering customers. You selected the chicken you wanted and one of the clerks would take it, squawking and flapping, out of the cage. He would carry it back to the rear of the market where the "shochet," the Kosher slaughterer, killed it with a neat straight-edge razor slit across the neck and hung it head down to let it bleed. Then it was plucked clean of feathers, wrapped in a newspaper, and handed to you.

9. **H. Koblick.** 1010 Fillmore Street. This sta-

Mr. Koblik sold us our comic books (1919).

tionery and book store was where I bought my comic books. They were large books, square in shape, with stiff cardboard covers in color. Barney Google and Spark Plug, his horse, were great favorites; an ostrich named Rudy occasionally appeared in his books. Other popular comic characters were Moon Mullins, Mutt and Jeff, Ella Cinders, the Katzenjammer Kids, Gasoline Alley, The Nebbs, Toonerville Folks, and The Gumps. *Bringing Up Father* starred not only Jiggs and Maggie, but Dinty Moore and his corned beef and cabbage restaurant. My personal favorite was *The Bungles*, featuring George Bungle, who was repeatedly being bitten by neighborhood dogs and saying "whooie" as he spun around in circles tussling with them.

10. Schubert's Bakery. 1014 Fillmore Street. Mouth-watering aromas floated out of this small bakery all the time. The specialty was displayed in the window: flaky macaroon tarts with jam filling under a baked hardtop crust. Two other popular treats were Hawaiian Delight, a combination of chocolate cake, crushed pineapple, and lots of whipped cream, and Burnt Almond Cake, toasted nuts sliced and spread in generous amounts on whipped cream piled on top of a white cake. Also fresh whipped cream puffs, dusted with confectioner's sugar, and chocolate eclairs as good as any in town at six for twenty-five cents.

11. Congregation Keneseth Israel. 935 Webster Street. One of the Fillmore District's two orthodox synagogues. The other was Congregation Anshey Sfard at 1032 Golden Gate Avenue (now on Clement Street). Keneseth Israel was founded by religious immigrant Jews who wanted to follow strictly the precepts their families had lived by in the Old Country. They had split away from another group which founded the Beth Israel Congregation, a conservative—that is, less orthodox—synagogue on Geary Street. The cornerstone for the Webster Street building was laid in

At Fillmore and McAllister Streets, 1930. Schubert's Bakery can be seen on the right.

Courtesy of the San Francisco Public Utilities Commission

1903. Congregation Keneseth Israel now holds services in the Jack Tar Office Building on Post Street.

Chaim Weizmann, later to become Israel's first president, spoke here in 1925 while on a fund-raising mission for Zionism. Jewish stars of the entertainment world, including Eddie Cantor, Jan Peerce and his brother Richard Tucker, and Morey Amsterdam, would come here to pray or to recite *kaddish*, the memorial prayer, on the *yahrzeit*, the anniversary of the deaths, of close family members. The late Hal March of TV's original "$64 Question" program, better known in the Fillmore as Harold Mendelson who clerked in his father's delicatessen on McAllister Street, attended Hebrew school here. So did retired San Francisco Judge Albert Axelrod.

12. White's Kosher Restaurant. 937 Webster Street. This restaurant was next door to the synagogue. Mr. and Mrs. Abraham White supervised a strictly Kosher restaurant, observing all dietary laws "according to the book." They served Kosher meats, poultry, and eggs, no dairy products at any time.

13. Schindler's Dining Room. 1207 Golden Gate Avenue. This restaurant was in the lower flat of a small Victorian house. Besides being preferred by some as more homelike—*haimish* in Yiddish—Schindler's was handy for the spillover diners from Diller's next door on crowded weekends and holidays. The food was good, and it was even a little cheaper than the more famous Diller's. One touch of class was an awning running from the entrance to the curb, although I can't remember ever seeing a taxicab drive up. Mr. Schindler was unforgettable. Wearing a white shirt and black bow tie, he acted as a combination greeter and waiter. He was tall and completely baldheaded, with dark eyebrows and a deep baritone voice—an early version of Kojak. At that time, he reminded me of "Bull" Montana, an ex-wrestler who was a silent-movie comedy villain. Mrs. Schindler supervised the kitchen.

14. Diller's Strictly Kosher Restaurant. 1233 Golden Gate. Diller's was the biggest, the best, and the most popular Jewish restaurant in the neighborhood —and the City. Dinner cost a *bissel* (little) more— seventy-five cents instead of the fifty-cent price at Schindler's—but it was worth it. On weekend nights Diller's was packed. Many Jewish families returning to the City from the popular Sunday picnics of that day at San Mateo Park or Alum Rock Park in San Jose would come directly to Diller's for dinner before going home.

Diller's later changed hands and became Kretsch's Kosher Restaurant without losing its high rating for Jewish-style meals.

15. Moshe Menuhin, Language Teacher. 1043 Steiner Street. Moshe Menuhin was the principal for a short time at our Hebrew school in the red-brick Aaron A. Alper Memorial Building, at Grove and Buchanan Streets. He had a little boy named Yehudi who played the violin—quite well. I have no personal memory of Yehudi, though I remember hearing that he had to practice on the violin a lot and could not come out to play with the rest of the kids. Some San Franciscans today speak of visits to the Menuhins at this house where Yehudi used to ride his scooter in the back yard. The Menuhins acquired the house from Congregation

Yehudi Menuhin used to ride his scooter in the back yard (1925).

Keneseth Israel, the Webster Street synagogue where Moshe once headed the Hebrew school. Visitors described it as bright, well-kept, and full of books. There were two practice pianos for daughters Hepzibah and Yalta—a baby grand in the living room, and an upright in the kitchen so that Mrs. Menuhin could oversee practice sessions while she was cooking. Visitors remember that Yehudi often had to wear gloves when he went outdoors. Yehudi and his sisters never went to a public or private school. Moshe tutored them in all their subjects except French. The house today remains essentially unchanged; it still has its original wood parquet floors and much of its original charm. The present owner, mother of a University of California faculty member and a peninsula doctor, remembers with

warm pleasure the day that Yehudi came over to visit and wandered around the old house recalling his early years there.

16. Golden Gate School. 1512 Golden Gate Avenue. The school has an annex now and a new play area, but the original school building still looked the same when I walked through it gingerly not too long ago. The former hard-top baseball "field" still tilts up about ten degrees toward Golden Gate Avenue. Third base was the corner of the concrete and brick building during the daily noon hour game we played with a tennis ball. The pitcher lobbed the ball on one bounce to the "batter" with a lot of breaking "English" on it. The batter attempted to hit it with his fist. The most exciting defensive position in the field was the deep outfielder. He stationed himself completely outside of the yard on Golden Gate Avenue, separated from the rest by the chain-link fence. Long soaring fly balls that cleared the fence were often caught in the middle of the traffic-heavy street. Screaming motorists slammed on their brakes in terror as they attempted to avoid running down a sprinting or circling future Joe Di Maggio.

Principal Effie Smith cracked students' palms sharply with a wooden ruler for disciplinary punishment. No one worried in those days about indignant parents filing suits to protest cruel and inhuman treatment. Every morning we pledged allegiance to the small flag in our classroom. We sang "Good morning to you, good morning to you, we're all in our places, with sunshiny faces" to the teacher and ate Graham crackers with our little bottles of milk. We bought thin, flat, chocolate-covered French nougat squares called "housie-housies" for a penny, as well as licorice candy whips, Tootsie Rolls, and jelly beans—all invitingly laid out in a glass case of candy smorgasbord at the little grocery store near the school. The grocery is still there but the housie-housies" are gone. After-school fist fights were scheduled, and settled, at Alamo Square Park, two blocks away on Fulton Street.

Our principal gambling vice was matching baseball cards, the ones with photographs of Pacific Coast League players on them. They came in the boxes of Home Run Kisses chews and Ruf-Nek candy bars that we bought at the ball games at Recreation Park. The cards had tear-off coupons that we saved to redeem for prizes.

17. The Practical Hat and Umbrella Works. 1132 Fillmore Street. My Uncle Louie's store was an ancient, dilapidated wooden structure even in those days. Uncle Louie cleaned and blocked hats and repaired umbrellas there. He had a small group of friends, unemployed or retired, who hung around the store and kept him company. Later, he married and moved into a house in the rear of the store with his bride, my Aunt Katie. "Those Wedding Bells Are Breaking Up That Old Gang Of Mine" was a popular song of the day. We had it on a record which I always played on our wind-up Victrola; it described exactly what happened to the gang at Uncle Louie's store.

I used to sit in Uncle Louie's 1917 black Dodge open sedan, which he parked at the curb in front of the store. It had a black cloth top and, for use in rain and wind, detachable snap-button side curtains with slivers of transparent isinglass for visibility and light. It had a notched hand throttle below the steering wheel, both a hand brake and stick shift protruding up high above the center of the floorboard in the front, and a foot starter that looked like a mine detonator. Uncle Louie had bought the Dodge new as a debonair and carefree bachelor. He was the first member of our immediate family to own a car.

18. Boston Lunch. 1123 Fillmore. A counter and stools ran the length of this narrow restaurant, which adjoined the red-brick streetcar barn. White porcelain letters spelling out "Boston Lunch" were glued on the window. The lunch counter drew heavy trade from the conductors, motormen, and carbarn maintenance men. I remember the crisp, well-browned waffles Boston Lunch turned out on the row of waffle irons in the window. Served with lots of butter and maple syrup, the batter must have been made according to a secret recipe, since I have never tasted waffles as good since. One of the special plates was three hot cakes, two eggs, and a large patty of sausage for twenty-five cents.

19. The Carbarn. Southwest corner of Fillmore and Turk Streets. The barn was used principally for the Number 22 Fillmore and Number 4 Turk and Eddy streetcars privately owned by the Market Street Railway Company. The two sets of rails which ran along Fillmore Street had spurs branching off into the carbarn. In those days the streetcars stopped at every corner with no skipping. The old power substation, across the street on the southeast corner, continues to generate current for the City's transit system.

20. The American Theatre. 1226 Fillmore Street. This was one of seven silent movie houses in an eight-block range. Of course, there was no TV then to cut down business. When people wanted entertainment

they went out. Fillmore Street was busy and bustling at night, and with seven movie houses, provided a wide range to select from. I remember that the American had been the Lyric Theatre. And my father recalls the construction of the Chutes amusement area on this same block immediately after the 1906 earthquake and fire. For a short time Fillmore became the City's combined version of New York's Broadway, Fifth Avenue, and Coney Island. My father describes seeing and hearing Sophie Tucker belt out songs on a Chutes stage.

At the American, the admission fee for kids under twelve was a nickel. Friday night was Country Store and Amateur Night on the stage. I remember desperately competing for one of the merchandise prizes, usually a shopping bag full of groceries. My "act" was a unique imitation of Charley Chaplin—done in a cowboy suit, including chaps and holstered toy revolver. I received no groceries; just a quick hustle off the stage after a few sympathetic handclaps.

21. The New Fillmore Theatre. 1329 Fillmore Street. This was the sister movie house to the New Mission Theatre, still in business in the Mission district. The New Fillmore was the aristocrat of the Fillmore movie palaces, and the only one that regularly booked the "pictures" immediately after they had appeared downtown on Market Street at the first-run houses. Live organ music accompanied the action on the silent screen. On weekend nights the half-block-long foyer and carpeted lobby were choked with waiting crowds behind red velvet ropes.

The Saturday matinee feature was Ellen Rose's kiddie revue, performed on the stage with regular weekly stars, usually either singers or toe dancers. Tommy Harris, now owner of Tommy's Joynt, the Van Ness Avenue beer and sandwich emporium, was one of the boy vocalists. Another was Joaquin Garay, later to become a local headliner and nightclub operator. During Christmas week the Rose troupe of tykes appeared in special evening performances of a Happy Yuletide show. Admission was a dime for kids under twelve. When I was still a gangling, overgrown eleven-year-old, I had to show a copy of my birth certificate as proof of my age to the cashier in the ticket booth.

22. George Haas & Sons. Makers of Fine Candies. 1355 Fillmore. This candy store, soda fountain, and restaurant was the elegant "confectionary" of the neighborhood, one of a chain in the City. It had all the classic touches—dark wood paneling and booths, black-and-white tile floors, a long marble-topped fountain, woven-cane-seat chairs, and waitresses and candy

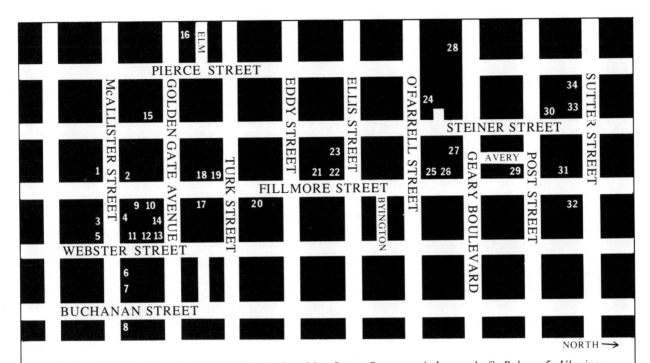

1. Dave's Barber Shop, 2. Cat & Fiddle, 3. Royal Ice Cream Company, 4. Langendorf's Bakery, 5. Ukraine Bakery. 6. Waxman's Bakery, 7. Heineman & Stern, 8. Jefferson Market, 9. H. Koblick, 10. Schubert's Bakery, 11. Congregation Keneseth Israel, 12. White's Kosher Restaurant, 13. Schindler's Dining Room, 14. Diller's Strictly Kosher Restaurant, 15. Moshe Menuhin, Language Teacher, 16. Golden Gate School, 17. The Practical Hat and Umbrella Works, 18. Boston Lunch, 19. The Carbarn, 20. The American Theatre, 21. The New Fillmore Theatre, 22. George Haas & Sons, 23. Princess Theatre, 24. Peacock Confectionary, 25. California Cafe and Bakery, 26. The Progress Theatre, 27. Congregation Beth Israel, 28. Hamilton Junior High School, 29. The Wagon, 30. Dreamland Skating Rink, 31. Temple Theatre, 32. Goldenrath's Delicatessen, 33. Sutter Theatre, 34. Iceland Pavilion.

clerks dressed in black uniforms with white lace trimmings like French maids in the movies. One side of the long front shop was lined with curved glass candy display cases. Haas made excellent chocolates and had a good trade in gift boxes. The soda fountain occupied the other side of the front shop, and the restaurant was in the back. Haas' ice cream sodas were probably the best in town. They were served in tall soda glasses in metal base holders. The bubbly foam header on the sodas tickled your nose. The "all-around chocolate" (chocolate ice cream and soda) was a real winner.

23. Princess Theatre. 1671 Ellis Street. The Princess was a bona fide vaudeville theater. It ran five feature acts plus a movie. Admission for kids was ten cents. An orchestra occupied the sunken pit behind a shiny brass rail for the vaudeville bill. On the back of each seat was a coin box holding a box of candy for five cents. Standard acts included unicyclists, jugglers,

tap dancers, acrobats, ballroom dance teams, magicians, ballet duos, and comedy acts that obviously were never going to play the Palace in New York. Occasionally a trained dog act appeared. Wilt Gunzendorfer and his band played in the pit, and occasionally on the stage. Gunzendorfer was also featured during the summers at Guernewood Park in the Russian River vacation area where we went for two weeks every year.

24. Peacock Confectionary. 1816 O'Farrell Street. The Peacock, run by A. Heubner, was one of those small bakery jewels. Two cast iron hitching posts with jockey figures, left over from horse and buggy days, stood guard at curbside. A bell tinkled above the entrance door when you opened it, and Mr. Huebner himself often came out in a white apron and coat to wait on you, and offer a friendly hello. Everything was lusciously tasty and "made from the best stuff," as my mother used to say. I particularly remember the layered pineapple-filled cakes with a thin chocolate frosting crust on top, decorated in a white-cap wave design; also a delicate cheesecake with a brown-baked soft top. In the showcases were artistic creations made of sugar for which Mr. Huebner had won awards at fairs and exhibitions.

25. California Cafe and Bakery. 1515 Fillmore. This was the place of tough decisions. The customer had to choose from great soft Parker House and hard-crusted German rolls, thick real cream puffs and eclairs, flaky layered Napoleons, strawberry and banana short cakes oozing lots of fresh whipped cream, snails, butterhorns, and bear claws. Custard, rich in eggs, was baked in thick, deep brown cups with just the right thickness of brown-and-yellow "skin" topping. These were all set out on a white-and-gray-streaked marble table top, along with other tempting desserts for you to pick from and carry back to your table.

26. The Progress Theatre. 1535 Fillmore. The Progress was another of the five-cents-for-kids movie houses, probably the smallest one. It had no balcony. Cowboy serials were the Saturday matinee feature attraction. I remember Art Acord and Buffalo Bill; Ken Maynard and his horse, Tarzan, and Yakima Canutt, the "world champion cowboy." Also Harry Carey, Hoot Gibson, Jack Hoxie, and Tom Mix and *his* horse, Tony. There were also William S. Hart, the original stone-faced actor, and Buck Jones and *his* horse, Silver. All films were backed up with the usual organ music, featuring the William Tell Overture during the chases.

27. Congregation Beth Israel. 1839 Geary Street. Beth Israel was the conservative synagogue of the district. The congregation was formed in 1872; it dedicated this steel and brick building in September, 1908. Past presidents of Beth Israel have included former San Francisco commissioner Ben Blumenthal, ex-newspaperman Harvey Wing, and former Superior Court Judge Isadore M. Golden, whose father served as assistant cantor. Cantor Joseph Rabinowitz was there from 1890 to 1943. His fifty-three years are believed to be the longest period of service in one synagogue for any cantor in the United States.

The congregation merged several years ago with the reform Temple Judea and now shares the modern building and facilities on Brotherhood Way near Lake Merced. The Geary Street building, still containing the original stained glass windows, *Bimah*, or pulpit, and

rows of wooden seats, has been leased in recent years.

28. Hamilton Junior High School. Geary near Scott. The school was built in 1875 and torn down in 1930. It stood next door to Girl's High School, now Benjamin Franklin Junior High. It was a San Francisco integrated public school, long before any of us heard of the word "integration." I do not know the percentage breakdown, but our student body was predominantly a mixture of white, black, and Japanese kids, reflecting the ethnic makeup of the portion of the Western Addition District from which it drew students. Post Street from Fillmore to Octavia was the City's main Japanese commercial strip, just as it is today, and Japanese families lived principally in that section bounded by Geary and Sutter Streets.

No racial problems existed at Hamilton that I can remember. Busing was not only unknown to us, but would not have made sense anyway, since most of us walked to an already integrated school from home. My contemporaries at Hamilton included Vernon Alley, the jazz musician; Municipal Judge Charley Becker of South San Francisco, and Herman Hittenberger, the San Francisco truss tycoon.

This building first appeared in the San Francisco City Directory for 1876-77 as the Geary Street Primary School. In 1906, after the earthquake and fire, it housed the City's municipal courts, then called Justice Courts.

29. The Wagon. Post Street between Fillmore and Steiner, corner of Avery Alley. This place served the best hamburger sandwiches in town, according to many San Franciscans. The fried-egg sandwiches were also rated high. The lunchroom was converted from an old wooden wagon that was roofed over and fitted with standup counters. It was entered via a porch and a couple of stairs off the street. The Wagon received heavy trade from the regular crowd of fans after the Friday night fights and the Tuesday night wrestling matches at Dreamland Rink, a half-block away. The hamburgers were fried on an open grill together with chopped raw onions which were slightly burned deliberately, and then served on thin slices of plain white bread. A sandwich, hamburger or egg, cost ten cents.

30. Dreamland Skating Rink. 1725 Steiner Street. The wooden arena here was demolished in 1926-27 and replaced with the present Winterland Arena. Dreamland was built as a roller skating rink, but was also used for boxing and wrestling shows. At different times during the Twenties, I sold the *Exam-*

iner and *Chronicle* newspapers and the *Knockout*, *Redhead*, and *Referee* boxing magazines just outside of Dreamland in the early evenings before the boxing and wrestling cards got under way. I can remember seeing professional fight cards made up of four-round bouts only. Since it wasn't until 1925 that ten-round bouts were permitted by state legislature action, I must have been about seven or eight years old when I first saw some savvy pro feint an opponent into position for a payoff punch.

I usually managed to get inside Dreamland as a paper and program vendor, or through a sympathetic ticket taker on a side door after the bouts started. The list of fighters I saw in action includes names that only fight fans from those days will recognize: Frankie Denny, the "Oakland Windmill" clown middleweight; Freddie Hoppe and Billy Adams in several of their Pier Six brawls; Tommy Cello, the sharpshooting North Beach lightweight; welterweights "Potrero Pete" Meyers, "K.O." Eddie Roberts, Virgil "Lefty" Cooper, and Fred "Dummy" Mahan, a main eventer before he parachuted from an airplane to his accidental death in 1939. He had been advised that a parachute jump might help him regain his hearing. The chute failed to open.

Others were Babe Marino, Frankie Klick, Matt Calo, Bert Colima, former welterweight champions Young Corbett III, Young Jack Thompson, and Jackie Fields, and Ray Pelkey, the trial-horse heavyweight. Prices for the fights ranged from one dollar for the gallery up to three dollars ringside.

Wrestling was then rated as a legitimate sport, not an exhibition show, and was given adequate straight news space and treatment in the press. Some of the well-known heavyweight wrestlers I watched groan and grunt at Dreamland were Renato Gardini, the pride of North Beach; "Strangler Ed" Lewis; Dick Schickat, and Joe Stecher, the "Scissors King." I also saw Stanislaus Zybysko and, later, "Jumping Joe" Savoldi, the ex-Notre Dame fullback whose "Flying Dropkick" finale set the stage for the hippodrome-type matches of today.

My father recalls when the National Theater, owned by the Grauman family, occupied the Dreamland site after the 1906 fire had destroyed Grauman's Theatre on Market Street. Al Jolson, just starting his career in those early post-quake days, was among the performers who appeared on its stage. At first a leased tent was put up; later it was encased in a roof-and-walls shell made of corrugated iron. The legendary story is that Jolson complained to the Graumans about the roof. When it rained, he said, the racket drowned out his songs and jokes. The Graumans responded by having a runway built which extended out from the stage into the audience. The runway was allegedly the model for what later become a standard burlesque prop for strippers.

31. Temple Theatre. 1745 Fillmore. This building, originally King Soloman's Hall, accidentally tumbled down into Fillmore Street in 1972 when wreckers were dismantling it. The old movie house, a nickel admission for kids, had a balcony of sorts with about three rows of hard wooden seats lined up in a horseshoe shape so that two sides faced each other. You had to look partly over one shoulder to see the movie screen from either side.

32. Goldenrath's Delicatessen. 1758 Fillmore. The District's international gourmet delicatessen offered everything from pâté de fois gras to enchiladas. Elegant Pacific Heights matrons could be found here rubbing elbows with McAllister Street *balabostas* (housewives). Now a liquor store occupies the site, but the weathered blue-and-white tile on the floor of the entrance doorway still spells out "Goldenrath's Estab. 1898."

33. Sutter Theater. 2103 Sutter Street. This movie house was formerly known as the Republic; later as the Uptown. The bouncing ball jumped on the screen and the audience sang "On the Bam, Bam, Bammy Shore" as the words ran across the screen and the South Seas music came out of the new talking screen. Knickered Bobby Jones himself took you around the course in a weekly short and explained how to play golf like a champion.

34. Iceland Pavilion. Sutter and Pierce Street. This was San Francisco's first ice rink and home of its first professional ice hockey team, the San Francisco Rangers. The Pavilion originally opened in 1916 as the Winter Garden, its ice skating rink "accommodating 1500 skaters without crowding." It had an adjoining dance hall known as Roseland. Professional ice hockey was received in San Francisco in the Twenties with roughly the same response as that which probably would meet introduction of jai alai in Nome—total indifference. Subsequent tries, with teams known as the San Francisco Tigers and the San Francisco Shamrocks, the latter based at Dreamland Auditorium, were equally unsuccessful.

6

The Chinatown Squad

One day in late March, 1921, at the old Hall of Justice on Kearny Street, San Francisco Police Chief Dan O'Brien called an old schoolmate into his office and assigned him to Chinatown to clean up the violence and killings that had been terrorizing the merchants and residents there for some years. O'Brien instructed his friend to select sixteen men to assist him. The former school chum was Detective Sergeant John J. (Jack) Manion; the chief had known him for thirty-eight years. Manion's assignment was to head up the department's Chinatown Squad, which had been formed back in 1875.

Then as now, Chinatown covered eight city blocks between Bush and Broadway, and three blocks up Nob Hill from Kearny to Powell. The narrow sidewalks overflowed with residents, merchants, shoppers, and tourists. Piles of merchandise, food, and produce in boxes and bales and stacked sacks of rice blocked passage on Grant Avenue, the major artery through the quarter, as well as on the sidestreets.

Narrow alleyways and passages that ran north and south through each block were rich in stores and shops that were soon to become rare, and thus all the more interesting for their old-country flavor. In the windows of apothecaries, for example, were displayed dried sea horses, snakes, birds, crabs, and strange herbs that were used in Chinese medicine formulas. Inside these Chinese drug dispensaries, as in the art and furniture stores and bazaars, you could see delicately carved woodwork and graceful teakwood chairs in which customers could sit while waiting for their prescriptions to be made up. The druggist would deftly and confidently select the ingredients he needed to fill prescriptions from unmarked drawers that lined the shop in row after row, and would weigh them on finely balanced scales.

Most of the fish and poultry stores were on Grant Avenue then, offering live ducks, geese, chickens, rabbits, and turtles. The Chinese shoppers preferred to buy these live and have them killed and dressed at the shops, or to take them home and kill them there. Windows were full of varieties of fresh fish, oysters, abalones, clams, and shrimp. Showcases just inside doorways displayed huge green frogs and guinea pigs. You might witness a dozen or more squealing hogs being carried into a small pork shop; inside you would find raw meat spread on open counters and sausages hanging overhead.

The confectioneries were crowded with glass jars containing sweetmeats, candied fruits and ginger, water chestnuts, sugared water lilies and other flowers, red and white sugar sticks, and thin-shelled lichee nuts. Still in existence were scattered shops stocking authentic Chinese treats such as shark fins, seaweed, bamboo sprouts, and eggs that had aged before being packed in mud and shipped from China.

And there were the smells. The odors emanated from the food shops and markets, from the restaurants, from the pungently treated camphor chests and other pieces of heavy carved wood furniture being carried in or out of stores. Occasionally the sweet, all-permeating smell of opium drifted out from a room or basement where a Chinese elder or two puffed a pipe and dreamed of their home districts across the Pacific. The notorious opium dens of the early days of Chinatown were gone by the 1920s. "Smoking rooms," their entrances often covered with wet blankets to absorb the tell-tale fumes, did exist. These milder meeting places, used by the elder addicts who could have died from withdrawal if deprived of their drug, were not usually disturbed by the Chinatown Squad.

Jack Manion's first task as head of the squad was formidable. He had to deal with the tongs which used hired gunmen to control and milk the gambling, narcotics traffic, and prostitution that existed in the Chinese ghetto. The tongs and their murderous henchmen

THE CHINATOWN SQUAD

also intimidated legitimate businesses operated by Chinatown merchants.

Chinese immigrants into the United States formed groups as protective, as well as fraternal, shields. Three basic types developed in San Francisco and other areas of California where Chinese communities were established. Family associations were composed of members of the same family, no matter how distant the relationship. District association members came from the same district of China. Finally, there were the fraternal organizations, or tongs, composed of immigrants from small families or isolated and lightly populated districts who needed to band together in order to create a substantial membership.

Practically all Chinese immigrants into San Francisco joined an association or tong which took care of the new arrivals' interests. Since the Chinese kept pretty much to themselves, largely because they were shunned socially and fiercely discriminated against economically, the protection they sought was against fellow Chinese who belonged to other associations or tongs.

Five of the six district associations in existence at the time formed the Chinese Consolidated Benevolent Association in the late 1850s. It was called the Five Companies by the non-Chinese in California. The Association was organized to protect Chinese in the United States against exploitation, oppression, violence, and extortion. It also acted as a court of arbitration for disputes between Chinese groups or individual associations.

In 1862, a sixth district association was added. Naturally, the overall group now became known as the Chinese Six Companies to outsiders. The name stuck even when a seventh district association was added permanently later. In the Twenties and Thirties, the Six Companies was considered the most prestigous and influential force in Chinatown.

As in many poor immigrant communities where poverty and economic exploitation are rampant, gambling, commercial sex, and other decadent means of making money took firm root in Chinatown. These activities retained their Chinese cast when they were imported. They were lucrative businesses, and it was inevitable that gangster elements should try to move in to control them. In San Francisco's Chinatown, several of the tongs entered this inviting field and struggled to dominate it. Gambling houses, opium dens, and prostitution came under their control, and hired blackmailers and assassins were used to intimidate the operations' owners and exact tribute, usually a certain percentage

In 1915, Jack Manion already had been a police officer for eight years. His Chinatown days were ahead of him then.

Courtesy of Sister Mary Clement Manion

of the profit. Six of the tongs became known as the "fighting tongs," an unknown phenomenon in China. The Suey Sings and the Bing Kongs were the two most powerful of the fighting tongs on the Pacific Coast. The hired killers and enforcers of the fighting tongs, originally called "hatchetmen" because they actually used hatchets and cleavers at the time, became known, for some unknown reason, as "highbinders."

Legitimate and respectable Chinatown businessmen and merchants, who belonged to family or district associations, often reluctantly joined one of the fighting tongs also. This was purely a protective measure against extortion or violence by the highbinders. Openly taking valuable merchandise out of stores, or threatening or molesting wives, daughters, and other relatives, were common practices. However, membership also carried certain risks.

The highbinder tongs maintained separate clubrooms for their gunmen, away from the main tong headquarters. There the assassins, usually from out of town, were entertained with women, liquor, and other amenities befitting their respected status. Highbinders normally travelled in threes and did execution jobs together.

Most of their killings were done at night, though they could and did kill their assigned targets any time. During the Twenties the weapon favored was a .38 caliber revolver, usually new. After the shooting, the highbinders would leave in different directions, dropping the guns they used so no evidence could be found on them in case they were caught running away. If this happened, they would testify that they were terrified bystanders, merely trying to get out of the danger zone.

One tong attempting to ignite a conflict with another might seek to harass the rival tong's gambling operation. A tong member would enter the rival tong's gambling place and put what appeared to be a folded five dollar bill on the table as a bet. If he lost, the bettor would not let the dealer, or game keeper, pick up the money on the table, insisting on paying five dollars from his own pocket. If he won, he would open the five dollar bill to show a $100 bill inside. If the game keeper refused to pay off, the bettor would bring the matter to the attention of his tong leaders, formally initiating a violent conflict.

In the early days of the fighting tongs, challenges were issued by the posting of a paper, called a *chung hung*, on Chinatown walls. The time and place of the battle would be given, and the opposing hatchetmen would show up for a bloody free-for-all. Subsequently, these challenges were replaced by offers of reward money to members for the killing of any member of another specified tong. This bounty system was a nerve-wracking, vicious practice that resulted in the terrorism of sudden ambushes at any hour of day and night, shootings in the back, swift stabbings by figures appearing out of doorways, and resignations by members from the tong named for attack.

A declaration of warfare in a *chung hung* posted on a back-alley wall in Chinatown carried far beyond the City. The fighting tongs divided up territories, just as Chicago gangs once did. All the gambling in Sacramento could be under one tong and all that in Fresno or Bakersfield under others. Intrusions into claimed turf were met by gun blasts and slayings.

When a killing took place, almost every member of the tong responsible automatically went into hiding. Only hired highbinder killers readied themselves for action. The slaying was a clear signal that war against the entire tong was on. All members of both tongs, not just the individual believed to be responsible for the outbreak, would be in danger of being shot down. Merchant members would barricade themselves in rooms and have food sent in, or brought in by their families. If they had to go out on business they hired one of several private but uniformed white "special" policemen in Chinatown to walk them to a bank or office, and back again.

A highbinder never attempted to kill when the slightest chance existed that a white witness was around. The danger that an outsider might identify someone or reveal some incriminating details was too great. Chinese witnesses would never talk because they feared, with good reason, that they would be marking themselves for death by doing so.

A Chinese who either knew or feared that he was marked for assassination could take advantage of the strict precautions highbinders took to avoid white witnesses. To prevent being ambushed on necessary errands, he would skirt Chinatown proper, using the streets that bordered it where whites would normally be walking. But sometimes even using busy Montgomery Street, in the Financial District, offered no protection. Nate Cohen, who operated a Chinatown plumbing firm on Sacramento Street founded in 1894 by his father, remembers one call he received to fix a heater.

It was upstairs in a corner rooming house at Commercial and Montgomery. When Nate knocked at the door, it was slowly opened just a crack while the occupant cautiously sized up the young plumber. Nate explained that he was answering their call. He was admitted by a young Chinese who was holding a 30-30 rifle in his arm.

"There were only four chairs in the room, all drawn up to windows looking down on either Montgomery or Commercial. In three of the chairs were three other men, also cradling rifles and staring out the windows. The guy who let me in showed me where the gas heater installation was and went back to sit down in the empty chair. There was no other furniture in the room. These guys were cold and had routinely called us to fix a heater which didn't work. I fixed it in about a half hour, the same guy who let me in paid me in cash, mumbled a thank you, and let me out. It was really weird. I never read about any one getting killed in that corner, although I looked the paper over eagerly every day for a while. Either the intended victim never came

Grant Avenue and Washington Street, about 1920.

Courtesy of the California Historical Society

along, or it didn't make the papers—which often happened.

"I sometimes wonder what these hit men would have done if the intended victim had walked by while I was in there. You know, no witnesses!"

Plumbing facilities and fixtures in Chinatown were favorite locations for disposing of pistols and guns used in killings, Cohen recalled. "We would get calls from rooming houses that the toilet water tanks were not working. We'd go there and find pistols and revolvers in the tank, some of them already rusty. The high tank toilets with chains were favorite dumping spots. We also found rifles stuck in garbage cans in the back of houses where we'd go to get at some plumbing installation."

On Manion's first day as head of the squad, the only tong highbinders ever captured in Chinatown for a

killing were arrested by the police, almost by sheer chance. Four Chinatown Squad members happened to be nearby when two highbinder gunmen, imported from out of town as was normal tong procedure, shot their target victim in his rooming house. The policemen heard the shots and apprehended the highbinders as they were fleeing down the stairs. Both killers were convicted of murder and sent to San Quentin. One was hanged and the other died in prison. It was the first time in San Francisco history that tong killers were ever caught, let alone punished.

Manion went into action against the fighting tongs immediately upon his appointment to the squad. His primary goals, on O'Brien's instruction, were to stop the killings and suppress all gambling operations. To stop the tong killings, Manion hit on a simple but effective approach that no law enforcement officer had ever used—or thought of using—before.

The Chinese associations, including the powerful gangster tongs, were great banquet-givers. They held feasts throughout the year, but the most spectacular gatherings occurred during the Chinese New Year holiday season. Big parties were held in San Francisco's world-famous Chinese restaurants. These restaurants represented the specialized cuisine of the five distinct schools of cooking. The food was prepared by highly skilled cooks and served in the seemingly never-ending series of courses. The Cantonese restaurants predominated because the majority of Chinese immigrants to California had emigrated from that area. Sweet and sour pork, steamed fish, and stir-fried dishes were Cantonese specialties. Hunan cuisine featured carp preparations; Peking cooking was known for duck, Chinese pancakes, and baked sesame-seed cakes. Szechuan restaurants specialized in crisp deep-fried duck, and the Fukien style mainly favored seafood.

Chinese would come into the City from Salinas, Sacramento, Watsonville, other California cities and towns, and from out-of-state communities as well, for a dinner arranged by the Louie Fong family, the Suey Sing Tong, or one of the many societies and associations with branches in Chinatown. These banquets were festive occasions and anticipated eagerly. They also served as a principal means of uniting all the family or district association members; matters of business and mutual concern were discussed during the course of the festivities. The Hang Far Low restaurant, upstairs at 723 Grant Avenue between Sacramento and Clay, was a favored site for many of the major banquets. Its fifty tables seated ten persons each.

Manion decided to apply pressure to the gangster tongs and their hired highbinder killers through a crackdown on the banquets. Manion and some of the squad members would show up the night a banquet was scheduled at one of the restaurants or banquet halls by one of the fighting tongs. He would station himself and his men outside the entrance and stop everyone going into the affair except those local members who were familiar to him as local residents and merchants.

"Where are you from?" Manion or a tough-looking squad member would demand coldly and gruffly, maintaining a stone-faced expression. Even if the visitor were a member of a family which worked in the vegetable gardens around Watsonville, he might be told he couldn't go in. It was a crude approach, and clearly unconstitutional, but it had a tremendous impact on the tong wars. It struck at a cornerstone institution of the tongs—the annual banquet in San Francisco's Chinatown, the largest Chinese community outside of China itself.

To be sure, Manion received complaints, both pleading and bitter in tone. But he stood firm and O'Brien backed him up. Then Manion completed playing his hand. He called in the heads of all the fighting tongs and said, according to a former squad member under Manion: "I want these wars stopped. I'm tired. I don't want killings in Chinatown. If there are any more killings here, I won't allow you to have a banquet here as long as you live."

Soon after delivering this ultimatum in 1922, Manion called another meeting of the heads of the fighting tongs and commanded, "No more opium. No more gambling. No more tong wars or attempted bribes or shakedowns, and no more slave girls. Step out of line and you'll not only be arrested—you'll be deported. Try me—and see."

Before a month had passed, there was a killing. This time Manion called a "peace conference." He was obviously annoyed and determined. He played his ace card. He put a peace treaty on the table and demanded that all the tong chiefs sign it. It was a pledge to end the killings, he said. After the last signature had been inscribed, Manion picked up the treaty and told them that what they had signed was an agreement to halt tong killings in Chinatown. They all could be deported on the charge of conspiracy to conceal a murder if one occurred, he told them.

That did it. Two slayings did occur in 1926 which temporarily interrupted the peace Manion had arranged, but these were caused originally by a dispute among two factions of the same tong. Other than these, San Francisco never had another Chinatown killing traceable to a tong war. Many tong disputes arose after Manion made the edict, but resultant killings occurred in other cities and towns. Merchants in Chinatown were no longer afraid to go out. While they had no assurance they would not be victims of a tong dispute if they went to another city or town, they knew they would be safe in San Francisco.

Manion's successful campaign against the tongs' use of hired highbinders in the City had spinoff benefits. It reduced the blackmail and pressure tactics that these musclemen had been using against merchants. Highbinders had been free to walk into a store, pick up a ring, and walk out with it. If the merchant did not belong to a strong tong, he was helpless. If he did, he would complain to his tong and compensation for

This is Manion's Chinatown Squad in late 1921 or early 1922, soon after he was sent up the hill from the Hall of Justice. Manion is seated in the center of the front row.

the ring would be demanded. If the merchant wasn't paid, a killing and another outbreak of tong warfare could result.

Manion's efforts to eliminate gambling were not as thoroughly rewarding as his campaign to eliminate tong killings, but they were highly successful. Only lotteries remained in operation when Manion was done, and even in that case, the actual number drawings were chased out of the City to Oakland.

The historic Chinatown gambling scene had involved four games, or "actions." They were Fan Tan, Pai Gow, Mah-Jongg, and the lottery. It seemed almost everybody in Chinatown at least played the lottery.

Fan Tan was a bean game in which the players would each scoop a pile of beans from a large bowl. A croupier, using a special stick, would rake off four beans at a time from the player's pile. The player would bet on whether the remaining number of beans in his pile added up to an odd or an even amount.

Pai Gow is the Chinese name for dominoes. In the version played in Chinatown, players bet on points and spectators bet on the players.

When Manion passed the word around Chinatown that the squad was about to move in on the gambling operations and shut them down, the Fan Tan and Pai Gow games were moved down to Colma in San Mateo County, just south of San Francisco. Automobiles, often big Buick sedans, would load up with passengers for the games at specific Chinatown locations and then would drive them back later. The transportation was furnished by the game operators.

Occasional "sneak" Fan Tan and Pai Gow games continued to be played in Chinatown, but without Manion's sanction. During the Chinese New Year holiday season, however, an unofficial understanding prevailed—the games could "go" during the ten-day period of festivities and feasting. Gambling back rooms that had been shut down, were spruced up for the brief but profitable fling. Plumber Nate Cohen could always tell when the Chinese New Year was approaching by the calls that came in from different landlords of the inactive gambling rooms who wanted him to come over and clean out the gas pipes so that heaters would function efficiently.

Mah-Jongg games were held throughout Chinatown, usually in walk in soda fountains and cigar stores. This ancient game is played with small marked tiles that are drawn and discarded until one player secures a winning hand. Players used sticks for money, just as chips are used in poker games, so that police could not arrest them for gambling. While Mah-Jongg didn't have enough action to satisfy an avid gambler, the parlors open to the street served another purpose. They offered the closest thing in Chinatown to open prostitution.

A few—but not many—houses of prostitution did exist in Chinatown, usually operating with four or five women. These houses did not go in for streetwalking or open hustling. Several of the houses catered only to whites. A Chinese man from out of town who wanted to find a woman for pleasure would usually head for one of the Mah-Jongg rooms. Chinese prostitutes could be found there, often playing in the games. The visitor would join in the game, reach an agreement with the woman, and she would get up and leave. The customer would never leave with her, but would follow her, about a half block behind, to her building and to her room.

The Chinese prostitutes were girls who had been bought in China, sometimes by a man, sometimes by an older woman, for amounts that usually averaged from four to five thousand dollars. They were brought over as concubines for illegal purposes under various guises, although sometimes they were really intended as legitimate wives for men already living in Chinatown. Many a tong war had broken out because a "slave" girl bought in China by a tong member had been talked into working, or even marrying, a member of another tong. Custom demanded that the money paid out for her be reimbursed to her original patron. If it was not, a killing usually followed, signalling open warfare on all members of the patron's tong.

Manion teamed up with Donaldina Cameron, the well-loved head of the Presbyterian Mission Home in

Chinatown Squad members show the press how they broke down a door to the Bing Kong Tong headquarters during a 1921 tong war, just before Manion was assigned to Chinatown to head the Squad. Sergeant Harry Walsh, Manion's predecessor, shows how with an axe. The other officers are Tommy Hyland (kneeling) and George Hipley.

Courtesy of San Francisco Public Library

Chinatown, to destroy this version of slave trading. He and his men would raid the houses of prostitution, and Miss Cameron would take the girls in to protect and rehabilitate them. She became known to them as "Lo Mo," the mother. Manion was credited with rescuing more than fifty Chinese girls from enslavement.

At the heart of Chinatown gambling were the lotteries. They were roughly equivalent in popularity to playing the horses, an American pastime that never captured the imagination of Chinatown gamblers of that era. So, although no "horse room" betting parlors existed, and no cigar-counter or bar bookies took wagers, hundreds of locations in Chinatown, often food markets and pork and fish stores, took lottery bets. The customers either came in to make their bets personally, or called them in by telephone.

With rare exceptions, whites didn't play the lottery in Chinatown, but some Chinese "runners" had white customers throughout the City. The runners formed their own regular routes, taking bets in stores, bars, and wherever the players might be. The Chinatown lottery agents and the runners who circulated around the City outside of Chinatown knew their customers well. There had to be a personal relationship since the lottery was illegal.

The lotteries operated much like Nevada Keno games. You selected your choices from eighty numbers. Twenty numbers were drawn for each game. If all your numbers were among them, you had a winner. The more numbers you selected, the higher your payoff would be on a win. Playing a "five-spot" meant that you had selected five numbers for that drawing. You could play any amount starting at about thirty-five cents and going up to whatever maximum the lottery company had established.

While Manion was never able to eliminate, or even substantially reduce, the popularity of the lottery among the people of Chinatown, he did manage to force the drawings out of the City. The half-dozen lottery companies then in business decided to hold their drawings out of Chinatown and away from Manion's surveillance and jurisdiction. Several of the companies first moved their drawings to Chinese laundries in other sections of the City, but all of them eventually wound up holding their drawings in Oakland. This cross-the-Bay location caused some inconvenience, but nothing more.

Lottery agents in Chinatown usually operated in a little office at the front of a store or shop. They never filled in the lottery "tickets," the thin, square pieces of tissue paper printed with the Chinese characters for 1 to 80. It was too much of a risk, because they could be used as evidence for gambling charges. Instead, as the agents talked to walk-in or phone-in customers, they would write all the number selections of each bettor in a book. Most customers followed the Chinatown habit of playing the same groups of numbers each day.

All the lottery companies held two drawings every day except Sunday, one in the afternoon and one in the early evening. For every lottery betting location in Chinatown there was a marking room somewhere, usually outside of Chinatown and away from the Chinatown Squad's turf. Agents would phone in all the

numbers in their books to this room about an hour and a half before the scheduled drawing. Dial-phones were not in use then, so agents placed calls through the Chinese-speaking operators in the telephone company's unique red and gold pagoda exchange on Washington Street.

In the marking room, along with several employees was a telephone and a case of fresh lottery tickets. As the numbers were received over the phone, one employee would call them out to another, who used a brush and ink to write the number selections of each bettor on one of the square paper tickets. As soon as this transfer was completed, someone would hurry down to the Ferry Building and board a ferryboat for Oakland and the lottery drawings.

After the drawings, the courier would return with the results to the San Francisco room. A machine would be used to punch holes for the winning twenty numbers on unmarked tickets from the case. These result sheets would be delivered to the agents and to any customers who wanted one. A strict code of honor insured that winners were paid off. A failure to pay off a big win could have resulted in a bloody tong war.

Manion and his men could not eliminate the illegal lottery play. Even if they had been able to read the Chinese characters, numbers in a book were not sufficient grounds for an arrest. The only real harm the police could do the operation was to locate the marking rooms and raid them, or arrest runners carrying lottery tickets. If a runner was intercepted on his way to Oakland and his tickets confiscated, the company sustained a double loss—that from the losing tickets never delivered, and that from paying off the winners whose numbers were registered in the Chinatown agent's book.

Still, arrests of agents or runners were difficult to make. They knew the movements of the squad members down to the time they went to dinner. Even when the squad managed to find an operating marking room, a seemingly sure arrest would be upset at the last minute when the runner would eat the betting slips just as he was about to be taken into custody.

Sometimes Manion's men made extra efforts to "knock over" a lottery agent in one of the Chinatown stores. One squad member recalled being slyly taunted by an agent who worked out of a corner vegetable store on Grant Avenue between Clay and Washington Streets. "We knew he was doing a hell of a business and we couldn't catch him," this ex-officer told me.

"He was laughing at me in his own way. I finally got up on the roof of his building from another building. There was a box up there with all the phone lines in the building connected through it. I got an interceptor set with earphones and hooked it into the box so I could listen in on all the lines going through. I knew approximately what time he was calling in his numbers to his marking room, about seven o'clock. So I started to listen in to different lines each night at the same time. I finally found the line where I could hear a lot of numbers being read off. It was in Chinese, but I knew enough Chinese then to make out what he was saying.

"So the next night, early enough before the time he had to call in his numbers for the early evening drawing, I was on the roof and hooked into his line. I waited for him to ring the room. There was no dial system in those days. I waited until he called the Chinese telephone company office where only Chinese women and girls handled calls. He asked the girl in Chinese for his number and I got it and wrote it down. The next morning I had a Chinese friend of mine in the telephone company find out the address for that number. It was in a Chinatown hotel. That afternoon we went to the room, arrested the men there, and confiscated all the tickets.

"It was more a matter of personal satisfaction. We booked him and the other men on several charges, including possession of lottery tickets. They each put up the usual ten or twenty dollars bail money to get out, never showed up in court, and had their attorney forfeit their bail to pay the fines when they were found guilty. It was the usual thing."

Even these perfunctory arrests and convictions became difficult. Some smart lottery owners began to use the Chinese characters meaning food items rather than numbers on the lottery tickets. When tickets were seized from a runner, or the record book of an agent in one of the shops was taken, literal translations for the markings revealed such household staples as pork or rice, even though they really were code identifications for lottery numbers. The arrested men would claim that they were only recording or delivering orders for food.

Manion and his squad policed Chinatown with the strong determination to eliminate gangster control. During his twenty-five years on the job, Manion earned the support of the Chinatown businesses and residents. "The Chinese Six Companies supported Manion," one old Chinatown hand reflected, "everyone did. They were as safe as they could be. They could roam around without worrying anymore."

"Manion stayed on in Chinatown even after Dan O'Brien left and Bill Quinn came in as Chief of Police. Quinn knew he couldn't pull Manion out, even if he wanted to, because the Chinese community wouldn't let him."

In November, 1939, an effort was made to oust Manion from Chinatown by so-called "progressives" in the district who wanted to "open up" Chinatown— that is, bring it into keeping with the liberal image San Francisco had possessed since Gold Rush days. They wanted to "wink" at the state 2 A.M. closing law for bars, permit them to employ "B-girls" who solicited customers to buy drinks, and relax the strict surveillance and suppression of gambling. The Chinese business community and church and social service organizations rallied around Manion as though he had been one of their own—by then he almost was. The attempt at squeezing him out failed miserably.

The officers on Manion's squad worked in pairs, four men covering Chinatown on each watch. Even if they didn't wear uniforms, there was no doubt who they were. Predominantly Irish, as was the entire San Francisco police department then, they were big, rough, tough-looking cops who used the inherent authority of their concealed badges to demand and command respect and, when necessary, fear. They wore somber suits, woolen shirts or sweaters to combat the early morning chill on the late patrol shifts, and the bulges under their coats made by their holstered Police .38s were easily discernible.

Like every effective law enforcement unit, the squad had its own network of "pigeons" who fed the men information in exchange for privileges and freedom from harassment. It was an exchange that seemed to work out for the benefit of everyone involved except the law violators. The most grateful beneficiaries were the residents of Chinatown who were able to walk its few streets without fear of violence or intimidation.

Federal agencies would often come to Manion for assistance because he and the Chinatown Squad members could do things and get away with them that they could not do—in the 1920s and 1930s, that is. For example, when federal narcotics agents had reason to believe that some opium had been stored in a building, or that it was being used in some room or apartment, they would ask Manion to enter and search the suspected premises. "We didn't need a warrant or anything," one squad member explained years later. "We just broke into the joint and frisked everything in there, and if we found anything, we'd book them in on it and name the federal agents as among the arresting officers."

"We used to keep axes, and crowbars, and sledge hammers stored in a wooden box we had wired to a telephone pole on Waverly Place between Sacramento and Clay Streets. We'd go and get a couple of axes and crowbars and bust in on 'em.

"Nobody challenged our actions in those days, and the good people in Chinatown supported us. If I wanted to go into a building and I thought something was wrong, I'd knock on the door and say, '*Hoy mon. Um cha!*' [Open up! Policeman!]. If there was no answer, I'd say, '*Fa de la!*' [Hurry up!]. Well, if nothing happened then, I'd kick the door in. They'd all be in bed. I'd walk right through the joint. Nobody ever hollered. Nobody said a word.

"You couldn't do that today. They'd sue. It would cost you a fortune."

Another retired member of Manion's crew reminisced about some of the squad's tactics: "These young killers were lodged in clubrooms apart from the regular tong headquarters. The Suey Sings, for example, had their headquarters on Grant Avenue, across from the Kuo Wah restaurant, but Suey Sing highbinders were on Jackson Street.

"When it got rough, we'd close up these side clubrooms and we'd pick them up and put them in jail. They had to put up a thousand dollar bond to get out on bail.

"But you couldn't do any of that nowadays. In those days, we were really the law. We did illegal things, but the Chinatown merchants were tickled we were there to protect them and prevent violence.

Manion probably knew of the rough but effective methods used by some of his men to maintain order and suppress violence before it could happen. Although there were stories about his own aggressive conduct when necessary in years past, his interest in Chinatown went far beyond mere enforcement of the laws and the maintenance of peace. Perhaps the most poignant description of Manion and his ties with Chinatown is given by his daughter, Sister Mary Clement Manion of the Order of the Sisters of Mercy.

"He has been called the Mayor of Chinatown, and in an unofficial way he was, but to me he resembled more a seigneur of the manor with a touch of King St. Louis of France—quite an attribution, I know—and in many respects different from the reality. He was genuinely interested in all the people of Chinatown, as much, if not more, in the law-abiding citizens as in the

Manion with some of the narcotics and opium pipes recovered by the squad in making arrests (1930).

Courtesy of San Francisco Public Library

law-breakers. At least once or twice a week he would have a kind of open house, in which any of the Chinese people could come to him and ask help or share problems. Sometimes it was a parent with a recalcitrant son or daughter; sometimes an elderly person hurting physically, emotionally, financially. Once a month, on report card day, he went to the local schools to talk with students referred to him by principals and teachers as needing a talking to. It was gratifying, as the years went by, to see many of these children later visit him, especially after his retirement.

GOOD LIFE IN HARD TIMES

The squad found opium and narcotics concealed in strange places. Here Manion holds a false-bottom bucket that was used (1928).

Courtesy of San Francisco Public Library

"A born psychologist, he knew the psyche of his people, so much so that the Chinese really felt he knew the language, for often when present at meetings of the Six Companies and the participants would lapse into Chinese, he would seem to know what they were talking about. Daily he spent many minutes pretending to read page by page, and column by column, the Chinese language newspapers hanging outside the newspaper office. He had a special feeling for the traditions of the Chinese, their rituals and taboos.

"When I was very young, my father would often take me to Chinatown, and I loved matching my small stride with his long one as he walked through the streets. I didn't like it much at all when the small children we passed would call him 'Daddy.' That was his name with many of the younger Chinese, especially the young ladies whom he had rescued, who had resided with Miss Cameron, and later led constructive lives in the community. He was godfather for many of them, a role he took seriously. Many of these adopted daughters were frequent guests in our home, and some shared Christmas dinner with us for many years.

"The hours he devoted to duty were remarkable. Except on Sunday evenings (and even then at times) he would always return to Chinatown after evening dinner at home, returning finally around midnight or later. He would invariably go to the district on his so-called day off, as many of the more nefarious plots were hatched and executed when he was supposed to be away."

One ex-squad member under Manion said, "At 9:30 every morning he'd be down there in Chinatown or at the office in the Hall of Justice across the street. At dinner time, he'd go down to Tadich's on Clay Street. Then he'd stay on the job until twelve o'clock at night when the watch changed. The only time he'd go home early would be at four o'clock Sunday. Nobody in the police department ever put in the hours he did.

"And he died a pauper, with patches in his pants. If he had ever taken anything, it would have been all over Chinatown. There were too many people who would have nailed him to the cross if they could."

Some years before his retirement, Manion sought to leave his post in then peaceful Chinatown, but a barrage of protests and pleas from Chinatown groups and leaders to the Chief of Police overcame any plans to re-assign him. When retirement day finally came in 1946, Chinatown's leading organizations and leaders presented Jack Manion with a scroll inscribed, *"Woo Que Bo Mun"*—Guardian of Peace, Protector of Chinatown."

During his thirty-nine years in the police department, Manion attended mass daily at Old St. Mary's Cathedral at California Street and Grant Avenue in Chinatown. He did this even after his retirement, until he could no longer walk easily. After services he would wander the streets and alleys he knew so well to exchange warm greetings with old friends, and some young ones who remembered him as Min Bok, Uncle Manion. Merchants near the Cathedral claimed they could set their watches by seeing Manion come out in the early morning after mass.

He died in March, 1959, when he was 82 years old. The mourners included his family, several former police chiefs, Chinatown leaders, and Chinese friends from all levels of the pagoda-topped section he knew so intimately. Also at the Requiem High Mass at Old St. Mary's in Chinatown were several surviving members of his old Chinatown Squad. And that was the only day that they could remember that Jack Manion came out of St. Mary's later than usual from morning mass.

7

Swimming, Anyone?

If you were a kid and had twenty-five cents in the Twenties or early Thirties, you could swim in a privately-owned indoor pool in San Francisco any time of the year, ignoring the fog, rain, and cold whipping winds that often startle arriving tourists in the summers. In 1929, if you had seventy-five cents, you could even paddle around in the lush surroundings of a luxury hotel pool on Nob Hill. The admission fees included a swimming suit, a towel and a locker.

Between 1920 and 1936, there were three private indoor pools in business in the City, plus the elegant, tiled Fairmont Hotel Plunge which opened in 1929.

Lurline Baths at Bush and Larkin streets, dated from 1894 and lasted until 1936. Out in North Beach, the Crystal Palace Salt Water Baths pool at 775 Lombard Street opened in 1924 and shut down in 1956. The cavernous and historical Sutro Baths complex near the Cliff House at the ocean beach, with seven separate pools, had been launched proudly by Mayor Adolph Sutro in 1896. It managed to survive until 1966 with gimmick injections, including an ice skating rink, basketball courts, and a Hawaiian "Tropical Beach," complete with thatched-roof "huts," vines, and striped table umbrellas. However, the last Sutro pools were closed down in the early 1950s.

When sunshine did pour over the entire city, it reached the ocean beach and warmed the "world's largest outdoor swimming pool." Fleishhacker Pool, at the end of Sloat Boulevard, was one of the finest municipal pools in the country. Adjoining it were the ocean beach and a vast expanse of Recreation and Park facilities, including an excellent zoo, and an elaborate children's playground complete with a miniature train ride and a huge wading pool. Opened in 1925 with the Men's National Amateur Athletic Union Swimming Championships as the feature attraction, Fleishhacker's

offered great promise. It was never realized. The weather was often bitter cold. There often was a clammy fog. Strong winds carried sand from the ocean beach and surrounding knolls into the pool. To cap it all, high maintenance cost for the enormous pool strained the Recreation and Park Department's budget, and in 1971 the pool was closed.

Two small outdoor pools were also operated by the City in two neighborhoods, but they were largely overrun by kids and swimming classes during the limited hours they were available. Like Fleishhacker's they were not open at night.

Out on Nineteenth Street, near Valencia, was the Mission Pool, better known to generations of San Franciscans as the "Nickel Baths." It is still operating and a dip there still costs a nickel for kids. Thirty yards long and ten wide, the tank was always jammed on weekends when the sun was out. That happened frequently out there in the Mission District of the City's limited "warm belt." The five-cent charge for both kids and adults included a suit, towel, and locker.

The North Beach Pool at Lombard and Mason also cost a nickel. This pool was wider than the Nickel Baths, but had a concrete wall and walkway splitting the tank into two sections.

For seventy years, Sutro Baths was one of the Bay Area's prime attractions for both residents and tourists. Built into the side of a cliff at the northern end of San Francisco's ocean beach, it was worthy of a site in The Land of Oz or the more current Disneyland. In fiction or fact, Sutro's definitely rated the classification "unusual" at the very least.

Adolph Sutro was a German engineer who had made his fortune in the late 1860s and '70s by building a tunnel to drain the flooded shafts of the famed Comstock Lode silver mines in Nevada. When he was

95

GOOD LIFE IN HARD TIMES

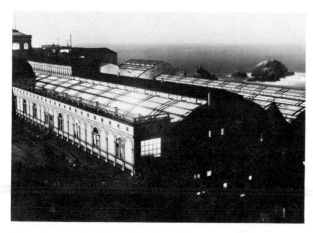

The glass roof of Sutro Baths, above Seal Rocks and the Pacific, was a striking San Francisco evening landmark when the lights were on.

rich he came to San Francisco. His particular kind of benevolence has stood the test of time. He is still considered to be a wealthy man who chose to contribute part of his fortune to the pleasure of the public in the city he had come to love.

Sutro planted more trees in San Francisco than any single person in the City's history. He purchased land on Mount Davidson and what is now Sutro Forest and covered them with trees; later the City acquired the wooded tracts. The Sutro Baths swimming pool complex was Sutro's final major building project for the San Francisco public. He started planning it in 1888 and offered a $500 prize for a design. The site he purchased for the pools was a three-and-a-half-acre parcel of sloping land on a rocky promontory south of Point Lobos, around the corner from the Golden Gate. It lay just below Sutro's summit parcel and cottage looking south over three acres of ocean beach. Sutro spent more than one million dollars on the elevated grounds to this mansion, which came to be known as Sutro Heights. On the rocky land he installed statuary, a stable of horses, sweeping lawns, and elegant landscaping. Many of the mansion's plants and trees were moved down to the Sutro Baths complex when it finally opened in 1896, two years after Sutro had been elected the City's twenty-first mayor.

The Market Street Railway Company ran two of its lines seven miles across the City from the Ferry Building directly into the open mouth of a vast wooden terminal barn at Sutro Baths. This high-domed roof covered the last half-block of track rails. A sloping pedestrian tunnel led directly down from the streetcar terminal to the head of a wide stairwell which led in turn to the booth and turnstiles for the Baths and Museum. When you walked down the steep and worn wooden stairways into Sutro's, it was like descending into a huge greenhouse. The air was damp and hot. The plants and trees in tubs and boxes sometimes reached up to touch the high ceilings.

Sutro Baths consisted of seven pools, a museum, and several restaurants inside what was reputed to be the largest glass-roofed building in the world. The museum housed a conglomeration of memorabilia and collector's items in a setting that would have served admirably for a production of *Arsenic and Old Lace*. There were aged stuffed and lacquered birds and fish, many of them in glass display cases. There were Egyptian mummies, stuffed apes and bears, and an enormous anaconda snake wrapped around a jaguar in a death-fight scene frozen inside an elaborate glass cabinet. There were wooden cigar store Indians, rickshas, and a giant stuffed musk ox with the initials of various visitors carved on its side.

From the level of the museum and the promenade, where a band had once played every Sunday afternoon, stairways went down into the gigantic main amphitheater. This was the core of Sutro's dream palace of pleasure, entertainment, and culture. Tier after tier of seats lined the east side of the hall, facing the windows which looked west out onto ocean. At the bottom level, some eighty feet below the colored glass domes were the pride of the labyrinth: the seven separate swimming pools. Each had a different water temperature. They ranged, with ten-degree gaps, from ice-cold to a steaming warm eighty degrees. A favorite "let's see you do this" dare among the hordes of kids scampering around the pools was to dive into the "hot" pool, climb out, race down to the small ice-cold pool, and dive in there. An almost cutting sensation was experienced as the ice water covered your warm skin. I sometimes wonder how many of our gang died before their time, due to early heart attacks stemming from this mad folly.

Spectators could enter the museum and watch the swimmers for ten cents. The swimming charge was fifty cents. This fee included rental of a suit, locker, and towel. None of the public pools allowed swimmers to bring their own suits. They insisted that pool-owned suits be worn to insure that sanitary standards were maintained. Most of the suits were floppy looking, and

Five of the Sutro pools as they appeared in about 1900. A sixth pool for diving was constructed later at the far end of the main pool and the "ice cold" pool is not visible off to the right.

Courtesy of the Marilyn Blaisdell Collection

usually gray in color with white stripes around the bottom edges. Women's suits had a skirt, often stretched from innumerable launderings. Men's suits had half skirts in front until about 1925. The suits at Sutro's were black, and the very ritzy Fairmont Hotel Plunge featured a comparatively stylish royal blue number. Usually, the name of the pool and a number were stenciled in white paint on the chests of the suits, but again, the elegant Fairmont used emblem patches. Swimming trunks for men were taboo in the Twenties. When trunks did come in, in the mid-Thirties, the Crystal Palace management, for one, required men in

An interior view at Sutro Baths (about 1900).

Courtesy of San Francisco Public Library

Going down one of the staircases to the dressing rooms at Sutro Baths. Plants were everywhere. (About 1900.)

Courtesy of San Francisco Public Library

Part of the Tropic Beach at Sutro Baths in 1935. Visible are a volleyball court, ping pong table, and barbecue facilities.

Courtesy of San Francisco Public Library

The Sutro Baths entrance in 1935. The bright lights, the Tropic Beach, and the modernized entrance and flanking towers were part of an attempt at modernization by the grandson of the founder, Adolph Sutro.

Courtesy of San Francisco Public Library

trunks to wear suspenders. It was feared that the trunks would fall off otherwise.

Some of the divers from the elegant Fairmont swimming club went out to Sutro's periodically "because it was a fun place." They would drive the guards and custodians to frustration by jumping twenty feet off one spectator balcony down into the ice cold pool. "We jumped when nobody was in the pool," said Ted Needham, a former champion diver for the Fairmont. "The bottom of the pool was round like a bowl, so it wasn't too dangerous for us either. We'd get in and out fast, but they used to raise bloody murder about it to Phil Patterson, our coach."

The seven Sutro pools collectively held almost two million gallons of water, practically all of it sea water that crashed in at high tide from the ocean just outside the Baths building. The water came swirling in through a unique tunnel that had been cut out of the cliff rock. It filled a catch basin and, after being allowed to settle, was pumped into all the pools except the tiny "ice cold" one, which used fresh water. A small amount of fresh water from a spring outside also went into the catch basin. The pools were drained constantly and the water was piped far out to sea so that it would not be re-used.

Sutro's publicity claimed that ten thousand bathers could be accommodated in the seven pools. The main pool was L-shaped and publicized as "the world's largest indoor swimming pool." It was seventy-five yards long and had a rectangle of approximately fifteen yards branching off at one end. It was maintained at the normal water temperature. The five small twenty-five-yard pools, lined up in a row, were heated to the different temperatures. The eighty-degree tank was popularly known as "the soup bowl." The little "ice-cold" pool was isolated off to the side near the dressing rooms, logically so because it was suitable for use only by polar bears, physical culture zealots, and goofy kids.

High above the pools was a hatchwork of steel spanners and tie rods, hanging lamps, and the seeming thousands of glass panels comprising the roof. Huge, thick steel I-beams supported all this, dropping down and piercing the walkways at different levels, and even entering the water of the main pool at several points.

Two levels of balcony seats rose high on two sides above the checkerboard of pools below. Below them were two tiers of what seemed like miles of dressing rooms. A wide promenade for spectators and strollers fronted the upper tier. These rising levels were all edged with wood matchstick-style railings and linked vertically with stairways.

Approximately 7,500 spectators could be seated in the balconies, and it was claimed that 25,000 persons could be held "comfortably" inside Sutro's if the room on the promenades and walkways was accounted for. Embellishing the pools themselves were nine springboards, seven toboggan slides, three trapezes, thirty swinging rings, a raft, and several high diving platforms, most of them in the big tank. National championship swimming meets had been held in the Sutro pool and Duke Kahanamoku of Hawaii had made his first mainland appearance there and broken the world's 100-yard record. And it was in the main pool at Sutro's that I made my first and last appearance as a speed swimmer, in the City Junior High School Championships. I was swimming for Hamilton Junior High in the twenty-five yard dash. The only reason I was entered was because our school swimming team was ridiculously small and the swimming coach, who coached every other sport as well, wanted to have somebody in each event. I seem to recall that if you owned a swimming suit and could float for thirty seconds you were on the team. I had never been in a meet race, had only one practice on the day before when I had been desperately recruited, and was scared to death when I lined up with the other entrants—all firm-faced, lithe, and obviously superbly trained young Weissmullers.

I crouched when they crouched on the edge of the pool, steely eyes on the finishing "line" only seventy-five feet away. However, I also swallowed hard as I noticed that we were kind of high above the water, for me at least. It looked like a long way down just to get into the water. The starter's pistol cracked and I dived in just like the other kids did. The only problem was that nobody had ever shown me how to do a shallow racing dive.

It seemed as if I went down and down. I finally managed to turn upward. I thought I'd never make it to the top. I came up choking and spitting salt water. When I finally could clear my head I heard cheers as the winner crossed the finish line and the others followed. I splashed desperately toward the side of the tank, hoping I would make it. I climbed out and headed for the dressing room. I didn't see any point in hanging around to congratulate anyone. Yes, I have memories of Sutro's!

Over in North Beach, at 775 Lombard Street, was the Crystal Palace Salt Water Baths, which has been described as both a "big old barn" and a "real old bathhouse." In 1933, its name was changed to Crystal Plunge.

Actually, Crystal wasn't so old, and it was a long way from being as big as Sutro's. It was opened in 1924 by Edward Cerruti, Jr., who boasted of having come to the United States from Italy with only a dollar in his pocket. Nevertheless, he managed to buy up four pieces of North Beach property just off of Columbus Avenue. Cerruti was an ardent swimming devotee, so on this property he built a fifty-yard pool. He surrounded it with eighteen tub baths and shower rooms, steam and massage rooms, and locker rooms off the second-floor balcony circling the pool. He also built a dance hall on the second floor which could accommodate two to three hundred people; this he rented out to clubs and for private parties. Three years after the pool opened, in 1927, he bought an adjoining lot and installed a back-up reservoir tank and forty-eight more tub baths.

When Cerruti opened his pool, he started looking around for a swimming instructor and pool manager. He called a young man somebody had told him about, who was doing the same job at the City's YMCA. Twenty-five-year-old Charley Sava came over to take the job and became "Mr. Crystal Baths." Sava even lived in a room at the Lombard Street building.

In 1926, two years after he went to work for Cerruti, Sava started a women's swim team at Crystal and began to develop his own method of coaching and training. Hard work and persistence paid off when the Crystal women's teams under Sava won eight consecutive national championships, a record never equalled. Sava and his "girls" dominated U.S. women's swimming for almost a decade. He turned out national champions and Olympic stars who brought the swimming world's attention to San Francisco as never before or since. Marian Gilman swam in the 1928 Olympics in Amsterdam and Eleanor Garatty went to the 1932 Games in Los Angeles. The list of Sava-trained swimmers is long and spans more than twenty years. Ann Curtis, Joyce McCrae, Joan Mallory, and Barbara Stark all made headlines. There were other national champions on the Crystal teams; Sue Curtis, Marilyn (Sugar) Sahner, Patsy St. Claire, Helen Hall, Barbara Jensen, Marian Falconer Pontacq. Sava also trained and coached divers Patsy Elsner and Vicki

Roy Woods just after stepping off the Bay Bridge lower deck on his 1937 jump.

Courtesy of the San Francisco Examiner

Menalo, later to become an Olympic champion as Vicki Draves. Carolyn Schuler won the 100-meter butterfly for the United States in Rome in 1960, eight years after Crystal had closed.

Besides springboards at the deep end, Crystal had a diving tower with three platforms of ascending heights. It was the only indoor high-diving tower in the City, except for a makeshift one out at Sutro Baths. The Sutro tower was not only somewhat jerry-built, but it also had a danger factor. Bathers swam around everywhere, and slides and a raft cluttered the water in the main pool below the tower.

The top platform of the Crystal tower was twenty-six feet high; below were twelve- and eighteen-foot levels. Still, the tower had its shortcomings. The major criticism was that it lacked a runway. "You took two or three steps and off you went," recalled diver Ted Needham.

One diver who used the Crystal high platform to practice in 1937 wasn't too concerned with the length of the runway. His name was Roy Woods and he was, to use an old Western phrase, a stranger in town. Woods wandered into the Lombard Street spa one day in early March, paid his money, slipped on a swimming suit, and soon was practicing dives from the twenty-six-foot tower. All his dives were the same—a back jack-knife, the best one for jumping off bridges.

That was exactly what Woods had in mind. He told lifeguard Norman Hanley that he was going to be the first person to jump off the new Bay Bridge. Next he asked Charley Sava to manage him and train him for his jump. Sava, probably with tongue-in-cheek, got rid of him by suggesting he go over and see Phil Patterson at the Fairmont. Patterson gave Woods the brush-off too, but told Ted Needham, who was then a Fairmont lifeguard and National Interscholastic Diving Champion from Lowell High School, to show Woods whatever courtesies he could around the Plunge. Woods practiced off the ten-foot springboard at the Fairmont and became friendly with Needham.

Woods made his jump on March 22, 1937, diving 185 feet into the Bay from the lower deck of the Bay Bridge. Wearing a football helmet and a steel-ribbed corset under his swimming suit, he jumped off backward as he had practiced from the Crystal tower platform and the Fairmont high springboard. He went into his jack-knife as planned, but about half-way down a strong and sudden gust of wind caught him. He floundered in the air, "flapping strangely," and hit the water awkwardly on his shoulders and back with his legs spread. The splash sent spray high into the air." It was estimated later that he hit the water at a speed of about sixty miles per hour. "It felt like I had hit concrete," Woods said later from his hospital bed.

A launch was standing below the bridge by prearrangement. In it were Woods's mother and wife, Ted Needham, and reporters and photographers from the San Francisco *Examiner*. The *Examiner* and Hearst's Metrotone News had reportedly arranged with Woods for exclusive coverage of his stunt. Needham, whom Woods had invited along for just such an emergency, dove from the boat into the chilly water when Woods's inert form bobbed to the surface, head down in the water. He reached Woods and held his head above water until the launch could be maneuvered into position to take both of them aboard.

This was Woods' last jump. He had broken his back and was paralyzed permanently from the waist down. Bizarrely, he had chosen a 185-foot height for his

Roy Woods (with helmet) being pulled out of the Bay after his jump from the Bay Bridge. With him in the water is Ted Needham, the Fairmont Plunge diver, who rescued him.

Courtesy of the San Francisco Chronicle

185th and final dive. Woods, it developed, was a professional stunt diver who had jumped off many bridges, including the Brooklyn Bridge twice. He had been hoping to get a contract from the Golden Gate International Exposition officials to dive off the soon-to-be-completed Golden Gate Bridge during the run of the Exposition in 1939. Instead of a contract, he wound up with a career-ending injury and a citation for walking illegally on the Bay Bridge. To top it off, according to the *Daily News* story, the *"Examiner* cameras missed the actual splash which had been planned for a feature play, because of the opposition paper's craft."

Someone had tipped off the rival morning *Chronicle's* city desk to the *Examiner's* plan for an exclusive on the stunt. The *Chronicle* had sent its own boat out with photographers and reporters, apparently blocking from the *Examiner's* floating photographer the view of Woods hitting the water. The crowning blow to the *Examiner* came when its launch wouldn't start after Woods had been fished out of the water. The *Chronicle* boat was first into the City with photographs and the detailed story. It was an hour before the stranded *Examiner* party returned to the waterfront and Woods received proper medical attention.

The *Chronicle* city desk had phoned the California Highway Patrol to report that an *Examiner* photographer was walking on the upper deck of the bridge and taking pictures. The caller suggested that the photographer ought to be arrested for breaking the law prohibiting pedestrians on the bridge. The patrolman dispatched from the Bridge's Toll Plaza arrived too late to prevent the *Examiner's* Johnny Florea from taking pictures, but the photographer was charged later with violating the no-pedestrian rule.

The Crystal pool held about 300,000 gallons of salt water. The Bay water was piped in directly from a pier installation near Fisherman's Wharf a few blocks away. A holding tank, as big as the pool itself, had been built on the second floor above the pool. The algae was allowed to settle before the water was run through large chlorine treatment containers and into the pool. The water flowed into the pool in a five-foot cascade at the shallow end. Little kids could get under it in the two-and-a-half-foot deep level. There was a four-foot ledge under it where they could sit and let the water pour smoothly over their heads, shoulders, and backs.

The admission fee for swimming, or for a tub bath, was fifty cents. Kids under twelve paid twenty-five

The water came in to the Crystal pool from the Bay through a five-foot cascade at the shallow end. (About 1936.)

Courtesy of Charles Sava

cents to swim. The pool was open from eight in the morning until ten at night every day, except for a dinner hour from five to six. This meant you couldn't spend the entire day there for one admission fee. On some Saturdays and Sundays four to five hundred bathers swam in the Crystal pool.

Despite Cerruti's enthusiasm and Sava's success in bringing Crystal national and international fame and publicity, the pool and baths were never a financial success. Starting in the mid-Thirties, the business was leased out by Cerruti, and later his widow. Throughout this period Sava continued to train his teams while managing the pool. In 1946, Sava teamed up with Ernie Smith, the broadcaster and former swim star, to lease the pool. They in turn leased the pool to the Recreation and Park Department during the daytime hours for free swimming classes. In 1952, Sava continued the lease for a year with a new partner, Dr. Henry Domeniconi, a North Beach dentist.

It was a losing battle. Although the City was paying $15,000 annually for use of the pool and Sava's services six days a week, Sava and Domeniconi paid Cerruti's widow, Norma, an annual rent of $16,000. And there were other expenses. Adult patronage kept declining. Groucho Marx for free on the television screen offered too much competition. "I've got to get out before I go broke," Sava told a reporter. "Just put me down as another of TV's victims. I was doing okay before TV came along."

Sava and Domeniconi gave up their lease in 1954 and another operator, Robert Pedersen, tried to make a go of it for more than a year, also unsuccessfully. In 1956, the City building inspectors condemned the Lombard Street structure because the roof was leaking. The wooden ceiling beams had rotted and the entire roof had to be replaced, the inspectors said. Pedersen ran up the white flag, and Sava offered to buy the property from Mrs. Cerruti, but was unable to raise the $90,000 she asked. The pool closed that same year and eventually the property was sold by Mrs. Cerruti for $120,000. The empty building was demolished in 1958.

103

SWIMMING, ANYONE?

The original Lurline Baths swimming pool at Bush and Larkin Streets in 1899. It burned down in the 1906 fire and was rebuilt on the same corner.

Courtesy of Marilyn Blaisdell Collection

It was the end of Crystal, but not Charley Sava. Early in 1977, he was still developing future stars as a swimming coach and instructor at the City's Larsen Pool on Nineteenth Avenue in the Sunset District. He had the same enthusiasm he exhibited more than fifty years before when he reported in at Crystal Palace Salt Water Baths.

Lurline Baths at Bush and Larkin Streets was the City's oldest public swimming pool until it closed in 1936. It was built in 1893 and opened the following year, two years before Adolph Sutro unveiled Sutro Baths. The original wooden structure burned down in the 1906 earthquake and fire and was replaced.

John D. Spreckels of the prominent San Francisco family was the president of the sponsoring Olympic Salt Water Company. The company announced it had been "formed with the view of supplying the people of San Francisco with pure ocean water for bathing pur-

poses." To fulfill that promise, the company installed a six-hundred-foot "Iron Pier" pipe on the ocean beach south of the Cliff House, built a red-brick pump house behind what later became the Playland amusement area, and pumped salt water some eight miles across the City to the Lurline Baths and other downtown customers. In the basement of the new "immense natatorium" on Bush Street, two eight-horsepower boilers kept the water at an even temperature suitable for the fifty-yard pool. The water, the Olympic company announced, would be changed daily at 10 P.M. when the pool would be emptied and cleaned.

There were springboards down at the ten-foot deep end. Available were tub baths with salt or fresh water, hot and cold shower baths, a Russian steam bath with needle showers, special "parlors" for men and women, a barber shop, boxing and fencing rooms, and a "cafe" for refreshments and meals. "Ladies' Day" was on Tuesday and Friday mornings, with "hot air hair dryers for women bathers."

The post-1906 pool featured two marble slides with water flowing down them, one on each side of the pool. The Bush Street slide, near the pool entrance,

GOOD LIFE IN HARD TIMES

A lazy day at Fleishhacker Pool, about 1925.

Courtesy of the California Historical Society

was about fourteen feet high and gave you the longest ride. The one on the other side of the pool was the steepest and most popular, but proved to be dangerous and was closed down in the Twenties.

The charge for swimming and the usual suit, towel, and locker was only twenty-five cents at Lurline's. The pool was concrete and had a tile gutter and rope runner around the edge to cut down falls by youngsters. Huge chandeliers hung over the pool. Dressing rooms were on the balcony and lockers in the basement. Ted Needham, the ex-Fairmont lifeguard and diver, remembers the first time he went down to Lurline's with his older brother.

"I was a little dinky kid and they had these little lockers you hung your clothes in. 'Darn it,' I figured, 'Now how do I get in there and change my clothes?' I did it too! I remember struggling around in there, with my brother laughing at me."

Only one major public outdoor pool existed in San Francisco, but it was the "world's largest swimming tank," able to accommodate a 220-yard straightaway race. Unfortunately, it was located at one of the coldest spots in the City. The Herbert Fleishhacker Municipal

Swimming Pool, at the end of Sloat Boulevard near the ocean beach in the southwestern corner of the City, opened in 1925. Five thousand bathers entered on the day it was opened to the general public, three thousand of them kids. They "kept the waters churning all day." Twelve lifeguards were on duty. Fifty Marbolite electroliers installed around the pool were expected to absorb fourteen percent of the moisture in the air. A few weeks earlier, the City had hosted the Men's National Amateur Athletic Union Swimming Championships at the new pool.

The pool was one thousand feet, or about three city blocks long. It was thirty yards across at its widest point. The pool was so huge you could not identify your mother if you were at one end and she were at the other. It held six million gallons of water and had a modern chlorinating system. Rowboats were tied up in the pool for use by the lifeguards if necessary. Life preserver rings were hung on the metal ladders of the pool, ready for a long toss.

The pool bathhouse, with dressing rooms and hundreds of steel lockers, was done in Italian Renaissance style. It had a green glazed tile roof, was 450 feet long, and was probably the finest bathhouse ever built for a public pool. Two tunnels led from the bathhouse building directly to the ocean beach. Two dining rooms were on the second floor, one looking out west to the beach and the Pacific, and the other looking eastward over the pool and nearby Lake Merced. The cement walks around the pool were wide and ideal for kids chasing each other. In case one of the little ones slipped and had an accident, a branch of the City's emergency-hospital service was in the bathhouse building, staffed by a doctor and a nurse.

The giant pool was purposely tailored for diving. Its deep end had a fifty-feet square under the high tower that was fourteen feet deep. Every couple of months, the fourteen feet decreased to about ten or eleven feet because sand coming in with the salt water pumped from the ocean accumulated on the bottom. Some of the sand that piled up at the deep end drifted down from the rest of the pool where bathers, coated with sand from lolling on the nearby ocean beach, dunked themselves without showering. When the pool was cleaned every three or four months, laborers would shovel the sand out.

The publicity for the pool said that a heating system maintained a water temperature of seventy degrees "at all times." Nevertheless, except when the sun was shining brightly, which happened rarely in that part of the City, every gallon of that water was cold, cold, cold. Your teeth often began chattering even before you climbed out to be hit by the chilling wind that usually swept in from the ocean.

During the pool's first two months in business, more than forty thousand adults paid twenty-five cents, and almost sixteen thousand children fifteen cents, for a rented bathing suit, two towels, locker space, and a swim in the pool. On weekdays, kids under twelve were only charged a nickel.

Adjoining the pool were sixty acres of landscaped lawn, walks, and baseball fields. There too was a children's playground, second only to the one at Golden Gate Park in size and facilities. Six free public tennis courts were built between the pool and the playground. They were never too crowded in the Twenties and Thirties because tennis had not yet attained the popularity it later did. Opposite the large wading pool in the Children's Playground, was the Delia Fleishhacker Memorial Building, a lounge and comfort station for use by mothers and their small children.

Finally, there was the zoo. Financier Herbert Fleishhacker, then president of the Park Commission, had subsidized it as a gift to the City. Fleishhacker had originally donated ten acres and about a dozen animals. By 1924 the zoo had six hundred animals and a staff of twenty-one keepers.

The pool proved to be a mistake. No matter what technological marvels are installed to beat the climate, in San Francisco, an outdoor pool is impractical during all but a few months of the year. "Half the time you were diving through the fog, and you couldn't see the pool or the water," one former champion diver said. "You couldn't train out there, the weather was so bad, even though it was the only good diving tower in the City."

The huge Fleishhacker installation was an economic monster. The costs for upkeep and maintenance were astronomical relative to the paltry amount of income the pool brought in. Also, the pool suffered the woes that struck many local recreational facilities during the Twenties. More families acquired automobiles after 1925. People went out of the City and out of the Bay Area more frequently for recreation and fun. The out-of-town beaches and resort areas, which had more sunshine and the appeal of fresh scenery, were simply more attractive. The opening of the Bay and the Golden Gate Bridges in the late Thirties accelerated this trend and hurt Fleishhacker's business even more. Regular users of the pool dwindled to small groups, such as policemen trying to "keep in shape." It finally got to the point where, as veteran Recreation and Parks Department official Doug Martin phrased it, "a $500 gross income for the pool was a great year."

A chain-link fence was installed around the pool in the late Forties in a vain attempt to increase revenue for the pool. Too many "freeloaders" had been using the

Fleishhacker Pool in November, 1928.

Courtesy of San Francisco Public Library (Gabriel Moulin)

GOOD LIFE IN HARD TIMES

A diving exhibition at the formal opening of Fleishhacker Pool (April, 1925).

pool without paying, coming in from the ocean beach, or simply slipping their clothes off in the adjoining recreation areas and lawns and diving in. But the fence proved useless. Not only did kids sneak under it, but it made the pool seem more like a huge, deserted reservoir than ever before.

The fatal blow came from nature in January, 1971. A storm battered the ocean beach trestle supporting the outfall pipe which carried the used pool water out to sea. A break in the pipe resulted and the estimated repair costs were judged to be prohibitive in view of the poor receipts from the pool. The pool was closed finally that month. It was reopened briefly, using fresh water from some wells in the area, but it proved too difficult to keep clean and was closed for the last time in June, 1971, some forty-six years after it opened.

The last word in San Francisco's public swimming pools was the Fairmont Plunge. It opened in 1929 in

the luxurious Nob Hill hotel, which has sheltered world notables and celebrities since the turn of the century. Today the Plunge is the centerpiece of an exotic eating and drinking rendezvous in the hotel. The white and blue tile and the underwater lights are the same. The black and white checkerboard tile walkway around the pool with an octangonal diamond design is still there, and there is water in the pool. But instead of swimmers, a barge carrying a dance band floats in the pool.

The band would probably have felt right at home back in the Thirties at the Plunge. Wednesdays were "exhibition" nights. Floating about during the entertainment were little boats, decorated to look like gondolas and manned by lifeguards outfitted as gondoliers. A fake bridge arched across the small pool to enhance the illusion of Venice and its canals.

Although we were not aware of it at the time, the Plunge apparently was not as public as we thought. Our gang of teenage kids used to go down to the hotel on Saturday mornings for the "good deal" we had heard about. Seventy-five cents for a suit, towel, locker, and fresh-water swimming as long as you wanted in the fanciest pool and surroundings we had ever been close to. Not cheap for us, but it was the first time most of us had ever dared to go into a classy hotel. Our regular recreation and game area was an unpaved stretch of St. Joseph's Avenue in front of Calvary Cemetery in the City's Western Addition District. The Fairmont had a glamorous appeal for us.

"Actually, the Fairmont was very exclusive when it first opened in 1929," one former employee said. "You had to have a membership card, and the initiation fee ran from fifty to seventy-five dollars. Then it went public, but it still had a loosely enforced membership system, so that if somebody came in and we could tell that we didn't want him in, we'd say, 'Do you have a membership card,' and they'd leave. We'd only challenge those we didn't want in. Others wouldn't even be asked.

"At first it was a dollar and a half to swim. Then it dropped to seventy-five cents. It was really snobbish. The ordinary guy wouldn't be comfortable. Actually there was nothing for him to do. He couldn't jump off a tower, because we didn't have any. The pool was tiny compared with other public pools available, so there was always a lifeguard right on top of you, watching your conduct. And there were no really cheap food and drinks to buy."

The Plunge supervision was efficient and strict. All the lifeguards were either divers or swimmers who competed under the Fairmont colors in amateur events. In the early Thirties they were paid twenty-five cents an hour for the lifeguard duty and there was no trouble in filling the jobs. Work was scarce in those Depression days, and that hourly wage was standard. The lifeguards were more concerned that the pay might make them professionals and ineligible for amateur competition than they were about the amount.

The pool was, and is, only twenty-five yards long and twenty-five feet wide. There were ten-foot and three-foot diving springboards at the ten-foot deep end of the pool then. The crystal-clear fresh water was tested three times a week. Sheets of green canvas were stretched under a low pipe rail which ran around the pool, edging the walkway and serving as a protective splash shield. Still, swimmers coming out of the pool would sit on the rail and their wet suits would drip down on the other side to the hardwood floor which covered the rest of the room. Several heavy stone benches were placed around the pool for the swimmers. The rest of the room was furnished in an elegant country-club style. An outdoor terrace, visible through huge glass doors added to the impression of an elegant country setting.

Former diver and lifeguard Ted Needham, now a top professional photographer in San Francisco, compared the Plunge with the Cocoanut Grove in the Ambassador Hotel in Los Angeles. With its hardwood floor, palm trees, and rattan furniture theme, the comparison was rather apt. There were times when the Plunge resembled a Southern California movie set, lacking only the zany four Marx Brothers. Needham recalled one night when he was on guard duty at a dance party given by a San Francisco social club. The doors between the ballroom and the pool room were left open and the tables around the pool were being used by the revelers. It was a lovely, romantic setting.

"I was seventeen years old," Needham mused, "and we were carrying billy clubs. Our uniforms were white ducks and a white sweatshirt. We had a hole cut in the pocket for the billy club. I weighed a hundred and thirty pounds, and the managers said, 'Don't ever pull that billy club out of your pocket unless you're really going to use it.' Well, can you imagine anybody doing that with some big moose? So you're walking around, and you're running up to a guy and saying, 'Don't throw the trees in the pool, please!' And the guy

says, 'Ah, beat it, or I'll throw you in.' And a couple of times that happened. They really gave you a rough time.

"This night was a really horrible experience for me. I can't remember the name of the club having the party, but they started throwing the potted palm trees into the pool, shoving furniture in, and they really got out of line. So I pulled the billy club at someone. Well, the guy took one look at me, and two of them grabbed me. There was a telephone booth right up by the entrance from the hotel corridor. They jammed me into it and laid the booth down on its doors. I'm inside the booth and I can't even see out. The glass doors were the only way you could see and they were on the ground underneath me. I mean I was in total confinement.

"So I reached into my pocket, lying on my back, put a nickel into that damn phone, push it down, and I phone the manager of the hotel at the desk—the night manager, Mr. Woods was his name.

"I said, 'Mr. Woods, this is Ted Needham, the lifeguard down at the Plunge,' and I said, 'they're tearing this place apart.' And he said, 'For Crissake, stop 'em!' I said, 'I can't.' He said, 'Why can't you stop 'em?' I said, 'I'm in the phone booth.' He said, 'Well, what the hell are you doing in the phone booth?' I said, 'I'm flat on my back. They put the phone booth down.' Well, they called the police and everything else, and calmed that one down. But talk about being embarrassed!"

The ceiling above the pool had iron support rafters below a huge skylight. For aesthetic reasons, a false ceiling of billowing blue and gold drapes hung below the iron rafters to hide them from view. Occasionally, the fold of drape just above the ten-foot springboard would be torn by practicing divers who playfully grabbed and yanked it while in the air at the peak height of a dive. This gave an extra little twist to their dive pattern. Ted Needham was especially adept at this.

On one occasion, Phil Patterson, the Fairmont diving and women's swim team coach, came into the Plunge and noticed that the fold over the high board had been ripped again. He insisted that Needham and another diver, who usually "double-bounced" him, repair the tip. In diving parlance, "double-bouncing" means that a second person runs out on the springboard just as the diver comes down on it after his hop. The added weight depresses the board further. Then, just as the board is about to spring back and catapult the diver up into the air, the "double-bouncer" dashes back to the base of the board. This suddenly removes the extra weight to be thrust upward and gives the diver extra height. The system merited one of those Rube Goldberg drawings. Needham and the other diver had used this technique to get high enough to grab the ceiling drape.

"Patterson insisted that we go up with a needle and some sail thread and sew the rip up," Needham recollects vividly. "Well, we put a ladder up along the wall and we went up into the rafters.

"When we're up there, the other guy holds my arm while I lean way out and down to try to pull this thing together so I can sew it. We're hot and wringing wet from the humidity in there.

"Then it happened. I slipped out of this guy's clutches. And, of course, people are all swimming down there, and I go right through the whole damn thing, and everybody thinks I came through the roof. They didn't even know I was up there.

"Crash! Down I came. Women screamed. Nobody, luckily, was hurt, but I just missed hitting the diving board. That accident really made a big hole in the drape ceiling, and that's how we got a new green cloth ceiling right away. Later, they took the cloth ceiling out entirely and left the rafters and skylight exposed."

The Plunge was extremely popular in the summertime. Although the pool was only twenty-five yards long, often three lifeguards would be necessary because so many people would be using the pool. On a particularly nice day there might be two hundred people in the pool, according to Needham. The diving boards would be closed off when it became that crowded. "No diving, because they'd kill each other," Needham said. "And boy, the noise! You wouldn't believe the noise."

Although the Plunge was only twenty-five yards long, the Pacific Amateur Association held several swimming meets here. It simply increased the number of laps to be covered in the races. Phil Patterson's forte and interest, however, was in the divers. Helen Crlenkovich, Frank McGuigan, Elton Stone, Patty Elsner, Patty Robinson, Dick Keating, and Ted Needham were among the many top performers he trained and who represented the Fairmont in national and Pacific Coast championships.

Patterson's swimming and diving team members were featured at the Wednesday night exhibition shows at the Plunge. Patterson used this weekly event, free

to the public, to give his divers and swimmers experience in performing before an audience. One popular act, a Houdini-like escape stunt, was performed by Fairmont lifeguard Wally Moeller. He would be tied into a sack and dropped off into the deep end of the pool. After a seemingly interminable and silence-shrouded time while the suspense increased and gasps of concern emanated from the audience, Moeller would suddenly bob up on the surface, gasping in dramatic fashion. He would wave modestly at the applauding crowd. Actually, Moeller had a knife concealed in his trunks and after waiting a suitable length of time, he would simply cut his way out of the sack.

Comedy diving acts were staged by the popular Bay Area team of Clyde Diaz and Norman Hanley. Another popular act was the plunge for distance. Competitors would swim under water for approximately three lengths of the pool. For a short time, kayak jousting contests were staged, but they were abandoned because the pool was too small for maneuvering.

The Terrace Room and Plunge became the "in" place for high school and college graduation parties. Normal procedure included a quick change from tuxedo or evening gown to a swimming suit and back again, with a hot shower and an hour of running and thrashing about in between. Nothing is impossible when you're seventeen.

Although the Plunge gave the Fairmont the distinction of being the only first-class hotel in San Francisco with a swimming pool, and its swimming club brought it national publicity through the sports pages, it was never a profit maker. After Patterson went into the Army in 1942, the swimming team and the divers were soon mothballed and even the publicity dividend was gone. When Patterson was mustered out in 1946, the Plunge was history. Ben Swig had bought the elegant but deteriorating Fairmont in 1945 and started an extensive renovation and construction program. Swig decided to convert the Plunge into an attractive South Seas bar and restaurant with a built-in lagoon, ending the novel, but costly, swimming operation. The Tonga Room is now considered one of the City's most attractive dining and drinking spots. The only splashes heard there now are from ice cubes or when a drunk occasionally falls in the pool.

With choices ranging across the City from the plush elegance of the Fairmont on Nob Hill to the sands of Fleishhacker's at the beach, San Francisco swimmers have never had it so good since.

The Fairmont Hotel Plunge in 1929, shortly after it opened. Potted palm trees were added later.

Courtesy of the San Francisco Examiner

8

All Aboard for the Office

During the Twenties and Thirties the Bay Area boasted one of the most efficient and enjoyable mass-transit systems ever implemented in the United States. The heart of the system was a spiderwork of ferryboat lines stretching across San Francisco Bay from Marin, Solano, Contra Costa, and Alameda county piers and terminals, and converging at two points in San Francisco—the Ferry Building downtown and the Hyde Street Pier, just west of Fishermen's Wharf.

Residents and past visitors who can go back in memory to those years will recall the pleasant trace of adventure somehow always present on the ferryboat crossing. A simple daily commute to the office was more than just a rapid-transit zip through a tube under the Bay or a ride over a bridge in a bus or carpool. The ferryboat trip across the Bay—whether in bright, glistening sunshine, through mysterious thick fogs pierced by warning whistles and horns, or against the driving wind and rain pelting the windows of the boat as its bow plunged up and down through surging rough water and waves—gave a stimulating tang to a normally dull part of the day's routine or activity.

Every weekday thousands of commuters came streaming into the City from Sausalito, Vallejo, Richmond, Berkeley, Oakland, and Alameda aboard the ferryboats to their jobs in San Francisco in the mornings, and then headed back home for dinner at the end of the day. A smaller crowd of San Franciscans followed the same routine in the opposite direction.

Boats going over to the Oakland Mole or the Key Pier from the Ferry Building carried a large number of University of California students enroute to the Berkeley campus. Most would congregate in groups to talk or visit, while some would go off by themselves inside, seeking a shielded corner of the deck in order to study, finish a neglected homework assignment, or do some last-minute cramming for an examination that morning.

Ferries also served the Oakland and Richmond transcontinental train terminals. To cross the Bay on the way to a hospital, the theater, or a Sunday picnic, the ferryboat was the way to go in those days. And some people rode the ferries for the sheer pleasure of it, cruising the Bay on weekends and holidays at bargain rates—the passenger fare was a nickel between San Francisco and the foot of Broadway in Oakland.

As the hours passed, the passengers changed. As noon approached, for example, elegantly dressed women would appear on the ferries en route to the City to attend fashionable luncheons or to take in downtown theater matinees. A little later, sporting types, some with Damon Runyan character accents, could be seen on their way to the City to catch a train, a bus, or a streetcar down to the Tanforan Race Track in San Bruno. They would spend the crossing studying their racing forms and tipster sheets and exchanging views on how to make the day a winning one. And after the thick commuter rush hour at the end of the day, theater-goers and sports fans, on their way to boxing or wrestling bouts or basketball games, would come over to the City and catch the late boats back.

Bowlers competing in intercity leagues used the ferryboats at night. One favorite story concerned the late Elmer (Red) Irwin, one of San Francisco's all-time great bowlers. Irwin had an expensive habit of occasionally throwing his bowling ball and bag off the boat in disgust while crossing back to the City from Oakland after a particularly bad scoring session on the lanes. One night, when he and his teammates were on the way back across the Bay, the boat suddenly lurched heavily because of a mechanical foulup. One of the bowlers immediatly shouted, "Everybody to the lifeboats! We've hit a pile of Irwin's old bowling balls!"

On weekends, especially on Sundays, the Northwestern Pacific boats to Sausalito usually carried hikers with knapsacks on their backs. Other rail passen-

ALL ABOARD FOR THE OFFICE

Sausalito passenger-ferry pier and rail terminal in 1927. The auto-ferry slips are at left.

Courtesy of Roy Farrington Jones

ger lines with ferryboat operations were Southern Pacific, Santa Fe, Western Pacific and Key System. The decor of the boats differed with the lines, creating a colorful array of red, white, yellow, and orange boats on the Bay.

Romances, friendships, clubs, and year-long card games developed on board. The rides went at a leisurely pace as the paddle-wheeled "walking beam" or the propeller-driven ferryboats churned in smooth or choppy waters between landings and slips. The vistas from the open decks and through the windows were often breathtaking. Brisk and invigorating breezes hit you if you went outside, and sometimes you were dampened by wind-whipped salt spray.

On stormy trips when the fog was a dense, opaque blanket and the wind was strong and bitterly cold, the squat ferryboat progressed with a lurchingly up-and-down motion. The waves slapped against the hull, protesting sounds of creaking wood cut through the other noises, and the normally smooth pulsations of

the engines seemed to be off-key and straining. Horns blared, whistles moaned, and bells jangled nervously and constantly as passengers mentally placed themselves alongside the captain in the wheelhouse peering into the blank wall of mist ahead. On extremely cold mornings under these conditions, it was both physically and mentally comforting to have one of the seats near the warm wall of the engine room. But a few hardy outdoor types were always aboard who enjoyed sitting outside on the open deck, no matter how strong the wind was.

A friendly and pleasant camaraderie arose among the "regulars" on the peak-hour morning and afternoon trips. Most commuters in those early days recall that this cheerful mood made the daily travel to work an enjoyment rather than a chore. The restaurants and the stand-up counters aboard served good food. The corned beef hash, apple pie, and coffee served on the Key System boats were hailed by regular riders as being unequaled anywhere. Some of the boats had small bars on board before and after the Prohibition years. Most had snack bars and soda fountains, well-stocked news and cigar stands, and bootblack stands. Some of the older ferryboats even had potted palms and stained glass windows on the upper deck. Pinball machines, coin-operated baseball games, and iron-claw games with inviting prizes lying on a mound of colored candy and peanuts helped passengers while away the short ride.

On the peak-hour commuter runs, an unwritten and undocumented system of seat reservations was observed. It was based on seniority, and assured a "regular" of his preferred seat. The seat was left vacant until he arrived. A stranger who made the mistake of sitting in it would receive disapproving frowns and often a polite comment explaining the unwitting breach of the traditional etiquette.

Large squares of board were kept in racks or under the benches on both decks for use of the card players. They balanced the boards on their knees and replaced them when they pulled in on "the other side." If there were not enough of the boards to go around, newspapers were spread out on the knees of the players.

Christmas crystalized the closeness of the commuter groups. The ferryboat companies and the crews competed in decorating their boats with the greenery, fluff, and symbolic ornamentation of the holiday season. Trees were set up on decks. Novel displays were designed and put together on board. Passengers exchanged gifts on the day before Christmas. Crew

A ferryboat restaurant.

members, some of whom had made the daily commute trip for several decades, received gifts in recognition of their services during the previous year. Some crew members, ranging from the masters and mates to deckhands and coffee-shop waiters, represented the third generation of families which had begun serving aboard the ferries back in the nineteenth century. All in all, many of the trappings and traditions aboard the ferryboats on San Francisco Bay were reminiscent of those popularly thought to exist in an exclusive London club —but without the membership dues.

The early-morning boat commuter who had to be at the office usually headed for the restaurant or the stand-up counter on the main deck for a cup of warming coffee. It was a nickel a cup and you could get refills and take them out on the deck to enjoy the crisp fresh air on the trip over.

Veteran commuters knew all the nuances and angles about riding on the ferryboats with the maximum comfort and minimum effort. Window seats on the boats were the most desirable, but the experienced rider knew which windows on which boats had leaky casings and would let water in on rainy days and evenings when the wind pounded the drops against the side of the boat. Puddles would form on the seats or on the floors, rolling up and down as the boat tilted and bucked through choppy water.

The seasoned rider also always was careful to check for discarded wads of chewing gum on the seats, floors, or other places where clothing and shoes might make contact.

When the fog was thickest on the Bay, the cacophony of whistles, bells, and horns was constant and varied, coming from every type of craft afloat, from steamships to tugs and sailboats. This pageant of sounds led to confusion at times for the ferryboat pilots and captains. One particular morning sometime in the Thirties the ferryboat crossing back to Alameda was carefully proceeding at quarter speed through an exceptionally heavy fog which made visibility practically zero. A sudden sound of "blaw" off to the right was strange to the captain in the pilot house, but he rang the bell in the engine room instructing the crew to hold the ferry idle in compliance with the other craft's one-toot signal. When he heard "blaw, blaw," still off to the right but closer, he was puzzled; this was not the signal that should have followed. While he was wondering what might be out there, the mysterious caller sounded off three times, "blaw, blaw, blaw." Ordi-

ALL ABOARD FOR THE OFFICE

The upper deck cabin of a ferryboat in the Thirties.

Courtesy of Southern Pacific

narily three toots meant back up. A little alarmed, the captain answered with the boat's whistle three times, "whoo, whoo, whoo," ordered the engines stopped, and waited nervously. Suddenly out of the fog blanket directly in front of the bow appeared a small motor boat, moving slowly. Soon behind it under tow came a barge with a lone cow standing on it. As the barge floated by, the cow looked up at the captain and said "blaw" rather weakly. The exhausted animal had been trying valiantly to answer all the whistles and toots on the Bay, and was very, very tired.

One of the public relations problems at the Ferry Building was the operation of the State Belt Line Railroad at the peak morning commute hours. Hun-

dreds of office workers hurrying off the boats and rushing to board the streetcars at the Ferry Building loop were frequently cut off by a locomotive and long string of freight cars slowly passing in front of them. Usually several minutes went by before they could cross the few remaining feet to the loop boarding stop and attempt to make it in to their desks on time. The State Harbor Board received constant complaints.

The scenario for a typical trip from the Ferry Building during the evening rush hour starting just before five o'clock was familiar to every regular commuter. The waiting room would fill up quickly and seats on the massive curved-back wooden benches were at a premium. The cigar, candy, popcorn and magazine stands did a brisk business. A music box against the wall often filled the room with music; its stacked "musical pie" records which shifted into position as the selection buttons were punched, were visible through the glass window.

The Ferry Building and a busy San Francisco waterfront (late Twenties).

Courtesy of the California Division of Highways

ALL ABOARD FOR THE OFFICE

Upstairs on the second floor of the Ferry Building the wooden benches in the cavernous waiting room, which was dotted with potted palms, were also jammed with commuters turning the pages of their late afternoon newspapers. A ticket-collecting gate and a shiny brass-rod fence cut off one end of the waiting room from the tunnel passageway leading to the entrances to berthed ferryboats.

When an arriving ferry had docked and the last of the debarking passangers were on their way to the streetcar loop outside the Ferry Building, a heavy sliding door in the downstairs waiting room was rolled back by a leaning terminal worker. The crowd that had bunched up behind the door then hurried into the cold,

drafty, black-tar-covered passageway and made a zig-zag dash into the slip where the boat was tied up. The gangplank had already been lowered hydraulically into place, and embarking passengers walked down the slight incline onto the main deck of the ferry. Already aboard, on the two wooden-floored alleyways running through to the front end of the main deck, were flat-bed carts with high, spoked wheels, loaded with freight, mail sacks, and passenger baggage. The carts had been

The Alameda *arriving at Oakland Pier on a commuters' run, October, 1938.*

The upper-level waiting room in the Alameda Pier, in the Twenties.

Courtesy of the Louis Stein Collection

pulled on board manually, or by small, rubber-tired motor runabouts.

You could walk directly ahead into the sparsely decorated main-deck interior. Rows of maroon-colored benches on each side of the boat were divided into two sections by metal casings which shielded the huge paddle wheels. Watertight doors gave access to the wheels for repairs or servicing. Or you could climb a stairway from the front or rear decks to the more elaborate, attractive, and warmer cabin deck. Women and children almost always went directly up there.

During the boarding process, the wooden pilings of the slip occasionally groaned in protest as the ironbark guardrail around the belly of the ferry pressed against them in response to the surges in the water below. Meanwhile, the deck hands would make the usual preparations to cast off. When everything was ready the signal would come. A bell would clang, a whistle would screech, engines would start rumbling, and the boat decks would shiver. The paddles would begin to turn slowly, picking up momentum gradually and churning up a white, frothy wake as the ferry slid out into the open water.

One popular spectator entertainment during the short crossing was watching the operation of the four-story high "walking beam" engine which powered the boat's two outside paddle-wheels. A floor-to-ceiling metal casing vertically ran through the center of both the main and cabin decks. Known as a "fidley," it contained the massive iron and steel arms of the engine. They moved up and down in a sweeping circular motion, linking the boat's cylinders, main rod, and crank. Through openings in the fidley on both decks you could watch the impressive swings of the huge metal arms only a few feet away. This box-seat view was a fascinating treat for small, wide-eyed children who were held up in their parents' arms to watch.

Arrival at the slips at Oakland, Alameda or Sausalito also involved another little scenario played out on each docking. First you felt the crushing impact of the bow against the weathered, blackened piling that

ALL ABOARD FOR THE OFFICE

showed scattered white blotches of seagull droppings. This was followed by the familiar groan of strained timber, the jangle of chains being lowered, and the drip of bilge water as the ferry eased in. The boat often took a beating on arrival in rough weather, veering from side to side while it reversed its engines. If the docking was violent and the boat rolled about, crashing up against the squeaky wooden slip, queasy passengers would sometimes get seasick.

The usual series of bells jingled topside. The bowline loops were flung over the piling hooks and the slack taken up on the deck as the lines were played back and forth around the deck cleats. Within a few minutes, the gangplanks were lowered, the hand lines dropped, and the crowd surged to the line of track terminals and the waiting trains, each set of tracks marked with a long sign listing the destination stations on that route.

The ferryboat lines were constantly attempting to add to the comfort and innovations they provided to their passengers, and sometimes to meet competition. In March, 1928, the Golden Gate Ferry Company, which operated between the Hyde Street Pier in San Francisco and Sausalito, in competition with the Southern Pacific runs from the Ferry Building, announced that "in line with the Golden Gate policy of keeping pace with the times," it was equipping each boat with radio-reception equipment. Four loudspeakers were placed on each boat, one at each end on both decks. Patrons were then able to "enjoy all the latest music and offerings of all local broadcasting stations." The system was also used to pass orders to the officers on the boats and to broadcast any emergency calls from the shore to passengers who might be aboard.

Later that year there seemed to be indications that the passenger-ferry business was falling off, but a revival two years later in 1930 produced a record—almost sixty million passengers, including those in automobiles, crossed the Bay that year.

In the early 1930s, six companies operated passenger-ferry service out of San Francisco's Ferry Building. The Southern Pacific had routes to the Oakland Mole and the Alameda Pier, both about three-and-a-half miles away. It fed its own steam and electric lines to points near and far. From the Mole, S.P. steam trains left for north, east, and southern destinations, and electric cars departed for points in Oakland, Berkeley, San Leandro, Emeryville, and Albany. The Alameda Pier had only about a quarter of the Mole's

The Golden Bear, *flagship of the Golden Gate Ferries' San Francisco-Berkeley direct auto-ferry service, prepares to dock. (1927)*

volume of traffic for its electric cars, which ran only to the city of Alameda.

The Southern Pacific also owned the controlling interest in the dominant auto-ferry business on the Bay. The Southern Pacific-Golden Gate Ferry Company had resulted from a 1929 merger of S.P.'s auto-ferry routes between San Francisco and the East Bay with several other lines. The S.P. routes ran to the Oakland Pier slips adjoining the Mole passenger train terminal, to the Alameda Pier, and to the landing at the foot of Broadway, the historic Oakland Harbor or "Creek Route" some six-and-a-half miles from the Ferry Building. As late as 1932, horse-drawn drays were carried along with automobiles on boats to and from the Broadway landing, and S.P. said it carried one million foot passengers on the route that year at five cents each.

The major company involved in the merger with Southern Pacific was the competing Golden Gate Ferry Company. Its fleet of twenty-six yellow auto ferries, each with a capacity of eighty-five to ninety cars, traveled from the Hyde Street Pier in San Francisco near Fishermen's Wharf to Sausalito and Berkeley. Also using the Ferry Building slips was the Monticello Line, acquired in 1927 by the Golden Gate

GOOD LIFE IN HARD TIMES

Autos lined up to board the Southern Pacific auto ferry in Oakland in the mid-Twenties.

Courtesy of Southern Pacific

Ferry Company. It had the longest scheduled ferryboat run on the Bay—thirty miles to Vallejo, an hour-and-forty-five-minute voyage which was a great sightseeing bargain. A foot passenger could make the three-and-a-half-hour round-trip cruise to Vallejo and back for a dollar. Fare for an automobile and driver was a dollar-and-a-half one way, and an additional fifteen cents apiece for up to four passengers. The Northwestern Pacific auto ferries ran from the Ferry Building to slips at its main passenger terminal and dock in Sausalito.

By 1931, the Southern Pacific-Golden Gate auto-ferry operation was handling more than six million cars a year, about three times California's total motor vehicle registration. About a thousand workers were on its payroll; this increased another two hundred during the summer months when traffic was heaviest. In the Thirties it ran an all-night service from San Francisco to Oakland, Berkeley, and Sausalito.

Besides Southern Pacific, three other railroad lines ran passenger boats out of the Ferry Building. The white Northwestern Pacific boats, with their familiar circle emblem showing a lone redwood tree with Mount Tamalpais in the background, delivered travelers and commuters to Sausalito. From there, the railroad operated its Marin County service and Redwood Empire line trains north. The other two railroads were Western Pacific, terminating at its own train departure pier in Oakland, and the Santa Fe, terminating in Richmond until 1933, when it agreed to run its passenger trains through Oakland and out to the Southern Pacific ferryboat service.

The formidable orange fleet of the Key System fed its transbay ferryboat passengers into its elaborate train and bus transit network in the East Bay. Key's Oakland terminal pier, built shortly after the turn of the century, reached out three miles from the Oakland shoreline into the Bay. It brought the Key boats' departure point closer to the Ferry Building than that of any competing line, a substantial advantage. The electric-powered Key ferries made the crossing in fifteen minutes, as compared with eighteen for the Southern Pacific. This three-minute edge at each end of the trip was increased by the longer layovers required by the S.P. boats in Oakland to handle train passengers and their baggage, as well as U.S. mail sacks. The Key System was strictly a commuter operation. A dividend result for Key was that it needed only two boats to offer the same service Southern Pacific gave with three, a definite expense saver.

The Key Pier was built on two miles of earth fill and one final mile of wood trestling. Six Key interurban lines fanned out from the eastern shoreline end of the pier to Oakland, Berkeley and Piedmont, with trains of from one to nine cars at the peak commute hours. The olive-green cars of the Sacramento Northern Railway trains also came in at the Key Pier, and their passengers used the Key boat service to San Francisco. The pier's waiting room was noted for its potted palms, banana trees, and interior fence of turned wooden rods.

The prides of the Key ferry fleet were the *Peralta* and *Yerba Buena* motor ships. Built to order in 1927, they had steel hulls and a special teakwood finish, and could carry five thousand passengers each. The pilot

houses were painted mahogany, in sedate contrast to the overall orange color of the boats.

Unfortunately, the *Peralta* was to prove to be a jinx ship. Not counting suicides, there had never been a loss of life through a ferryboat accident on San Francisco Bay until February 17, 1928. On that day, the *Peralta*, with less than a year of service, was headed east from San Francisco loaded with evening rush commuters. Just as it came opposite Yerba Buena Island, its bow suddenly and unexpectedly plunged deep into the chill waters which surged waist high over the outside forward deck. As usual, many passengers had crowded out there in order to be up front in the race for choice seats on the waiting trains at the pier ahead. One girl was immediately swept over the side. There were cries of "We're sinking," and panic spread over the 5:15 commute crowd. Some men and women dashed to the rail, climbed up, and leaped into the Bay. Others, inside, smashed windows and plunged into the water below. Most of the passengers on the forward deck rushed toward the stern of the boat, pushing and shoving frantically. Some of them joined other wild-eyed passengers struggling for the canvas life belts that were stored in overhead racks, breaking and splintering the wood supports as they dragged down the belts.

A Key Route train crossing the Key Route Pier shortly after service was started in 1903.

The Key System's Peralta, *which had nothing but bad luck (1926).*

Courtesy of the San Francisco Public Library

At least thirty passengers were washed overboard or jumped from the *Peralta* to the accompaniment of screams of terror and horror. The Key ferryboat *Hayward*, which was passing the *Peralta* on its way to San Francisco, quickly stopped and lowered a life boat. Two Navy launches were sent out from a Yerba Buena Island installation to rescue passengers thrashing in the water. Finally, the *Peralta* itself lowered a boat, which was manned by two commuters, a deckhand and a ship's officer.

Not all the passengers in the water were rescued. Five persons drowned. A subsequent investigation placed the blame for the accident on improper handling of the boat's water ballast. The rear tank should have been filled to compensate for the extra weight of the usual passenger surge to the front of the boat as the landing pier was approached. Instead, the front tank had remained filled from the trip over and the added passenger weight had been too much.

Five years later, the *Peralta* was involved in another Key System disaster. On January 21, 1933, at about ten o'clock at night, the sleek boat was tied up at the Key Pier when a fire broke out suddenly and soon spread along the entire width of the pier. The bright flames licking into the dark sky were clearly visible from the waterfront as well as many San Francisco and East Bay hilltops. When the blaze was finally quenched

hours later, the three million dollars in damages suffered by Key included fourteen electric cars and the completely gutted *Peralta*. The pier building had been completely leveled. Only one slip remained usable. Southern Pacific helped carry Key's passengers during the emergency period until the pier was rebuilt. The new all-steel and fire-resistant terminal building opened in October, 1934.

Finally, one independent auto-ferry service, the Richmond-San Rafael Ferry and Transportation Company, operated between Point San Quentin on the Marin County side of the Bay and Point Molate on the Richmond side. Its distinctive red-colored boats were easily recognizable until the early Thirties when they were painted the conventional white used by then on the other auto-ferry lines.

The auto-ferry operations had special problem wrinkles of their own. Sometimes drivers would walk around the boat, start talking to friends who were riding purely as passengers, and walk off with them. They would suddenly remember, and blurt out with embarrassment, "Hey, I forgot my car." In January, 1933, a story appeared in San Francisco newspapers about a possible suicide off the Lake Tahoe auto ferry of Southern Pacific. An abandoned car had been found on board when the motorship pulled into the Ferry Building slip. A few hours later, it was learned the driver of the car had absent-mindedly gotten into the car of a friend and ridden off to work.

Over in Berkeley, the three-and-a-half-mile causeway pier out to the auto ferry slips was extremely narrow, and Southern Pacific officials were always afraid that some day a drunken driver would swerve off into the water. As a preventative measure, crew members on the boats would keep a wary eye out for drivers who appeared to be unsteady. When they suspected someone, the traffic officer at the Berkeley pier would be alerted when the boat pulled in. The suspected tipsy driver would be flagged down by the officer and instructed to pull off to one side. The officer would reach in, take the ignition key out, and return it only when he was sure the driver was clearly sober.

When the collegiate football season's Big Game between California and Stanford was held in Berkeley, a bumper-to-bumper string of cars would line the entire three-and-a-half-mile stretch from the pier slips back to the foot of University Avenue after the game. Thirteen boats were usually in service on the twenty-four minute run to San Francisco.

ALL ABOARD FOR THE OFFICE

The new Key System Pier, rebuilt after the 1933 fire.

Courtesy of AC Transit

The Berkeley pier was known for its one-legged seagull, apparently no relation to the notorious "Peg-leg Pete" who followed the boats on the Oakland-San Francisco ferry lanes. This one was a land-based panhandler who had staked out a monopoly. He would beg food from parked motorists waiting for the boats, hopping up and down the line of cars and jerking his beak up and down in case anyone didn't get the message. If another seagull happened to land on the dock, Pete would chase the intruder away with squawks of outrage and warning.

Then there was Eddie, the Dumb Seagull, as commuters named him. Eddie used to hang around the Key pier in Oakland, but always had trouble actually landing. He was once observed on a cold day touching down on an ice-covered spot on the pier, skidding clumsily, and cracking up against a wooden four-by-four that edged the lip of the pier. His particular frustration was trying to set down in rainy weather on top of the gold balls which topped the flagpoles of the ferryboats. They always seemed to be too slippery for Eddie, and he apparently never succeeded in making a successful landing, although he kept trying. On one particularly windy and wet day, Eddie was observed making three separate attempts to land on the flagpole of a boat starting out for San Francisco. Failing twice but twice returning, he finally fell ignominiously into the water, witnesses reported, while commuter regulars gathered at the windows of another boat jeered.

The Northwestern Pacific's network of boats and trains serving Marin County commuters and residents had its own little world of travel and its own peculiarities. All Marin commuters to San Francisco converged from all directions on a single terminal, in Sausalito. The trip with the heaviest traffic was the 8 A.M. weekday boat, usually the huge *Eureka*, which

After the Bay Bridge was completed ferryboats continued to operate in and out of the Ferry Building (about 1938).

Courtesy of Southern Pacific

could carry 3,300 passengers. Four trains from different interurban runs would pull into the depot yard at 7:55.

The Northwestern Pacific management took more than a casual interest in their riders. Printed notes were distributed to passengers on any early morning run that obviously was going to be late in arriving at the Ferry Building because of a late departure of the ferry, fog on the Bay, or some other unforeseen circumstance. The note, much like one from a parent to a teacher at school, explained to a boss why the employee was late arriving at the office that morning.

During the summer months, jam-ups would occur on Sunday nights and Monday mornings involving automobiles using the auto-ferry slips on Bridgeway

Boulevard edging the Sausalito waterfront. A never-ending chain of cars stuffed with families returning to San Francisco and peninsula towns and cities from weekend or Sunday trips would stream into the single roadway entering Sausalito. From four o'clock Sunday afternoon to ten or eleven at night, the Southern Pacific-Golden Gate auto ferries would keep as many as fourteen boats in service to try to keep up with the traffic load backed up all the way out of town and up the winding hill to the north on Highway 101. At about 11:15 P.M., a sudden drop-off of traffic coming in would occur, when scarcely enough cars would arrive to fill a single boat. But on Monday mornings another gush of loaded cars would spill into Sausalito between six and nine as office workers struggled to get to work in the City on time.

Weekends, especially Sundays, also saw a heavy influx of hikers into Marin on the ferries and the connecting interurban trains to Mill Valley. From Mill

ALL ABOARD FOR THE OFFICE

The ferryboat San Leandro *on the last Bay ferry trip, July 30, 1958. The ferryboat model on the forward deck is being prepared to be dropped overboard.*

Courtesy of Southern Pacific

Valley trails led to Muir Woods, Mount Tamalpais, and the Dipsea Trail to Stinson Beach. Northwestern Pacific printed and distributed special "Hiking in Marin" and "Vacation" folders. The reported record Sunday crowd on the ferryboats was approximately 25,000 one weekend in 1920.

Not all the passengers on the Bay rode in regularly scheduled ferryboats. In August, 1934, a special trip was organized for fifty-two passengers on two barred and armored railroad coaches. These arrived at Tiburon on the north shore of the Bay in Marin County, where the coaches were rolled aboard special barges with tracks on the decks, and then pulled by tugs over to Alcatraz Island. Inside the coaches, chained to the seats in pairs, were "Scarface Al" Capone and other notorious federal prisoners being transferred to the maximum security "Rock" in the Bay.

These jumbo-size barges, capable of carrying up to fourteen freight cars, were a familiar sight to ferryboat commuters and passengers. Occasionally the connecting rods on a freight car would break as it was running onto a barge and the car would keep on going, dropping off the stern and into the Bay with a costly splash.

Besides the barges there were also self-powered freight ferryboats that could carry as many as sixteen freight cars on their low, flat decks. The Santa Fe, Western Pacific, and Northwestern Pacific railroads used these barges and boats to carry all their freight in or out of San Francisco, connecting up with their freight car terminal yards around the Bay. The Southern Pacific only barged a minor portion of their freight business this way with its special ferryboat *Transit*.

Nineteen thirty was the peak year for ferryboat

traffic on the Bay. After that it was all downhill as the automobile became more of a family staple and less of a luxury.

Improvements in the highways and roads drew more people out from the urban centers and the auto-ferry traffic, rather than the passenger trade, became the center of interest. More people began to use their cars to get to work on the boats and carpools were formed, taking revenue and riders away from the passenger boats.

When construction started in 1933 on both the Bay Bridge to Oakland and the Golden Gate Bridge to Sausalito and Marin County, the towers and girders that seemed to rise out of the Bay were recognized by hard-headed realists as a gallows for the ferryboats. When the trap would be sprung was only a matter of when the bridges opened.

Some people were afraid that the new Bay Bridge concrete towers would be a hazard to ferryboat traffic, but these fears proved to be unwarranted. Collisions turned out to be the least of the ferry enthusiast's worries. Within a few years there were more surplus ferryboats for sale than in operation.

The Bay Bridge opened for auto traffic in November, 1936, six months ahead of schedule. One widely trumpeted statistical estimate had it that approximately one million people traveled across the bridge in 250,000 cars, buses, and trucks in the first 108 hours of operation. Combined with the losses due to the car pools driving across, Key System and Southern Pacific suffered a drop of more than 3,300,000 ferryboat passenger-trips in the first year the Bay Bridge was open.

Meanwhile, the Golden Gate Bridge opened in May, 1937, connecting San Francisco and Marin County by automobile, bus, and truck. About the same time, the Southern Pacific-Golden Gate Ferries reduced their auto-ferry fares in a futile fight-back gesture. The Hyde Street to Sausalito fare was cut from seventy-five cents for an auto and driver to fifty cents with no extra charge for up to four passengers. The dollar and half trip to Vallejo for an auto and driver was reduced to a dollar.

Reducing the fares was really tilting at windmills. Less than a year later, in July, 1938, Southern Pacific-Golden Gate Ferries ended its auto ferry service on the Bay and closed the Hyde Street-Sausalito crossing. Twenty-two of its boats were put up for sale. It was bargain day for ferryboat buyers. The independently-owned Richmond-San Rafael line snapped up three steel-hulled boats at ten cents on the dollar.

With the sale of the other boats serving Sausalito, Northwestern Pacific operated the only remaining ferryboat service between San Francisco and Marin County. Its passenger boats travelled from the Ferry Building to Sausalito and Tiburon. Northwestern Pacific continued to carry automobiles on the open aprons of its Sausalito boats except during commuter hours. As many as six cars were carried on the aft deck, four on the forward deck.

But Northwestern Pacific couldn't make it either. In December, 1938, the railroad company applied to the State Railroad Commission for approval to abandon its Marin interurban train service. The following month, on January 15, 1939, Southern Pacific and Key System inaugurated train service directly to San Francisco from the East Bay over the Bay Bridge's lower deck. The new Union Terminal at First and Mission Streets, only a few blocks from the once-busy Ferry Building, had been dedicated the day before. The passenger ferryboat fleets of Southern Pacific and Key had made their last scheduled commuter runs out of Oakland and Alameda. A day earlier, by chance on reputedly bad luck day, Friday the 13th, a special committee of the regular 7:30 A.M. boat riders from the Alameda Pier decked themselves out in somber clothing and silk hats to serve as "pallbearers." Robert Lowenstein, who had commuted for fifty-seven years on the ferryboat route from Alameda to San Francisco, served as chairman. Passengers boarding the *Piedmont* for their last commuter trip were handed crying towels by the committee members. About midway across the Bay, a ferryboat model was solemnly paraded around the boat on the shoulders of the pallbearers and then dropped overboard in a final tribute.

Perhaps the fact that the model did not sink to the bottom of the Bay as planned, but bobbed up later and was scooped up by a Coast Guard cutter, was prophetic. Thirty-seven years later—in 1976—a rejuvenation of large scale, 24-hour ferryboat service for commuters on the Bay was being readied. The service was to be from Marin County to downtown San Francisco. Ironically, the sponsor was the Golden Gate Bridge and Highway District, operator of the span which had killed off the many ferryboat runs and the excellent complementing interurban electric train network that had served Marin residents for so long and so well. The bridge was being choked with increasing auto traffic during the commute hours and certain weekends, so in desperation the bridge directors turned to ordering 750-passenger, high speed ferryboats and building an expensive terminal and parking facility at Larkspur on Corte Madera Creek. The District had been preparing for this by operating a smaller commuter motor ship between Sausalito and the Ferry Building since 1970. Some Marin commuters had also been coming in daily since 1962 to downtown San Francisco with the privately-operated Harbor Carriers which ran launches between Tiburon and the Ferry Building, increasing service during the commute hours.

In 1939, the Key System's orange ferryboats which had not been sold off, began a short-lived comeback with a scheduled service to the Golden Gate International Exposition on man-made Treasure Island, built on the northern shoals of Yerba Buena Island through which the Bay Bridge tunnel passed. Additional ferryboats were leased from Southern Pacific and Santa Fe and painted orange. Crowds of visitors laced with Exposition employees were carried over from the Ferry Building in San Francisco and the Key Pier in Oakland.

The Key boats operated from 10 A.M. until 1:30 A.M. at forty-minute intervals. In 1940, when the Exposition opened for a second season, Key boats operated from San Francisco only. Buses to Treasure Island from the East Bay were substituted for ferryboats from the Key Pier. After the Exposition finally closed in ,1940, the familiar orange boats on the Bay were seen no more. The final burial of mass transit ferryboat service on the Bay finally arrived when the State Railroad Commission acted on Northwestern Pacific's application to abandon its Marin interurban train service. On February 28, 1941, the railroad's last electric trains ran in and out of Sausalito and its last boats made runs between the Ferry Building and Sausalito, as well as to Tiburon. The *Eureka* made the last scheduled San Francisco-Sausalito commuter run. It was a raucous, emotional party on the huge craft that ploughed through the wind-whipped water on what was described as "one of the stormiest days the Bay had ever known." The noisy and exhuberant passengers were met on their arrival in Sausalito by policemen who patiently recovered from them intended souvenirs of the occasion, including life belts and dishes. Before that funeral day, some valiant, but fruitless, protests and resistance moves were staged by groups of Marin commuters and diehard ferryboat and railroad buffs. A

The dedication of the East Bay Terminal, First and Mission Streets, San Francisco, January 14, 1939.

Courtesy of AC Transit

representative protest gesture appeared in the last news bulletin issued by the Save-the-Trains-and-Ferries League in Marin County before it ran out of funds. The editorial was titled,"Ride a Bus Just Once," and read as follows:

Have you ever tried the bus? We believe every commuter should—just once. Now is the time to put the buses to the test. The weather is rainy and you will have to wait at some street corner where there is no shelter, but every bus traveler has to put up with that.

Find out for yourselves—now, not later, what your chances are to get that continued story read. Try the ventilation of a bus. Take a deep breath near the end of the journey. Try again.

Where is the deck where you can take a short, brisk stroll in the fresh air? Try the seats—are they wide enough for comfort? Maybe you will have to stand up. Does standing up in a bus all the way to San Francisco improve your disposition?

Ask where the restrooms are located on the bus. Perhaps the bus carried card tables for the convenience of its passengers, perhaps not. If the bus has some place where you can get a cup of coffee and something to eat, now is the time to find out.

Unfortunately, no official poll was taken of the Marin commuters back there in 1940 to see if they did find out.

The San Leandro *on the last regular Key System ferryboat run to the Ferry Building in January, 1939. The* San Leandro *was later acquired by Southern Pacific.*

Courtesy of AC Transit

Almost thirty years later, in 1969, the Marin Transit District polled commuters as to the mode of travel they would most prefer. Ferries came in first. Buses came in last. Survivors of the Save-The-Trains-And-Ferries League must have smirked a little, especially when they read about the plans of the Golden Gate Bridge and Highway District to buy some ferryboats and begin commuter service to San Francisco.

After the 1941 demise of the San Francisco-Marin County ferryboat service, only two regularly scheduled lines continued to operate on the Bay, attempting to ignore the roar of traffic on the two bridges. Even they were only postponing the inevitable. The San Rafael-Richmond auto-ferryboats shuttled between Marin and Contra Costa counties until 1956, when the $20

million Richmond-San Rafael Bridge was completed by the State and opened to traffic. Southern Pacific's limited passenger boat runs from the Ferry Building to the Oakland Mole, where the railroad's main-line trains continued to roll in and out, kept churning a wake under the Bay bridges until July 30, 1958. On that day, the ferryboat *San Leandro*, bulging with misty-eyed old-time commuters, officials of the S.P., politicians, photographers, reporters, and the perennial attendees at all such historic events, made the last "official" crossing to the Ferry Building. So ended ninety-five years of uninterrupted ferryboat commuter service on the Bay.

The new, sleek, jet-powered ferryboats running between the Ferry Building area and the Larkspur terminal in Marin County under the sponsorship of the Golden Gate Bridge administration were in service by early 1977. They revived at least a semblance of what was once a pleasant interval for tens of thousands of Bay Area residents in the daily grind of each workday.

9

Care of Mother Tusch— U.C. Berkeley

In August, 1935, we churned across the Bay from San Francisco on ferryboats and then rode to Berkeley on the electric trains. We were entering freshmen at the University of California and foresaw nothing but pleasant days ahead. Actually most of that school year was very pleasant, although beginning in March some of the press headlines were somewhat disturbing. "Shadow of Hitler over Europe," one said. Another read "Communists Riot in Spain." The prediction of Webb Miller, European correspondent for the United Press, that "War in Europe is inevitable" was printed in the *Daily Californian* student newpaper.

Miller should have foreseen war in the Pacific as well. I scrimmaged that fall against a big, raw-boned sophomore football center named Bob Herwig, later a pro star with the San Francisco Forty Niners. The next time I got that close to Herwig was on the muggy island of Guadalcanal in the Solomon Islands when we wound up in the same company of U.S. Marines.

But that August back in '35, we were light-heartedly reading the published list titled "Frosh Do's and Don'ts." It included such meaty admonitions as, "Most houses, both sororities and fraternities, like rushees to have a fair knowledge of bridge, dancing in the case of sororities . . . but if you don't, be cheerful about it."

Room and board in private houses around the campus ran between twenty-five and thirty-five dollars a month. Rooms could be had for eight dollars single or ten double.

The Sip and Bite Sandwich Shop on Telegraph Avenue, a few doors down from Sather Gate and Allston Way, offered "quality food prepared and served by experienced hotel men." They were identified as "Albert, formally of Mark Hopkins Hotel," and "Mike, formerly of Athens Athletic Club." Vienna Meat Loaf with vegetable and potato was

twenty-five cents. Hamburger steak, Spanish-style, also with potato, was fifteen cents. The full-course steak dinner ("a dinner what is a dinner") went for thirty-five cents. This must have been quite a change for Albert if he really was from the Mark Hopkins Hotel.

Drake's Restaurant, around the corner from Telegraph on Bancroft Way, was generally rated as having the best food around the campus as well as a pleasant atmosphere. Breakfast cost fifteen to twenty cents, lunch thirty to thirty-five cents, and dinner fifty-five to seventy-five cents.

In beauty shops, you could get a shampoo and finger wave for sixty-five cents, and a manicure for thirty-five.

Roos Brothers California Shop on Telegraph was selling shirred-back suits for twenty-five and thirty-two dollars and tuxedos for twenty-five. Gabardine suits were big that year. "The demand for gabardine suits has swept the country" one ad said. Robert Atkins in San Francisco had them in green, blue, and black for thirty dollars, and in Oakland you could buy either a single or double-breasted one for twenty at Foreman and Clark, Twelfth and Washington.

If you were really with it, you could wear the "official" garb for your class. Moleskin pants and "dink" caps, the visored skull caps, were the proper attire for freshmen, and frosh women were supposed to wear green. Blue-jean trousers, available at $1.45, and hickory-striped shirts were prescribed for sophomore men, and red was the color for second-year women. For junior men it was cords and blue shirts, and blue the color for the femmes. Finally, proper dress for senior men was cited as cords and hats, with white dresses and hair bows for the graduating women.

About twelve thousand students registered for classes at Cal that fall, ten thousand of them under-

The University of California campus in Berkeley in the fall of 1935, the year I entered as a freshman.

Courtesy of the Oakland Museum

graduates. The tuition charge was twenty-six dollars a semester for California residents, or fifty-two a year. A student-body card was ten dollars annually.

That fall I lived in a famous Berkeley landmark just off campus. Mother Tusch's was on Union Street, across from the main entrance to the Men's Gymnasium. The main house was a modest, shingled, wood-frame dwelling; in back was a small cottage which I rented with three roommates. Hanging down above the porch entrance was a sign with "The Hangar" spelled out in silver letters. Above the sign was fixed a wooden propeller from a vintage airplane.

The house was actually a private air museum loaded with souvenirs and gifts sent to Mrs. Mary Elizabeth Tusch, the landlady, from flyers she had befriended. It had all started when she began inviting student pilots over to the house on Union Street for a home-cooked dinner when they were lonely cadets at the University's training school during World War I. When I lodged there the small house was packed with everything from a piece of strut from the first plane of the Wright Brothers to the helmet worn by Charles Kingford-Smith in the first flight across the Pacific. Besides the hundreds of autographed photographs of flyers who called her "Mother" filling all available table, shelf, and wall space, signatures of celebrated aviators and explorers literally covered the walls and ceilings in two rooms. The signatures of General "Billy" Mitchell, Eddie Rickenbacker, Charles Lindbergh, Jimmy Doolittle, Admiral Richard Byrd, and Sir Hubert Wilkins could be found among those personally inscribed directly on to the walls inside the house. Glass cases housed some of the most valuable objects.

Mother Tusch's priceless collection of aviation history is now at the Smithsonian Institute's National Air Museum in Washington, D.C. The mementos were stripped from the Union Street house when Mrs. Tusch suffered a stroke and moved to the national capital in 1950. The wallpaper was even peeled off the walls so the famous signatures could be preserved. Mother Tusch died in Washington in 1960.

The Class of '39 was welcomed formally to the university at the annual Freshman Reception for all new students. Roger Bourke and his orchestra played until midnight in three large rooms of the Men's Gymnasium. The punch was plentiful and mild. Dignified and smiling University President Robert G. Sproul and Mrs. Sproul greeted us in the athletic setting which was strangely studded with large, white Grecian urns, potted bamboo, and statues.

The traditional evening Freshman Rally a short time later was held in the open-air Greek Theatre. The rally drew some eight thousand students into the chill night air and onto the cold tiers of stone lining the amphitheater. The four classes came marching down the aisles into the spectator area separately, after meeting at various rendezvous points around the campus. The freshmen led the way, carrying an effigy of the St. Mary's football team on their shoulders. St. Mary's was the first major opponent on the schedule. The huge student body band, resplendent in blue and gold uniforms, paraded noisily through the streets near the campus before marching into the rally. The mass singing by the classes was led by the university glee club. There was a tumbling team exhibition and a comedy skit. "Oski," Alpha Tau Omega sorority's bear-cub mascot, was present to entertain the rally crowd. Oski didn't get around too much anymore. He had been banned from appearing at football games because another bear-cub mascot had clawed a man on the field two years earlier. After the rally broke up, many of the crowd drifted down to the Men's Gymnasium for a post-rally dance with music furnished by Bob Beal and his Athens Club Orchestra.

The Greek Theatre was also the scene for the famous annual Pajamarino Rally held later that fall. First held on the campus way back in 1902, the rally was modeled on the "nightshirts parades" that the

Mrs. Mary Elizabeth (Mother) Tusch, my landlady and a University of California living landmark for decades, in a 1930 photograph.

Courtesy of the Oakland Tribune

older Eastern universities held before major football games. Each year a huge stack of wooden timbers piled in the open space in front of the stage was touched off in a massive bonfire that shot sparks up into the darkness. It was circled by arm-waving, dancing, pajama-clad students. The band played wildly, the glee club voices echoed off the back hills, and a pair of blue and gold pajamas went to a student for wearing the "gaudiest" nightwear. Grizzled Head Football Coach Leonard B. "Stub" Allison and Assistant Coach Frank Wickhorst delivered grim "fight talks." Dr. Harold B.

"Brick" Muller of the Class of '23, who threw the famous 68-yard forward pass to Brodie Stephens for the university's Wonder Team in the 1921 Rose Bowl game against Ohio State, spoke to the enthusiastic rooters.

No women played in the University band at these rallies. There wasn't much hope that any ever would after twelve coeds petitioned that fall to join the band. The band members voted them down 65-0. They even decisively turned down a request to allow women to rehearse with the band. The band members did approve one recommendation, however. It stated that the presence of women "would be detrimental to the esprit de corps and morale of the band." It was suggested that women form their own band.

That fall the annual men's Frosh-Soph Brawl was held at Hilgard Field on a Saturday afternoon. Several days before the event we dug a mud hole "grave" in the field and announced that we planned to pull the sophomores through it during the featured tug-of-war event. The other contests were the joust, relay race, tie-up and sack race. Each victory earned a point for the team; wins in pre-Brawl morning contests in basketball, softball, tennis, handball, and swimming were worth a half point each.

Our Brawl was to be a rough one because, for the first time, members of the previous year's freshman athletic teams were allowed to compete for the soph-

"The Hangar," Mother Tusch's house and museum, was stripped of its mementos for the National Air Museum in Washington in 1950. Zellerbach Hall occupies the site today, across from the Men's Gymnasium.

Courtesy of the Oakland Tribune

omores. They included the former frosh football team members who also formed the nucleus of the fifty-man Sophomore Vigilante Committee.

After a lapse of four years, the student body executive committee had decided to reinstate the requirement that all frosh men wear "dinks," the silly-looking blue skull caps with tiny yellow visors. The Vigilantes, wearing blue armbands with superimposed "V"'s, were charged with enforcing this ruling. Carrying wooden paddles and traveling in groups, the Vigilantes would do such things as wait on the steps outside of Wheeler Auditorium for the end of a crowded freshman lecture class. Stopping exiting freshman who were not wearing dinks, they would publicly whack them across the buttocks with the paddles.

I waited enthusiastically for the Brawl because I had had several run-ins with the Vigilantes. Known from the daily practice session to be a freshman football candidate, I was a natural target. Still, having spent almost two years out of school as a working stiff in the South-of-Market industrial plants in San Francisco, I was scornful of such "kid stuff." When the Vigilantes stopped me and demanded that I surrender my blue registration card because I had ignored several "warnings," I told them to get lost. Their normal procedure was to keep the vitally needed card until you showed up at a set time at a fraternity house to receive your "punishment."

The *Daily Californian* description of the Brawl was fairly accurate, as I remember it: "For the first time in years, the Brawl turned into a real scrap as frosh grabbed handfuls of mud from Hilgard Field and made a fighting charge against the sophomore battle line," the enthusiastic reporter wrote. "The men of '38 retaliated in kind and the battle raged until broken up by Big 'C' men, Brawl arbitrators." A description followed of a "free-for-all" occurring on the Sophomore Lawn where "most of the freshmen men were stripped of their clothes."

The Sophomores, expecially my Vigilante chums, really beat our—and my—brains out that day. The final tally was 6½ to 1. The tie-up was the only event we won. I eagerly took part in every event, and was frustrated every time. In the tug-of-war I was dragged through the sloshy mud hole we had dug ourselves. The kid on my shoulders in the joust was punched off with a well-placed thump from the padded end of a sophomore pole, and we both went face down into the oozing mud. It was a miserable afternoon.

That night the Brawl Dance was held at the Men's

CARE OF MOTHER TUSCH—U.C. BERKELEY

Gymnasium, where soft-colored lights beamed down from the ceiling. Large drapes hung downward, concealing the balcony seats. Sophomore Vigilante Don Mulford's twelve-piece orchestra played appropriate melodies for the day's activities such as "I Get a Kick Out of You," "Deep Purple," and "Little Man, You've Had a Busy Day."

The twenty-four sororities on campus pledged more than 230 women early in September, prior to the annual Channing Way Derby, which highlighted the pledge activities. The Derby started from the corner of Channing Way and College Avenue in a chilling fog at 6 A.M. The theme that year was "Crime Does Not Pay." Pledges were seated in improvised "electric chairs"; they jumped up quickly with appropriate screams as small surges of current were turned on momentarily. Other activities in keeping with the theme were held while Roger Bourke's orchestra played throughout the "ceremonies." Sophomore Eileen Davidson of Alpha Phi sorority was selected as the "Sweetheart of Sigma Chi" from a field of eight contestants.

Meanwhile, on the fraternity front most of the excitement during the "Hell Week" initiation of pledges focused on a Psi Upsilon pledge, Thomas Dawson '37. He was one of the approximately 450 new men who filled out cards indicating that they were interested in joining one of the forty-five fraternities on the campus. Following one initiation event, Dawson was revived only after a Berkely Police Department ambulance squad had worked on him for half an hour with an inhalator. He was then taken to Cowell Memorial Hospital and held overnight. One of the fraternity leaders said Dawson had rolled down a hill, clogging his nose and throat with grass, after taking part in strenuous push-up exercises. The police report said he tripped, fell down the hill, and got gravel in this throat. The Assistant Fire Chief and a doctor said it was a case of exhaustion. Dawson said nothing.

College football was really big in those days before the Forty Niners and the Raiders. Pro football was something they played back east, except for an occasional post-season appearance in the Bay Area. I remember seeing the barnstorming Chicago Bears, headed by "Red" Grange, the immortal "Galloping Ghost," play an "All-Star Pacific Coast" team headed by Ernie Nevers, Stanford's all-time great, at San Francisco's Kezar Stadium.

At the Saturday home games of California's Golden Bears in Berkeley, it seemed that the entire Bay Area

The Vigilantes would wait on the steps outside of Wheeler Auditorium. This picture was taken in 1934.

Courtesy of the Bancroft Library, University of California

poured into the narrow streets leading up to Memorial Stadium. Thousands fanned out on Shattuck Avenue from the S.P. and Key System electric cars arriving in strings from the ferry slips in Oakland.

If you got to Berkeley early enough, you probably tried to crowd into Dad's on Telegraph Avenue near Sather Gate for one of the rich, creamy milkshakes in the heavy bucket-shaped glasses that were served directly from the mixer to you. You could buy a three-gardenia corsage for your girl for fifty cents, delivered in Berkeley without charge. A diamond-topped rooter cap cost a dollar, and the pom-poms for coeds sitting in the special mid-stadium Cal cheering section were fifteen cents at the Co-op store in the Stephens Union building on campus.

The speeches at the rallies held on campus before the games sounded like the ones you heard Pat O'Brien mouthing from the screen as Knute Rockne at Notre Dame. Or perhaps they were more like those in the college movies starring Jack Oakie and Arline Judge.

GOOD LIFE IN HARD TIMES

For example at the first football rally of the season, about three thousand shouting, boisterous rooters were told by Coach Allison, the rugged, wrinkled former Navy man: "I'd go to hell for this gang. You're going to have a team to be proud of. Hoist the flag and follow through. Don't throw down the flag and howl if we lose. You'll never see an alibi. If we must, we're going to take it and keep our traps shut. We'll make errors. But everybody learns from experience and nobody will out-fight this team!"

We roared in agreement, and "Stub" smiled his appreciation.

Also at the rally, "Brick" Morse '96, known as the "perennial freshman," reminisced about football in the "Gay Nineties." He talked about the days when football games were won "by damaging the first eleven players and then proceeding to beat the remaining ones."

The huge turnout at the rally resulted in part from an editorial that appeared that day in the *Daily Californian*. "It is up to the students to let the football team know that they are behind it from the first kickoff and are never going to let it down," the paper said. "With that kind of spirit behind them, the boys in blue and gold jerseys will be a long way along the road to success."

When the Bear varsity team headed south for Los Angeles at the beginning of November for the UCLA game, a special tour for rooters on the Southern Pacific cost $17.50 round trip. It included a room at the elegant Biltmore Hotel, and taxis to and from the station. That same weekend one student was killed and nine others injured in four automobile accidents stemming from trips to Los Angeles for the game. One of the injured had fallen asleep at the wheel after driving all night. He woke up cut and bruised on the front steps of a church, his car having glanced off a light pole. He sold the wrecked car before returning to Berkeley.

Enthusiasm for the Big Game against Stanford was exceptionally high in that year of '35. The day before the game, an estimated 2,000 Cal students rioted for two hours through the streets of Berkeley following the annual men's smoker rally in the Men's Gymnasium. The riot started when students began stopping passing cars and attempting to push them into the gymnasium. The street near Sather Gate became blockaded with stopped cars. Attempts were made to derail two street cars; the ropes holding the trolleys were cut. Alerted police rushed to the United Artists Theater on Shattuck Avenue to prevent a rumored invasion attempt and

were showered with barrages of eggs. The same scene was then repeated at the California Theater. Nine people, six of them university students, were taken into custody and later released at the Berkeley police station after being reprimanded. But most of the Bay Area expressed its Big Game spirit less raucously. Some of the bridges offered Big Game toll reductions, and the hotels advertised dancing on Big Game night.

That fall must have been an interesting and startling experience for one of the fraternity pledges, Randy Hearst, who had attended summer session classes. His name was mentioned in a social note in the Loose Ends column in the *Daily Californian* shortly after the term started. Just six days later, a story in the student daily quoted a radical student leader as stating, "We're going to try to end Hearst's rotten influence on this campus at last."

The target of this verbal attack was, of course, young Hearst's father, Publisher William Randolph Hearst. This threat was one of many coming from left-wing campus groups. They were a response to the publication of a series of scathingly anti-radical articles in Hearst's San Francisco *Examiner*. "The dictates of Moscow have been given ready response by radical student groups at the University of California," the opening article warned. In the reply from the leftist student groups, university students were encouraged "to boycott Hearst Newspaper and radio stations and theaters which show Hearst Metrotone News . . . because William Randolph Hearst stands for un-American principles."

Six weeks later, an editorial in the *Daily Californian* demonstrated that in those golden years of the mid-1930s, not love, but college football, could conquer all. Titled "In the Flesh," it reported that the elder Hearst had been seen in a box at the Los Angeles Coliseum the previous Saturday, accompanied by movie stars Marion Davies and Dick Powell, cheering for the Bear varsity in its game with UCLA.

"For once in their lives," the editorial commented, "3,000 Berkeley students found themselves agreeing with Mr. Hearst." Noting that the publisher had left the game early into the fourth quarter, the editorial concluded mellowly: "In spite of this one shortcoming, we feel it is our duty to report that Mr. Hearst really is a mortal who wears a bright blue overcoat and drinks Coca-Colas."

Nineteen thirty-six was a leap year, and that meant a February 29 Big "C" Sirkus. This leap year tradition dated from 1896, when a group of fussy students asked

CARE OF MOTHER TUSCH—U.C. BERKELEY

A 1937 Frosh-Soph Brawl scene outside Hilgard Hall.
Courtesy of the Bancroft Library, University of California

the State Legislature for a day off to clean up the messy campus. The day had developed into a festive, rather than a custodial, occasion, and had been held every four years since then with the exception of 1900, which was not a leap year. The profits of the Sirkus went to help injured members of the university's athletic teams, and it was always a rootin', tootin' affair.

A cavernous 300-by-150-foot Big Top tent was pitched over a section of Edwards Field and connected with the west entrance to the Men's Gymnasium so that the milling hordes of students and visitors could pass freely between the tent and the gym. Colored flags and pennants were draped all around Edwards Field. The tent was jammed with concessions. The highly-publicized five-cents-a-dance "nickel jig," with Don Mul-

"In the tug-of-war I was dragged through the sloshy mud hole. . . ."

The Channing Way Derby for sorority pledges started early in the morning. The theme of the 1938 Derby was a model Indian village.

Courtesy of the Oakland Tribune

ford's orchestra playing, was staged in the gymnasium at night. Other concessions included penny pitching, egg- and dart-throwing booths, a ducking pool, and a rat race. There was also a pie-throwing contest. You could stuff yourself with "Sno-cones," whipped cotton-candy floss from paper scoops, "Karmel" corn, hot dogs, ice cream, peanuts, and popcorn. Beer was sold. Anything harder you had to bring yourself and drink on the sly.

The tent hullaballoo went on from two in the afternoon until one the following morning. It shut down from five to seven P.M. to allow the concessions to regroup and the smoke to clear. On Sirkus day, 1936, at 12:30 an explosion on Charter Hill above

campus signaled the start of the parade. A gigantic, half-mile long, two-and-a-half-hour procession of ninety-two floats snaked through the streets of Berkeley. An estimated thirty thousand spectators watched the Big "C" Sirkus Parade along its route, which ended at the Campanile on campus. Prizes were awarded by the Sirkus Queen to the outstanding floats.

Later that spring, shortly before our freshman year ended, the American Student Union organized a nationwide, one-hour-long "Peace Strike" in colleges and high schools. The 11 A.M. rally at Sather Gate drew about five thousand students, faculty, and outsiders—the largest single group in the country to participate. Socialist Party leader Norman Thomas, the perennial candidate for President, was the main speaker. Although traffic was blocked at Telegraph and Allston Way for an hour, and despite the presence of a considerable number of uniformed Berkeley policemen no incidents occurred. "Not an egg was thrown," a press report noted.

"Young men have the power to make or break war," Thomas told the cheering crowd, which overflowed onto the campus. Other speakers came from the American Students Union and the Young Communists League. Still, the Berkeley campus was not the pacesetter then for riotous student demonstrations that it was to become later with the Free Speech Movement.

Things were not so quiet that day on other campuses. Down south at UCLA in Westwood, crosses were burned on lawns the night before the demonstration, and a flurry of circulars reading "The Klan Rides Again" littered the campus. At the University of Kansas, striking students were greeted with tear gas bombs. Scuffles broke out and the meeting of three hundred demonstrators scattered.

I have a bag of assorted other memories and events of that year in Berkeley. For instance, there was the morning that "Bojangles" Bill Robinson danced for more than two hours on the floor of the Men's Gym. The great black entertainer was headlining the stage show at the Golden Gate Theater in San Francisco that week, and graciously agreed to cross the Bay and demonstrate his skill to the tap dancing classes and any other students that cared to drop in. Robinson had no music accompaniment as he danced. He didn't need any. He made music with his feet. Talking gently, explaining carefully the steps and routines, the slender dancer held the crowd of hundreds of students entranced as he glided across the hardwood floor. Periodically he would burst out in a spurt of rapid-fire motion, with his toes and heels cracking off the wood with machine-gun sounds.

I remember well the lazy afternoons I spent in the classroom of Professor David Prescott Barrows in rickety South Hall, listening to the ramrod-straight old general tell our Latin American history class about the Allied Expeditionary Army he took across the frozen steppes of Siberia in 1919. It was about as far afield as you could get from Latin America, but the booming-voiced, jumbo version of the "Esky" character on Esquire magazine covers told a damned interesting yarn.

Memory-stirring names appeared in Berkeley that year. Amelia Earhart spoke at the Berkeley City Women's Club. The aviatrix had a cousin, Beatrice Earhart, who was an economics major at the university. And there was a young Stanford sophomore basketball star from San Francisco's Galileo High School who attracted a lot of attention when he

appeared against the Bear varsity. He was Angelo "Hank" Luisetti and he was to become an all-time great.

Many a campus romance began at the Mixer Dances, the "afternoon moonlight specials," held on Thursdays from 2:30 to 5 in the Women's Clubrooms at Stephens Union. Admission was ten cents with a registration card for dancing to the music of Benny Goodman, Kay Kyser, Glenn Miller, and Tommy Dorsey and their bands—on records, of course.

Nineteen thirty-six was also the year of "Rainbow Isles in the South Seas." This all-color travelogue drew standing room only for its spectacular run of five repeat performances within a few months at Wheeler Auditorium. The narrator and producer, Rodman C. Pell, personally gave scholarly and dull descriptions to accompany the routine film. The *Daily Californian*,

A 1937 view of Telegraph Avenue from Bancroft Way to Allston Way. Today this area is Sproul Plaza.

Courtesy of the Louis Stein Collection

puzzling over the film's popularity, finally ran a photograph of a scene showing two bare-breasted "Tahitian maidens" and asked in the caption with the photograph: "Can this be the reason?" Whether it was or not, the final showing was sold out extra early.

The mammary display in this photograph was rather risqué for any daily newspaper then, let alone a university publication. Some concern was expressed about possible reactions. However, something else in the same edition of the campus paper was of far greater interest to the university administration. Student Editor Larry Resner had written an editorial stating that students were now recognizing "the chaos and discontent bred by capitalistic society." Resner said that he personally was "firmly convinced of the right of the radicals and the shallowness of the general student body." So the eyebrow-lifting picture of the Tahitian maidens was ignored while administration chiefs worried about the effect of the sentiments Resner expressed on future contributions to the university from the "capitalistic" alumni. Resner escaped possible disciplinary action of any consequence, since he was graduating and it had been the final issue for the paper.

The capitalistic spirit was by no means inhibited by Resner's article. For example, two enterprising students brought a trailer house up from Brawley in Southern California, parked it on a lot at Channing Way and Dana, and announced they would rent it out

for fifty dollars for the year, throwing in the use of a car for the first semester. Complete with bathroom and shower, two-burner stove, carpeting, and green curtains, the trailer came with an arrangement for an electricity connection to a neighboring home for $1.50 a month.

On the ferryboats to and from San Francisco, you passed under the light-bathed towers of the Bay Bridge then under construction, which reflected brilliantly in the dark blue waters. Already in place was a skeleton web of girders reaching out from the Oakland shoreline toward Yerba Buena Island. In 1936, the first span was being hung on a suspension cable looped between towers.

People were nostalgic about the ferryboats even then, as the bridge took shape. "There goes another tradition," a young *Daily Californian* columnist, Phyllis Kimball, lamented. "Half the glamor of going Dining in the City lies in the cooling, restful interims on the ferry . . . when you can disentangle yourself from Four in the Front Seat and go upstairs . . . to play the slot machines or have a coke, or look at the bridge."

On football Saturdays, you probably tried to crowd into Dad's on Telegraph Avenue near Sather Gate for one of the rich, creamy milkshakes. This is a 1930 view.

Courtesy of the Louis Stein Collection

10

Remember the Rose Bowl?

On a Saturday night between April and September in the Thirties, you might have gone dancing in Marin County under the stars in a redwood grove. There has never been a lovelier setting for dancing in the Bay Area than the Rose Bowl. It was set in a grove of soaring redwood giants in the heart of Larkspur. Its waxed, glistening hardwood floor was pierced by massive redwood, and smaller buckeye, bay, ash, and maple tree trunks. The floor shimmered under strings and clusters of strategically placed bulbs, Chinese lanterns, and floodlights. Sheets of red, blue, amber, and green illumination swept over the dancing couples below. A bubbling creek ran under a portion of the floor and could be seen outside, just off Cane Street. A few fallen leaves lay scattered about the floor, giving a further rustic and authentic touch to the outdoor scene.

Thousands of dancers, ranging from high school students to senior citizens, packed the half-acre floor every Saturday night for the twenty-two weeks of the season, which started right after Easter. They came from all over the Bay Area. Their cars jammed the two-lane roads into and out of town. They loaded the auto and passenger ferries which rumbled by each other on the Bay, passing Alcatraz Island, "The Rock." The trip to Larkspur in the summer, on the wind-whipped and sometimes fog-shrouded upper deck of a huge ferryboat, with occasional blasts from the fog horns sounding like honking geese, was an exhilarating way to start off a promising evening.

During the Thirties when my friends and I went to Larkspur for the Saturday-night dances, the towers for the Golden Gate Bridge were still being constructed. To get to Larkspur, we crossed to Sausalito, either boarding a passenger boat at the Ferry Building at the foot of Market Street, or driving to the Hyde Street pier to take the auto ferry. A few cars could be taken on the

longer run from the Ferry Building, but there was no sound reason for going by car that way.

If we took a streetcar down to the Ferry Building for a five-cent fare, we got off in front of the clock tower at the end of the terminal loop of rails. The waiting room for the Sausalito passenger ferry was just inside some shiny, gold-colored metal grillwork. At one of the marble-counter ticket windows outside, we always bought a one-way boat and train ticket to Larkspur for fifty-four cents, hoping to "bum" a ride back to the City after the dance with friends who had come over in cars on the auto ferry. If we didn't succeed, it meant leaving the dance early, since the last electric train with a connection to a ferryboat left Larkspur at about 11:30, an hour and a half before the Rose Bowl dance ended.

The thirty-two-minute ferry trip to Sausalito was not just a Saturday night commute to us. It was a voyage, with all the rewarding pleasures of boat travel, even if on a minor scale. There was the invigorating bite of the cold wind sweeping in from the Pacific. You were obliged to lean somewhat into it to stay upright when you went outside from the upper deck's warm and cozy enclosed cabin. Two life boats hung from their davits on each end of the boat above the open lower deck, ready for launching. Sea gulls followed the boat and swooped down low, coaxing passengers to toss food morsels into the air for them to snatch.

Other attractions conjured up what we imagined to be the pleasures of sea travel, an enclosed restaurant on the upper cabin deck, for example. A bottle of beer, with crackers, was fifteen cents. "Eastern" beers and ales were more expensive—twenty cents. Coffee was ten cents, as was a slice of apple pie (fifteen cents with cheese and twenty cents à la mode). If you had not eaten before you left the City, you could get a bowl of

The glistening dance floor was pierced by tree trunks and overhung with branches. (Early Thirties.)

Courtesy of the San Francisco Public Library

"Exposition Clam Chowder" for fifteen cents, a roast beef sandwich with mashed potatoes and brown gravy for twenty cents, a minced ham or cheese omelette for thirty-five cents, or a hamburger steak with sautéed onions and fried potatoes for forty cents.

Reinforcing our Walter Mitty image of being aboard a seagoing cruise ship were the stacks of life jackets under the curved seat benches. Illustrated instructions on how to put them on when abandoning ship were visible in glass frames on the walls near the outboard windows.

Smoking was permitted on the lower deck and in a separate, low-ceilinged little alcove inside the upper deck men's room. The sins of youth in those days were smoking and drinking. Marijuana and other narcotics were things you usually knew about only from reading Sax Rohmer's novels about "the insidious Dr. Fu-Manchu," or perhaps Frank L. Packard's detective stories about the underworld of yeggs and other crooks.

Sometimes we would bring a bottle of bourbon or gin and pass it around surreptitiously on the open, swaying cabin deck (the ninety-eight-cent fifth of Five O'Clock Gin was a popular buy). The passing of the bottle seemed to serve as a symbolic signal that we were really taking off for a devil-may-care Saturday night of fun, frolic and, hopefully, sin.

The seven-mile train ride to the tiny Larkspur station from Sausalito took only fourteen minutes despite four stops. The Baltimore Park station came just before Larkspur, but we never got off there, although it was closer to the Rose Bowl. We preferred to follow a favorite walking route from the Larkspur station through town, with bar stopovers.

If Suren Hagopian could borrow his brother's 1932 blue Model "A" Ford convertible roadster, we skipped the rail trip and avoided the pre-midnight Cinderella deadline for catching the last train out of Larkspur. Instead, we would take the Southern Pacific-Golden Gate auto ferry from the foot of Hyde Street to Sausalito, and drive nine miles up and down the high, switchbacking two-lane mountain road, then part of Highway 101, from Richardson Bay, through Corte Madera, and on into Larkspur. There were usually five of us crammed into the car, with three in the front seat nudging the stick gear shift, and two in the rear rumble seat. We usually shined up the convertible in the afternoon with auto polish and wax. And Suren would pinch his nostrils together and imitate Al Jolson's voice singing "the stars are going to twinkle and shine, tonight about a quarter to nine," from a popular song of the day.

After arriving in Larkspur, we would head first for the Blue Rock Inn bar on Magnolia Avenue across from the station. A few beers or Tom Collins' there, and we would walk one block up Magnolia to Cane Street and the crowded, smoke-filled Bob's Tavern on the corner. It was the closest bar to the Rose Bowl, some forty yards up Cane Street. There was another

REMEMBER THE ROSE BOWL?

"Thousands of dancers . . . packed the half-acre floor."

Courtesy Marin County Historical Society

bar on Magnolia, just across the street from Bob's, which was painted a calamine pink. It was named the Rose Bowl Chateau and we usually patronized it during the dance intermissions.

Mixed drinks were twenty-five cents, a bottle of local beer fifteen. Nobody ever asked our age, and most of our crowd were four or five years under twenty-one, the drinking age minimum. You rarely saw girls alone in the bars. "Singles" bars were unknown in our day, although we would have considered it a great idea.

When we arrived at the Bowl, there usually was a long waiting line up to the box office. Admission was fifty cents. There was one entrance and exit gate. During the dance, if you wanted to go out for booze, beer, hamburgers, romance or other activities, an invisible ink stamp was pressed on the back of your hand. To get back in, you put your hand under a special ultraviolet lamp at the entrance which made the stamp visible. You couldn't transfer the stamp to a friend's hand by contact to save an entrance fee; we had tried that unsuccessfully.

The dancers and oglers at the Rose Bowl were a mixed bag. Besides the college students looking with pseudo sophistication at the eager-eyed high school kids, there were the older secretaries and nurses, prime

Ernie Heckscher led his band with a guitar at the Rose Bowl in 1938. The "C" banner indicates it was "Cal Night" that Saturday.

Courtesy of Ernie Heckscher

targets in our set for hoped-for amorous episodes because they usually had apartments in the City. Then there were the local mothers and a few fathers planted on the wooden bench that extended around the outer edge of the floor. They were chaperoning teen-aged daughters, who in turn were being propositioned for walks among the trees outside, auto rides, trips to the nearest bar, or other less innocent pastimes by partners blissfully ignorant that they were under sharp surveillance.

One member of our group, now a sedate San Francisco industrial executive with a home in Hillsborough, recalls one disastrous stroll in the darkness behind the Bowl. He was quietly and eagerly leading a newfound

friend in search of a quiet, secluded spot in the darkness when he stepped through a low glass greenhouse of the Niven Orchid Company just behind the dance pavilion. The shattering crash of the glass and frenzied scramble to get the hell out of there ended his romantic adventure for that night.

There was a small bar in the Bowl which sold beer and soft drinks, but no hard liquor. Uniformed members of the volunteer fire department, sponsors of the dances, were accredited deputies. They kept order and quickly and adroitly hustled away any unsteady dancers or nuisance creators.

The Rose Bowl dances were deliberately designed on a romantic theme. The leafy and star-studded open sky canopy above the floor, the strings of lights and colored lanterns, and the soft lighting during most of the dance numbers all contributed to the sentimental atmosphere. In those days you usually danced close together, cheek to cheek. Even the chaperoning moth-

"There was a small bar in the Bowl which sold beer and soft drinks."

Courtesy Marin County Historical Society

---

ers tolerated that. Much of the music was soft and dreamy—songs like "My Silent Love," "Lazy Bones," "Stars Fell on Alabama," "Deep Purple," and "Did You Ever See a Dream Walking?" were the hits of the day. There were also "fast numbers"—like "Shuffle Off to Buffalo," "You're the Top," "Forty-Second Street," and "Heat Wave"—which my friends and I usually skipped because we were lousy dancers and knew it. Besides, we didn't really go there for the dancing, although we knew others who did. For us the dancing was just a necessary preliminary.

When you were dancing closely in a tight, clutching embrace which, with good fortune, would lead to more intimate things later, you had to be careful and not keep your eyes closed too long during a dreamy number.

You could crash into one of the massive and unyielding redwood tree trunks with your partner, rudely spoiling the mood you had been working so hard to create. Another mood interrupter occurred sporadically when the Interurban Service electric cars whooshed by on the rails just outside the Bowl, causing the dance floor to shiver.

Mrs. Evangeline Kelly Swineford, of Fresno, one of the female violinists in Ernie Heckscher's band, remembers the first dance she played at the Rose Bowl. "I had not realized that the Northwestern Pacific Railroad tracks were adjacent to our dance stand. Right in the middle of a number, a train came roaring along, causing the stand to shake violently. Naturally, I thought the worst—a major earthquake."

On the bandstand, "Cap" Larsen, the smiling and red-cheeked secretary of the Larkspur Volunteer Firemen's Association, served as master of ceremonies. Nattily uniformed, wearing a visored Navy-style white cloth cap on which "Larkspur Rose Bowl" was spelled out in gold letters topped by a fireman's badge, Cap made announcements and delivered special messages. He was the Johnny Carson of the Rose Bowl, you might say.

Couples at the dance would ask Cap to announce their engagements, eliciting surprised whoops from unsuspecting friends. And couples who had met for the first time at the Rose Bowl would have him report their wedding anniversaries. In the early fall, he would announce the scores of Bay Area college football games that had been played a few hours earlier on Saturday afternoon. The band would loudly break out with the school songs of the winning teams to accompanying shouts, cheers, and applause of some in the crowd, and the good-natured boos of others. Some Saturday nights were dedicated to specific colleges—U.C., Stanford, Santa Clara, St. Mary's, or perhaps the University of San Francisco. Colored pennants and banners of the college were draped around trees and hung on the fences and bandstand of the Bowl. Triangles outlined with colored light bulbs, each triangle carrying in its center the name of a Bay Area college, were elevated above the Bowl fence. Students from the colleges concentrated beneath them.

At around eleven o'clock, during an intermission, a high-pitched siren would sound and Cap Larsen would announce that it was time for the Rose Bowl's famous firefall. The crowd would spread out from the bandstand across the floor and around the trees, facing toward the north end of the trellis-topped fence rimming the Bowl. The lights would be dimmed and the band drummer would beat out a long staccato roll. Cap would dramatically give the voice signal over the mike on the bandstand: "All right, Chief, let the fire fall!"

Suddenly a startlingly beautiful and brilliant cascade of vivid and glittering white silver sparks would drop in a wide, blazing stream from a straight line forty feet up in the sky and outside the Bowl. Lighting up the night, it would continue for fully twenty seconds. Simultaneously clouds of colored smoke mushroomed up behind the firefall. It was truly a dramatic spectacle in an outdoor scene, and always drew oooohs and ahhhhhs from those seeing it for the first time.

Four or five dance bands played at the Rose Bowl each season, usually young college groups from around the Bay Area. Ernie Heckscher and his band played there in 1938 and 1939. Ray Hackett, Paul Law, Walter Krausgrill, Ray Tellier, and Del Courtney headed other bands at the Rose Bowl before going on to more lucrative engagements. Old timers recall that Phil Harris was a drummer and vocalist there way back in 1918.

Heckscher played at the Rose Bowl right after graduating from Stanford. "I got married on the strength of the twenty-two week contract I received at the Bowl," recalled Heckscher in a conversation at the Fairmont Hotel. "The guys played for about ten bucks apiece. I had a fourteen or fifteen piece band then, so we cost about $200 a night, and we were the most expensive band they had up to that time. We built up a following at the Bowl, and at society affairs down on the Peninsula, and that's how we got our big break and went into the Palace Hotel."

The dances were sponsored by the Larkspur Volunteer Firemen's Association. They grossed about $50,000 a season and the profits were used to buy equipment for the town's fire department. It helped keep the tax rate low.

The first Rose Bowl dance was held in 1913 on a platform built under a tree in the redwood grove. The floor area was expanded several times in the following years. "Crowds averaged about 2,500 when we were going there," Heckscher recalls. "We broke the record with 4,200 in 1939. Biggest crowd they ever had."

Opening night was insured against rain. Heckscher recalls that the Volunteers employed a weather forecasting service in Denver. If the prediction was for rain on Saturday, the dance was postponed on Friday. This normally occurred only once or twice a season, he said.

During the Twenties and Thirties the Volunteer Firemen's Association was a political power in town. Membership was limited to about twenty members and was highly coveted. Vacancies only occurred when one of the Volunteers died or moved away. New members were voted in by the Association and, with few exceptions, were selected from the building trades. The skills of roofers, electricians, plumbers, carpenters and the like were not only helpful at fires, but also at the Rose Bowl for maintenance, improvements, and such chores as Willie Frizzi performed in operating the lights and firefall for the Saturday night dances. The Volunteers were all trained in first aid and voted themselves a dollar a day salary, or $365 annually. They answered all fire alarms when possible, and hired a chief and two firemen to run the department.

On Saturday nights, four of the Volunteers slipped on Larkspur Police Department khaki uniforms and

Couples who met for the first time at Larkspur would return to have their wedding anniversaries announced. (Pre-1920.)

Courtesy of Mrs. R. C. Doherty

acted as deputies at the dance. Their duty stations were at the entrance and exit gates, the check room, and the outside box office. Other Volunteers were deputized by the Police Chief to direct traffic. Any Volunteer missing attendance at a Saturday night dance was fined ten dollars.

Don Denton, a retired Navy petty officer and roofer, was on a waiting list for seven years before he was accepted into the Volunteers. He recalled vividly how the Volunteer deputies skillfully and swiftly steered drunks out of the Bowl and marched them part-way up nearby Rice Lane, just short of the back of the police station and firehouse.

"We'd tell them," Denton said, "look, would you like to take a train ride out of town like a good boy or would you like to be taken in to the jail cells right up the alley here?"

"As a matter of fact," Denton said with a smile, "the only time there was a call for the regular town police came when we had a noisy party ourselves at the home of one of the Volunteers after a dance. Some neighbors phoned the cops to complain about the racket. We still had our deputy police badges on when the squad cars pulled up. It was embarrassing."

In the Magnolia Avenue firehouse on the ground floor, Denton nodded toward two small, barred windows looking out on Rice Lane from a kitchen area and remarked, "There used to be two cells here, but we rarely had use for them." Then he pointed toward the center of the firehouse where a circular safe embedded flush with the concrete floor was visible. "We used to bring the cash receipts from the dance up here every Saturday night. We'd put them in the safe until Monday morning when we deposited them in the bank."

At one o'clock the band would play "Good Night, Sweetheart," and the dance would be over. We returned to San Francisco by ferryboat in the dark early morning hours. Rows of lighted windows reflected on the swirling waters as the ferryboats followed their courses to and from Hyde Street or the Ferry Building. The dark tarpaulin of fresh sky would often be dotted with stars. A bright moon sometimes competed for attention with clusters of lights that marked out the shape of the City back of Yacht Harbor and the Marina Boulevard shoreline.

On foggy nights, though, there was no use going out on deck or peering through the windows, because you couldn't see anything. Listening to the deep, hoarse blasts of fog horns, the whistle toots and hisses of escaping steam, and the clanging of ship bells above decks was the only diversion outside as the pilots sounded off to each other. And the warnings were not just symbolic, or merely intended to charm the passengers—there was no radar aboard in the mid-1930s.

In 1957, with attendance and receipts dropping off rapidly at the Rose Bowl dances, largely due to the competition of television and movies, Larkspur taxpayers voted to pay the costs of the fire department on their tax bills. The Volunteers then turned over to the town government about half a million dollars worth of fire engines, pumps, and other equipment. The Volunteers kept the dances going until 1963 when attendance was so low that they closed the Bowl and sold the property to a developer. The Rose Bowl dances had lasted exactly half a century.

There is now a historical museum on the upper floor of the firehouse on Magnolia Avenue. Featured among the old photographs, handbills, and printed material from the former Volunteers are display advertisements and mementos from the Rose Bowl dances.

"The Volunteer Firemen's Association is probably the most cherished institution we ever had in town," said Doug Archer, a young Larkspur fireman and history buff. Born and raised in Larkspur, Archer established the museum and is principally responsible for its collection, which he is still trying to augment. The Association is still alive and well; it annually stages a Firemen's Ball, using all the profits to purchase equipment needed by the department.

In San Francisco, a rather bulky memento of those days is moored at one terminal of a former Saturday-night route to the Rose Bowl. It is the 3,300 passenger *Eureka* ferryboat, which once cut through the tides between the Ferry Building and Sausalito. It is now berthed at the San Francisco Maritime State Historic Park at the foot of Hyde Street, the former auto-ferry landing just below today's Ghirardelli Square. Once the largest double-end passenger ferryboat in the world, the *Eureka* remained in service on the Bay until 1957, when its crank pin snapped on a run between the Ferry Building and the Oakland Mole. The *Eureka* was also the last "walking beam" ferryboat to operate in the United States. Parked on its two main deck alleyways today at the Hyde Street berth are strings of cars of the 1920s and 1930s vintage. As tourists stroll by gazing at them, the cars seem to be waiting patiently for a signal to drive ashore. A signal that never comes.

As for the Northwestern Pacific line that carried ferryboat passengers to Marin County destinations, San Francisco has a memento of it, too. A statue dedicated to Colonel Peter Donohue, done by reknowned sculptor Douglas Tilden, stands in the red-bricked triangular island at Market and Bush Streets. Donohue, who died in his Rincon Hill mansion in the City in 1885, founded the predecessor of the Northwestern Pacific, the North Pacific Railroad Company.

I recently looked for a duplicate of the Hagopian Model A Ford roadster in the lines of cars on the *Eureka*. Somehow I knew I wouldn't find it. And I'm sure I never will—not that Model A! It's back there among the discarded calendar leaves.

11

Neptune Beach— "Coney Island of the West"

Beginning almost sixty years ago, and continuing for more than two decades, thousands of Bay Area and Northern California families, couples, and young people poured into the Neptune Beach amusement park and resort in Alameda, on the east shore of San Francisco Bay.

Huge 24-sheet Foster and Kleiser billboards advertised the 120-acre "Coney Island of the West"—a two-level spread of entertainment and recreation that has never been duplicated in the Bay Area. Neptune Beach was open every year from Palm Sunday to Labor Day. From shortly before 1920 until attendance started to fall off in the early Thirties, it was a favorite gathering place for every age group and every lodge and association staging a picnic or an outing. The park appealed strongly to children, so the family-trade volume was particularly high.

Neptune boasted two swimming pools with filtered salt water pumped from the Bay, and the largest and gaudiest set of rides and concessions on the Pacific Coast. Free band concerts, death-defying stunts, bathing-beauty contests, entertainment acts, and Easter kiddie revues were held during the season. The fireworks displays had spectators throughout the whole East Bay climbing the hills at night to watch. The park had huge picnic areas, a lavish dance hall with reflecting mirror chandeliers, a spacious dining room and cafeteria, a stadium, and a movie theater.

On weekends, crowds of twenty to thirty thousand adults and children were funneled into Neptune Beach from ferryboats, electric trains, streetcars, and buses, in private automobiles, and even on steam trains from Sacramento and other interior towns and cities. On July 4, 1920, the crowd count reached an all-time high of approximately 40,000.

Neptune Beach developed into the attraction it became during the Twenties under the guidance of

Robert C. Strehlow. Strehlow became involved with the park almost involuntarily. He was a nationally known builder and contractor for government buildings and expositions throughout the country. He had been the senior partner of Strehlow, Freese, and Petersen, the firm that built all the courts and many of the buildings at the 1915 Panama Pacific International Exposition in San Francisco.

After the Exposition closed, Strehlow was contacted by a group that had started an amusement park on the western end of Alameda's south Bay shore. This group's park consisted of a large office building, a bath house, an Olympic-size swimming pool, and a soaring entrance tower modeled after the Tower of Jewels that had dominated the San Francisco exposition. Business was slow and pocketbooks were thin, and the company realized that some rides and an amusement area were needed. At that point they contacted Strehlow, and convinced him to advance them the money to purchase three of the San Francisco fair's key attractions that were about to be liquidated—the Red Devil Scenic Railway, a valuable Denzel merry-go-round, and a shooting gallery.

When the company fell behind in their payments to him, Strehlow accepted stock in lieu of cash. By 1921, he was the senior partner and soon bought out the others in what was now called Neptune Beach, operating under the name of Alameda Park Company. Over the next few years, three sons, Robert Jr., Arthur, and Roland, and a daughter, Margaret, joined him in the business.

From 1922 until 1929, when the Great Depression was catapulted off the starting blocks by the crash of the stock market, Neptune Beach was aptly promoted as the "Coney Island of the West" by the Strehlows. In 1926, the Strehlows built the Neptune Court complex —twenty-eight apartments on the Central Avenue edge of their beach property. They lived with their families in three of them in order to remain close to the family business. The company also constructed thirty-six housekeeping cottages which were rented out by the day, week, or month year round. "Spend Your Vacation at 'Neptune by the Sea,' " urged advertisements. Families from Fresno, Merced, and other interior cities and towns in Northern California, many of them wealthy ranchers, rented the cottages for two or three months to escape the scorching summer heat.

During its five-month season, Neptune stayed open from 9 A.M. to 6 P.M. on weekdays and until ten at night on weekends and holidays. Admission to the park was ten cents for adults and a nickel for children under twelve. Many kids, teenagers, and even adults would go down beyond Neptune to Washington Park, strip down to a swimming suit, swim around the old pier on the edge of Neptune, and come into the grounds from the rear to save the admission fee. Others would wait until the tide went out and simply wade over, carrying their shoes and socks. Some youngsters would sometimes find a loose bar in the big exit turnstiles near Central Avenue and slip in. "The game of the day was to beat the Strehlows," Mrs. Arthur Strehlow recalled.

Neptune Beach opened its gates every year with an Easter celebration featuring King Neptune and his "court of mermaids and bathing beauties." The publicity releases promised that "scores of pretty girls in bathing suits and costumes will appear in the spectacle." Young Bay Area girls who dreamed of entering the Miss California contest worked hard to appear with King Neptune. In 1931 the feature act was the "hatching" of a big Easter egg from which little Tootsie Holt, child song and dance star, emerged as the Easter Bunny. Tootsie also did an Easter Rabbit Dance and sang.

While crowds of 20,000 to 25,000 on weekends were not unusual in the summer months, attendance on the Fourth of July would often exceed 30,000. Admission was free after 7 P.M. on the Fourth, thanks to a donation made by Alameda merchants. "They would line up for blocks to go in free and save a dime," said Andy Hynes, one of the key employees of the Strehlows.

Father Neptune, complete with trident and crown, always presided over a day-long string of free feature events and entertainment on the Fourth of July. The celebration climaxed with a super ninety-minute fireworks show which started at about 8:30, just after the summer dusk hour. Bombs, skyrockets, and "set pieces," the glowing displays of fire and light formed on a pattern of wires, were unleashed. The grand windup revealed a blazing American Flag in red, white, and blue. Besides the thousands gathered throughout the East Bay hills, passengers on the ferryboats on the Bay crowded onto the front decks to watch the showers of colored light and sparks exploding above the shoreline and reflecting over the dark water of the Bay.

The Strehlows flooded the Bay Area with free one-day passes. "The secret is to get people out," Arthur Strehlow said. "If you give the free tickets, they will spend from a dollar to a dollar-and-a-half a head. If you get a thousand people out, you will make out."

In keeping with that principle, Neptune Beach gave out free tickets on a lavish scale. The largest hand-outs were given on the many special days honoring industries, political groups, national ethnic societies, fraternal orders, and other promising revenue producers. On Milk Day, for instance, sponsored by the Alameda County Milk Dealers Association and the Cooperative Dairymen's League, thousands of free admission tickets were handed out and the event's chairman announced that anyone could use a milk bottle cap for entrance into the park. Free milk and free tickets for rides were distributed inside. The *Oakland Post Enquirer*, a Hearst newspaper, claimed to have entertained 35,000 kids and members of their families at Neptune Beach one Sunday. Free admission passes and tickets for rides, and free use of the pools were available all morning on that *Post*-sponsored day.

Annual picnics were big business at Neptune's vast grounds. In 1934, 10,000 Northern California Democrats held a picnic at Neptune. The Sons of Norway was the largest group to hold an annual Day-at-Neptune outing, with between eight and nine thousand people massed in one area. This was the one event at Neptune every year when people stayed late. The festivities lasted until midnight when the musicians at the lively dance in the picnic area clubhouse started to pack their instruments back into the cases. Although a lot of beverages were poured to quench dry throats and lubricate vocal chords for folk songs and a few scuffles did take place among vigorous celebrants, no special police were ever needed. The Sons of Norway leaders did their own policing and the festivities never got out of hand.

NEPTUNE BEACH—"CONEY ISLAND OF THE WEST"

This is a partial view of Neptune Beach looking in from the Bay side. The large pool and Kiddieland, both on the reclaimed marsh land, are in the foreground. (About 1930.)

Courtesy of Arthur F. Strehlow

The real secret of Neptune Beach's profitable and action-packed success during those highlight years of the 1920s were the crowds that took the ferryboats and special shuttle trains from San Francisco. "The San Francisco people supported Neptune Beach," concessionaire Andy Hynes recalled with fond memories of the prosperous years. "They would spend dollars; the East Bay people spent dimes. The people that came over on those special trains from San Francisco spent nothing but money."

Hynes recalled that around 1925, during Neptune's boom period, "Dad" Strehlow attempted to obtain permission to run launches directly over to the park from the Ferry Building in San Francisco. However,

the State Railroad Commission turned him down, ruling that the Southern Pacific had an exclusive franchise for that route.

Early arrivals at Neptune on Sundays and holidays were usually picnic groups anxious to secure one or more of the approximately twenty choice tables and benches alongside Neptune's lower level sand "beach." This was a long stretch of boxed land filled with white Monterey sand imported from the southern coastal county and replenished regularly. Using old newspapers they had brought along, the picnickers would wipe the early morning dew off the dark green tables and benches and settle in for the day. Many would play pinochle, some would just sit and chat, and the children would play in the sand. Each table could seat twelve persons, and there was enough room to spread out the enormous repasts that many families brought. "All these facilities were free and these people stayed put and didn't spend much money any-

Arthur F. Strehlow, who supervised the promotion of Neptune Beach, sent "traveling billboards" around San Francisco to increase lagging attendance at the amusement park. This stop was on Turk Street below Jefferson Square. (Early Thirties.)

Courtesy of Arthur F. Strehlow

where," Robert Strehlow, Jr., remembers wryly. Robert Jr. is the oldest Strehlow son, and the one appointed Neptune Beach superintendent by his father.

Not only did these no-spend visitors get the best tables, Strehlow said, but "they had an excellent view of all the free shows." These were presented every Sunday and holiday afternoon on a fifty-foot-square platform in the center of the main rectangle of sand. During the early Thirties, the platform was raised to a height of six feet to make it easier for everyone to see. Acrobatic stunts, boxing and wrestling exhibitions, bathing beauty contests, costumed dance groups of

various countries, and musical combos were among the entertainment features. Clusters of lights were installed on the corners of the platform for evening illumination.

On that platform Fay Lamphier was crowned Miss California in 1928. She went on from the "Coney Island of the West" to the real Coney Island in New York, where she won the Miss America title. Dave Shade, Young Corbett III, and Frankie Klick were among the outstanding boxers who engaged in exhibition matches in the temporary ring rigged up on the platform. And before he became Heavyweight Champion, Max Baer did part of his training here for his tragic fight with Frankie Campbell in San Francisco. (The much smaller Campbell, a brother of baseball star Dolph Camilli, was taken from the ring unconscious and later died.) Highly publicized contests, exhibitions, and unusual novelty events were presented on the platform almost every weekend. One Sunday afternoon, the Fancy Fox Trot Contest was staged, featur-

NEPTUNE BEACH—"CONEY ISLAND OF THE WEST"

ing "ten of the hottest stepping couples around the bay region."

A little beyond the platform, at one end of the sand area and in front of the Bath House, was a bandstand. Here the Neptune Beach band, dressed in bright red uniforms and caps with gold braid and tassels, blared out um-pah-pah music in free brassy concerts. The band director was appropriately named Schultz, as in the popular song going "Schultz is back again, with his oom-pah-pah, oom-pah-pah."

From the top of the Bath House, youngsters used a concrete double slide, with a divider in the middle, to drop down about thirty-five feet into the soft sand near the bandstand. Then they climbed back up on a flight of stairs for another go. The white sand extended all the way down beyond the far end of the park's main building, containing a cafeteria and a dance hall, to a children's playground. On busy weekends it was completely covered with a solid mass of lounging bodies, food baskets, spread-out blankets, striped rented beach umbrellas, and children with sand buckets and shovels. A taut high wire was frequently strung directly over the sand, spanning the 175 feet between the roofs of the Bath House and the dance hall for use by acrobats doing balancing acts. On one Sunday, "Aerial" Thompson thrilled an awed crowd by riding a bicycle on the wire.

In the main building, the ground-level cafeteria was well-equipped and could seat more than three hundred people for lunch or dinner. The food was tasty and well prepared by German cooks.

Directly above the cafeteria, on the second level, was the beautiful dance hall—or ballroom, as it was sometimes called by the management—with a special maple "spring" floor. The interior was decorated in rich colors, and huge lanterns hung down from the ceiling above the dance floor. Made of octagonal cardboard cut-outs, with silk windows diffusing the light, the lanterns created a soft, romantic atmosphere for the dancers. A band played music on Saturday nights and Sunday afternoons and evenings. Eddie Murphy, known as the Dancing Manager because of his habit of waltzing unaccompanied girls around the floor, was the popular ballroom supervisor.

A cocktail bar had been installed next to the cafeteria shortly after Prohibition was repealed in 1933, but it closed following a brief and unprofitable trial run. The large picnic and outing groups that came to Neptune usually brought their own drinks, and the normal daytime family crowd was not of the sporting type accustomed to seek out the day's social life at a bar. However, beer was sold at Neptune in 1933, with Acme leading sales. Rainier Ale, also known as "The Green Death" because it came in bottles of that color, was also popular.

Beyond the sand beach area were two outdoor pools that together formed one of the major attractions of Neptune. The weather was good for swimming and sunbathing all summer at Alameda. Although morning fog was common, it usually cleared away before noon and did not return until the evening. San Francisco mothers frequently brought children with colds over to Neptune to avoid the fog elsewhere and to take in the warm sunshine.

Back in 1927, the Strehlows began a dredging and filling operation on forty-three acres of Bay marsh to expand Neptune. Until then the Bay waters came up almost to the Olympic-size swimming pool which had been built in 1916, before the elder Strehlow became a partner. Surf bathing, with the Bay beach only steps from the pool and main park complex, was popular.

The highlight and centerpiece of the new land parcel rescued from the muddy flats was to be the largest swimming pool in the country, perhaps the world. Using a bulkhead against the Bay tide, Strehlow had the area around the new pool site filled in, creating

Neptune dining room, ballroom (upper level), and "beach" area. (About 1918.)

Courtesy of the Oakland Museum

The Neptune pool and one of the fountains. (About 1917.)
Courtesy of the Oakland Museum

a new peninsular block of land. The dredging crews initially could only make progress by working during low-tide hours.

Measuring 575 feet in length and 125 feet wide, the new pool ran parallel to the older Olympic pool. The two pools were meant to make Neptune Beach the outstanding swimming and water-sport center for both pleasure and competition in Northern California. The giant new pool was shallow, with a depth of from one to four feet, making it ideal for bathers learning to swim. A children's wading pool was built at its shallowest end, not far from the children's playground in the sand area. Between the two pools was a covered pump house which brought salt water from the Bay into both pools through a filter system.

The pool was often cleared of swimmers and bathers for special events. Outdoor motorboat races were held there on Sundays, "giving a new thrill to both drivers and spectators due to the small area that these speedboats must race in," the publicity releases said. "The participants are all eager to try this new idea of racing in a small confined area," the publicist wrote, probably with tongue in cheek. "The public is assured of sensational thrills, with spills a certainty."

The pool was used by Putt Mossman, the "world's champion stunt rider," who did a "Leap for Life" one Sunday afternoon, riding his motorcycle along a 150-foot runway at a speed of sixty miles per hour and leaping "motorcycle and all" into the pool.

The original 75-by-300-foot pool at Neptune Beach was the only Olympic-size one in the Bay Area until 1925, when Fleishhacker Pool was built in San Fran-

cisco. The old Neptune pool had a three-tiered sixty-foot-high diving platform and four poolside springboards. The water in a rectangular slice on the opposite side of the pool was only one to three feet deep; here children and nonswimmers could splash about behind a submerged wall that peeped out of the water. Two elevated centrifugal fountains gushed water down on delighted children and other bathers who grouped under them inside the wall. Six lifeguard chairs were in raised position around the pool, and competent guards were on duty constantly.

Championship swimming and diving meets were held here as well as special exhibitions and demonstrations. Johnny Weissmuller broke the world's 100-yard record at Neptune long before Hollywood had him swinging through the trees as Tarzan. Duke Kahanamoku, Arne Borg, Ann Curtis, Helen Crlenkovich and other reknown champions competed at Neptune. Norman Hanley and Clyde Diaz, the comedy diving team that entertained Bay Area fans for many years, performed on Sundays from the high tower and springboards. And Robert Strehlow, Jr. remembers that Jack Dempsey was paddling around in the pool when he was offered his first four-round fight in Oakland, before he became heavyweight champion.

Canoe-tilting contests had two-man teams maneuvering in the pool, one paddling and the other standing up with a padded-end jousting pole. And water polo matches were staged between teams from Bay Area clubs, including San Francisco's Olympic Club and the Stockton Rowing Club.

The fee for use of the pools was thirty-five cents for adults and twenty-five for children. Swimmers had to pay it even if they swam over from Washington Park in their bathing suits and sneaked in on the Bay side. They were required to wear around their neck or wrist a special numbered brass disc which they received when they paid the pool fee. It identified their locker in the Bath House where they returned to dress. Without this visible disc, they could be challenged and stopped from entering the pools by one of the security guards, off-duty policemen, and firemen hired by Neptune. The fee included a towel, wooden locker, and a Gantner and Mattern wool suit if you didn't bring your own. For an extra fifteen cents pool-users could rent a private room which could be locked.

The numerous food and refreshment stands around the park provided a wide range of edibles and thirst quenchers. "Sno-cones," scoops of shaved ice saturated with fruit syrup flavors like blueberry and cherry, were allegedly invented by an Alameda youth named Gordon Mills and first sold for five cents at Neptune Beach. There was pink, spun-sugar "cotton candy" and Orange Crush and Green River bottled soda. Black Jack gum was a best-seller with the kids, and Baby Ruth and Big Hunk were the popular five-cent candy bars.

"Coney Island Red Hots," hog dogs on steam-freshened buns, were consumed by the thousands at a dime each. These were a big profit item for the concessionaires. The buns cost ten cents a dozen and the hot dogs were a penny and a half each. On warm Sundays, twelve thousand rolls would be ordered from the Remar bakery and twelve thousand frankfurters from a sausage company. Also, in the "Syrup Room," twenty- to twenty-five-gallon bottles of orange punch and ten gallons of Hires concentrated root beer would be prepared. "Whatever was left over, we would give to the Salvation Army and the soup kitchens," said Robert Strehlow, Jr., who was in charge of purchasing.

Above all, Neptune's noisy, throbbing, and dazzling amusement area was responsible for luring heavy weekend and summer crowds from all over Northern California. Here were found the rides and games of chance and "skill." The most popular rides and the biggest revenue producers were the Whoopee and the Red Devil Scenic Railway.

The Whoopee, put up on the fill land reclaimed by the Strehlows from the Bay in 1927 and 1928, was a sensational, plunging roller coaster. Thrilled riders

talked about it long after they returned home. The only electrical power used was that required to take the four-passenger cars up to top of the first hump. From then on, the cars plummeted downward and were carried up to each following peak on their own momentum. Each car had twelve wheels assembled in a special way to prevent them from leaving the track no matter how violent or sudden a turn or lurch was experienced. "The ride just about took your breath away," Andy Hynes reminisced. "We did have one gal killed on a Fourth of July because she stood up at the top of a loop and was thrown out and broke her neck."

The Red Devil Scenic Railway, brought over from the 1915 Fair in San Francisco, was an exciting double-track course in the air with two trains of four to six cars racing each other. The trains were named "Red Devil" and "Green Dragon," and were painted in vivid colors with symbols to represent their exciting names. Each train was controlled by a brakeman who regulated the speed as the rushing cars whipped up and down and around. As the trains raced side by side, the passengers would lean forward and scream, attempting to help win the race. Many often stayed in their seats and paid another dime to a collector to go again.

The German-built Denzel merry-go-round was one of only two in the United States. Its sparkling center core of diamond-shaped mirror segments reflected the whirling circles of hand-carved and brightly painted wooden horses, beasts of the jungle, and creatures of the seas and lakes. These animals had been together for

The Whoopee ride at Neptune Beach.
(About 1928.)   Courtesy of Jerry Connolly

The electric railway in Kiddieland at Neptune Beach.
(About 1929.)   Courtesy of Jerry Connolly

some time, having originally run their never-varying circular paths at the San Francisco Exposition. A calliope played lilting whistle tunes to keep those wooden animals in good spirits; it was decorated with moving female figures that accompanied the music with cymbals and a drum.

The Jester's Palace, or Fun House, was redesigned many times during Neptune's history. Shortly after it opened it was hit by censorship and the social mores of the day. Complaints were made about the floor vents that blew up women's skirts as they entered. "The police department soon put a stop to it, saying it was too vulgar," Andy Hynes recalled. A glass-mirrored labyrinthine passage where you could get lost, an arcade with picture-viewing machines, and a long sweeping maple hardwood slide with several exciting humps were the attractions inside.

In the center of the upper park was the Whip, a body-shaking flat ride geared to give its passengers unexpected jerks during its run on the steel-decked raised platform, highlighted by swift 180-degree swings of the platform cars. On the lower level of the park was the Flying Airplanes ride, which swung its cars in a high wide circle around a small tower.

The Merry Mixup, a ride with thirty chairs suspended from a turning center pole, had a brief trial run in the shallow section of the big swimming pool. Riders had to wear swimming suits for the takeoff and landing on water. As the ride gathered speed the chairs were swung up into the air. The Mixup was moved up to dry land after only a few months of operation for safety reasons.

One well-advertised attraction was Neptune's Kiddieland. It had midget versions of the major rides in the park, including a Baby Whoopee roller coaster. It also had a motor boat ride and an electric railway.

All the rides in the park cost ten cents, except for those in Kiddieland where the fee was five cents for children under ten.

The games-of-chance booths, with their spinning numbered wheels splashed with color and flashing lights, and their discordant symphony of bells, buzzers, and clicks, were an irresistible magnet for many visitors to Neptune Beach. Andy Hynes was closely tied to this phase of Neptune's operations.

Hynes had been running an Alameda candy store and soda fountain where young Robert Strehlow, Jr., used to drop by to eat banana splits. Hynes made his own candy and Strehlow thought it was pretty good.

When the rent on Hynes' store was boosted and he muttered something about closing it up, Strehlow asked him to move his equipment to Neptune Beach and come to work there making chocolates for the boxes given away as prizes at the game booths. Hynes accepted the offer and soon had three chocolate dippers working with him and his wife for the Neptune candy kitchen. "We turned out about 375 pounds of chocolate creams daily, six days a week," Hynes said. "About a ton of chocolates a week."

In the succeeding years, whenever a game booth was given up by a concessionaire Hynes would ask to take it over. With the Strehlows' approval, he soon ran more than half a dozen booths. He became his own best customer for boxes of chocolate creams.

During the "fat years," 1920 to 1928, Hynes prospered. On the Fourth of July alone, each concession booth would bring him about $200 profit. One, with the catchy name of Housie-Housie, would net him between $300 and $400 each Fourth. Housie-Housie was the Neptune Beach version of what later was to become Bingo. It originally was known as Lotto back in the Gay Nineties before the turn of the century.

Hynes gave away yellow canaries as prizes in his Canary Cottage spinning wheel game. "I used to go out and buy an aviary," he recalled. "I'd buy the whole thing. About twenty or twenty-five canaries."

The Strehlows also operated several booths, including the Kewpie Doll game. Though this was only a run-of-the-mill spinning wheel with numbers to select, the prizes were unique and drew well. Every month Robert Strehlow, Jr., bought from one to two hundred kewpie dolls in San Francisco. He hired a couple of helpers to paint eyes, lips, and hair on the dolls. He bought bolts of Japanese silk in different colors and hired three seamstresses to make tiny, flared dresses with hoop skirts for the dolls. The dressed dolls, which cost Strehlow about a dollar each, proved to be a sensation. Today they are collector items.

However, the games, the lights, the clattering rides sweeping and diving above the park, the cries of the barkers, and the special events periodically held in the evenings did not prevent the daytime crowds from leaving for home when darkness began to fall. The Saturday and Sunday night dances managed to keep some excitement alive late on the weekends, but it wasn't enough. Most families, especially those with small children, would leave Neptune for home around five in the afternoon. The Strehlows tried every

NEPTUNE BEACH—"CONEY ISLAND OF THE WEST"

An aerial view of Neptune Beach complex in 1930.

Courtesy of Arthur F. Strehlow

gimmick and lure they could dream up to keep people at Neptune Beach after sundown, without any noticeable success.

Their efforts included the construction of a stadium with a midget auto and motorcycle racetrack, the Alameda Speedway, on several acres of the new land added to the park by the dredging of the Bay marsh. The stadium had seating for about four thousand spectators. The first midget auto races in Northern California were held there on Tuesday nights, and motorcycle races roared around the fifth-of-a-mile track on Thursday nights. Rodeos and circuses were booked into the stadium, Alameda High School used it for football games, and dance festivals, fraternal group ceremonies, and club soccer games were staged in it.

In 1928 the ballroom was enlarged, remodeled, and beautified. A broad promenade walk was built around the outside of the building from which spectators could watch the dancers through large windows that opened off the balcony.

Frank Russ, who coached the nationally famed Neptune Beach Swimming Club at the park, believed that Neptune Beach ultimately failed because this program of expansion was overdone. "Strehlow borrowed too much money and couldn't make the payments," Russ said. Andy Hynes blamed a combination of things. "It was the Depression and Strehlow's expansion ambitions that killed Neptune," Hynes said. "When the Depression started after the 1929 stock market crash, people didn't come over from San Francisco and they were the ones that supported Neptune Beach."

Arthur Strehlow did not agree with this assessment. He blamed Neptune's eventual slide into bankruptcy mainly on broader developments. "Business fell off with the increasing advent of the family automobile and the progressive elimination of the ferryboats as the bridges were being completed," Strehlow said. "New recreation areas were opening within easy driving distance on improved roads. Yet, during the Depression, strangely enough, Neptune remained popular. People would save up and come over for the weekend."

Strehlow also blamed at least part of the loss of patronage on the construction of the Naval Air Station in Alameda. "Sailors were seen more frequently at Neptune and mothers became fearful about their daughters going there."

The 1939 season proved to be the last stand for Neptune Beach and the Strehlows. That year the remodeled Neptune ballroom was converted into a roller skating rink. A false floor was laid over the spring hardwood dance floor and a new Hammond electric organ was installed. Advertisements glowed with praise for the "only skating rink in Northern California using organ music." You could skate every afternoon for twenty-five cents and for fifty cents at night. Uniformed instructors were on hand to give "novices an opportunity to learn the proper method of skating" in the special beginners' rink.

In September of 1939, a month before the fading park closed for the last time, the Strehlows bravely staged a "Jumbo Circus and Thrill Show" at Neptune Stadium. Featured were 187 performers, animal acts, and Billy Rose's reknowned elephant Jumbo. The publicity for the show ballyhooed Cal Owens and "his sensational act of walking upside down fifty feet in the air without a life net." The program also included such drawing cards as a car crashing into a brick wall, a human battering ram lashed to an automobile radiator and driven through a flaming solid-board wall, and a super car crash with one vehicle "somersaulting with a Hollywood daredevil ace at the wheel."

Neptune Beach finally closed in October, 1939. The opening of the dazzling Golden Gate International Exposition on man-made Treasure Island earlier that year helped to speed up the lingering demise of the "Coney Island of the West." By then, the bridges connecting San Francisco with Oakland and Sausalito had opened and the predicted decline of ferryboat service was quickly becoming a reality. Families now hopped into their cars and drove out of town more frequently and to more distant attractions. Public dependence on mass transit lines fell off. The gates at Neptune Beach were closed for the last time when the park's bondholders foreclosed.

The paint had faded, weeds had sprouted, and patronage had all but disappeared. Early the following year, in March, 1940, a public auction was held at the Neptune Beach grounds. The returns were meager, bitterly disappointing to both the Strehlows and their creditors. Less than five hundred persons showed up on the opening day of the sale, and most of them were gawkers or curiosity seekers. Bidders were scarce and the amounts offered were startlingly low. For example, $200 was the only bid received for all the buildings.

The merry-go-round with its electric organ and eighty-two carved animals, valued at $35,000, went to George Whitney of Whitney Brothers for $1500. The Whitneys said they would move it back across the Bay to their Playland-at-the-Beach in San Francisco. Elec-

tric heaters went for as little as fifty cents each, and 230 leather-upholstered folding chairs only brought five dollars. The Red Devil roller coaster was sold for sixty dollars to a junk dealer. At the end of the first day, seven hours after the sale started, Auctioneer Fred Newberg had taken in about $10,000 for Neptune equipment valued at $500,000.

The next day the Whitneys bought the Kiddieland electric miniature railway, with its engine, six cars, and two miles of track for $325 for their Playland. Three springboards from the Olympic-size swimming pool, upon which such national champion divers as Neptune's own Bunny Fergus had performed, were sold for six dollars each. The athletic equipment in the beach playground, including rings, bars, and trapezes, were purchased by a smiling bidder for $75. Their installation had cost $7500 originally. Swimming suits and water wings sold at "rock bottom prices."

The Kiddieland motor boat ride with six cars and the Baby Whoopee roller coaster each brought $50. The big wooden stadium that the Strehlows had built on a portion of the filled marsh was sold to wreckers for $260. The tower lights used for night events there went for $270. The Ferris wheel sale price was $275. The offers for the giant scenic railway and the reknowned Whoopee and its roller cars were so low that Auctioneer Newberg refused to consider them.

The third and final day of the auction was just as bad. Symbolic of the sad and ignominious end of Neptune Beach was the sale of the venerable German naval gun which had been in the park since shortly after World War I. It was sold for $40 and the buyer said he intended to melt it down for scrap metal.

Actual demolition of the facilities and clearance of the site started that same year, 1940, to make way for the construction of the U.S. Maritime Reserve Training Center. By 1941, the two swimming pools had been filled in and converted to a parade ground, just in time for World War II. In 1967, most of the former Neptune Beach property was returned to recreational use, this time as the Alameda Memorial State Park under the jurisdiction of the East Bay Regional Park District.

But during the 1920s and into the 1930s, Neptune Beach really was a Coney Island, a choice picnic and recreation complex, an outdoor swimming and aquatic-sports center, a showcase of entertainment and spectator thrills, and a favorite summer resort all rolled into one. Never again has such a park been seen in the Bay Area—and undoubtedly one never will be.

12

On a Sunday Afternoon

No freeways connected Bay Area cities in the early Twenties. To go to San Jose from San Francisco on the Sunday family drive, you drove along El Camino Real, Highway 101. You left early in the morning because the trip took a good two hours, and if you wanted to spend some time at the picnic grounds, you had to allow for the drive.

We usually stopped on McAllister Street below Fillmore to stock up with cold meats, bread and bakery goods, sweet butter, Kosher dill pickles and, with grimaces from some of us, pungent herring from the barrel. When we were going to my Uncle Harry's on East Santa Clara Street in San Jose, my mother would occasionally pick out a tender brisket to roast later for dinner, telling the butcher, "All right, Al darling, pick me out a nice one, now."

She would buy small portions of parsley, garlic, and onions at one of the little grocery stores, and here she would personally remove the wooden lid from the musty pickle barrel and dip down dextrously with her fingers to select the particular pickles she wanted. All her life my mother was a devout believer in having too much rather than too little. On these occasions she would also buy a substantial supply of smoked meats—tongue, salami, baloney—and frankfurters and garlic sausages.

Finally, all the food would be stuffed into bags and squeezed into the car between legs and against doors. The herring and the pickles would be carefully balanced on top so the juices couldn't spill or run. We would be off to the country!

The route we usually followed out of the City was Nineteenth Avenue and Junipero Serra Boulevard across the San Mateo County line into Daly City. At Vale or School Streets, we would swing left for a couple of blocks to Mission Street and then drive down through the small business area of Colma.

When we passed through Colma, my father would frequently mention the little town's fame as a former training site for professional fighters. Some major fights after the turn of the century were held there. Lightweight champion Battling Nelson had knocked out local San Francisco pride Jimmy Britt in eighteen rounds at a specially constructed arena built for the 1905 bout where Jefferson High School is now, at Mission and School Streets. Heavyweight champion Jack Johnson was knocked down by middleweight champion Stanley Ketchell in a Colma bout in 1909 before Johnson knocked out the little man in the twelfth round. San Franciscans Willie Ritchie and Abe Attell, Joe Gans, Ad Wolgast, Billy Papke, and Tommy Burns were other champions who fought in Colma-Daly City arenas or who used Joe Millett's training quarters at the foot of the hill below Colma.

Until 1927, a notorious traffic bottleneck existed on the stretch of El Camino Real which dipped down from Colma and ran between the rows of cemeteries that are still the traditional burial grounds for San Franciscans. (Burials have been prohibited in San Francisco since 1901.) Until 1927, El Camino Real was a two-lane road here, running parallel to the tracks for the Market Street Railway's Number 40 "Iron Monster" streetcars, which went to San Mateo. On Sunday nights, there would be an especially aggravating crawl up the Colma hill for family automobiles returning to San Francisco loaded with sleepy, tired, and cranky children. But in 1926 and 1927, the cemetery strip of highway was widened and the streetcar tracks were moved to the center of the road, and the traffic problem was solved.

Later, in 1929, our time to San Jose was cut down when two sections of the new Bayshore Highway were opened. They enabled us to speed down almost seven miles to the South San Francisco underpass from Army

155

Street in San Francisco. The first highway section had already been completed from the underpass to Fifth Avenue in San Mateo. An article in *Motorland* that year, heralding the new "speedway," said, "It is difficult to realize that we have actually reached the era of one-hundred-foot wide pavements" and "wide super-elevated curves negotiable at 40 miles per hour with a 'pull' to the outside. . . ."

Near the southern end of the cemetery-alley stretch, El Camino Real veered off to the right and up a slight grade to continue on to San Bruno. Branching off southeasterly to the left was a turnoff on to the old Mission Road. This road passed Molloy's, an old-time saloon across from Holy Cross Cemetery where Irish mourners would often gather to toast the loved one they had just laid to rest. Holy Cross was the first cemetery established in Colma, dating from 1887. Mission Road continued on to South San Francisco.

As you drove up the slight incline to continue on 101 south to San Bruno, you could see, in the nearby hills to the west, fields covered with Brussel sprouts, cabbages, cauliflowers, artichokes, turnips, carrots, and beets. These truck gardening farms were a rich source for San Francisco's congested produce market between the Financial District and the Embarcadero and Ferry Building. Hog ranches up in the heights are now covered by the Westlake development homes.

On the left hand side of the highway, looking toward South San Francisco and the Bay, you could see an imposing castle-like structure on a high hill. This was the Reichardt Duck Farm. A good part of its twenty-two acres were covered with coops containing thousands of quacking ducks. Reichardt's was the only major duck farm in the country east of Long Island. Chinatown restaurants counted on the farm for the main ingredient in such tasty treats as pressed duck and Peking duck.

During the mid-Thirties, the Baden Kennel Club could be seen a few miles further along on the left side of the highway. Turnoffs at Orange or Chestnut Avenues in South San Francisco were alive six nights a week with the headlights of cars and buses carrying dog racing fans and bettors to watch greyhound races. The card of eleven races began every night except Sunday at 8:15 during the racing season. Admission to the track was ten cents. Baden could also be reached from the new Bayshore Highway. Two public transit services ran there from the same block in San Francisco. Greyhound buses roared out from their Fifth and

Mission Terminal and Market Street Railway's No. 40 car started at Fifth and Market Streets and advertised "direct to grandstand" service to Baden on its way to San Mateo.

At San Bruno, we could see Tanforan Racetrack on the left hand side of the road. Soaring, shade-making eucalyptus trees lined the stretch of highway in front of the board fence topped with barbed wire which blocked off the view of the track and the racing thoroughbreds. A few steps from the road was the streetcar platform for the horse followers who came down on the Number 40 to chunk their dollars in at the betting windows.

Tanforan, now the site of one of the plethora of super shopping centers strung out all the way to San Jose and beyond, had a rich history. The land parcel on which the track was built had originally been part of the Rancho Buri Buri tract granted by the Mexican government to the Sanchez family. It was inherited by a Sanchez son-in-law, Toribio Tanforan.

The track was constructed and opened in 1899 by a group of prominent San Mateo Peninsula leaders headed by Dan "White Hat" McCarty. Many famous horses and jockeys had raced at Tanforan in the years since then under the colors of such notables as A. B. Spreckels, Leland Stanford, Charley Fair, and George Hearst.

The track was shut down and reopened twice before it closed forever. In 1912 betting on horse racing was made illegal in California after a series of scandals involving owners, trainers, and jockeys in fixed races. There was no horse racing at the track until the track was opened for several meetings in 1923 and again in 1930. Both times no betting was permitted. Gambling on the horses was finally resumed in 1933, when pari-mutuel betting was approved by the voters in a referendum election.

Auto races were also held at the Tanforan dirt track. I have a faint recollection of watching wide-eyed as the excessively noisy racing cars of the late Twenties roared around the mile track. I also recall that the famous driver Tommy Milton was competing in the race. Car racing at Tanforan went back many years. Faded clips can be found describing a 1909 auto race sponsored by the San Francisco Olympic Club in which a Stevens-Duryea 318 car won the 300-mile race at an average speed of almost sixty miles an hour.

Back in 1911, part of the Tanforan parcel had been called Selfridge Field. It was the takeoff point for what is claimed to be the first shore-to-ship airplane flight.

ON A SUNDAY AFTERNOON

That fellow in the middle coming this way is using the optional third lane for passing in either direction on El Camino Real. It had been made available by adding the asphalt lane at the right. This is near Mountain View. Fruit orchards border the highway. (Early Thirties.)

Courtesy of the California Division of Highways

Pilot Eugene Ely landed a biplane on the Navy's armored cruiser *Pennsylvania* in the San Francisco Bay after an eighteen-minute flight. Then Ely roared off again from the ship for a twelve-minute flight back to Selfridge. The year before, Louis Poulhan, a French flyer, had made the first air flight on the Pacific Coast at the track. He flew a Farnham biplane eight miles in eight minutes, reaching a height of seven hundred feet, while a large crowd of onlookers stood in the rain.

Tanforan had been used during World War I for a troop camp, particularly by the overflow from the Army's "California Grizzlies" artillery regiment at Camp Fremont in Menlo Park. More than twenty years later, directly following the attack on Pearl Harbor, it was used again as a concentration point—but this time

for the internment of Japanese-Americans in one of the country's less creditable actions.

Before arriving at Millbrae, you would pass the Lomita Park station, a Southern Pacific commute train whistle stop serving a subdivision by that name. Millbrae consisted of only a few scattered houses then on the hills leading up to the Skyline Boulevard road on the ridge above the Pacific Ocean to the west.

Eucalyptus trees lined both sides of 101 as you drove into Burlingame. The giant trees on the east side along the railroad tracks served as a windbreak, and provided shade during the morning hours.

When you passed through San Mateo, you went right by San Mateo Park on the highway. Many San Francisco and Peninsula families would picnic here on Sundays. All-day poker and pinochle games on the park's wooden tables were favorite recreation features. The northwest corner of the park was a baseball field, the home of the San Mateo Blues in the semipro California State League. They played there on Sunday afternoons. Right field backed right up to El Camino Real and was short, so that a hard-hit drive by a left-

*Looking north toward Colma and the cemeteries in 1916.
Yes, those are windmills—and a horse and wagon near them.*

Courtesy of the California Division of Highways

handed hitter occasionally would land on El Camino
Real itself. If you drove by in midafternoon, you could
see the games in progress and hear the shouts of the
fans. A small grandstand, with an admission fee of
fifty cents, circled home plate, but you could watch the
games from the edges of the outfield outside the park.
San Mateo Park is still a Sunday picnic area and the
baseball field is still there, although the State League,
where many major league ball players learned their
fundamentals, went out of existence in the early
Thirties.

The Beresford Southern Pacific commute station
came into view next. The small station was there until
1934 when the Bay Meadows Race Track was opened
near the railroad tracks. Bill Kyne, a well-known San
Francisco betting commissioner, built the track with a
syndicate he headed. Today another station house is
there, but the sign on it reads Hillsdale and across the
six-lane highway is a shopping center and residential
area.

As you drove up to the crest of the hill before
Belmont, where both the highway and the adjoining
railroad tracks bent to the right, a small hill rose

between El Camino Real and the tracks. It cut off sight
of the Bay to the east. In the Thirties, this hill was
leveled to provide fill for the continuing construction of
the new four-lane Bayshore Highway. The Bayshore
was started in 1924 when El Camino became crowded
with the increasing number of automobiles that families were acquiring, and fatal accidents were becoming
more common.

At San Carlos, from one elevated point on El
Camino Real, you could catch a startling, unexpected
glimpse of a memento of San Francisco's 1915 Panama
Pacific Exposition. More than thirty miles from its
original site in San Francisco's Cow Hollow neighborhood, known today as the Marina District, was the
Ohio Building, a replica of the Ohio state capitol at
Columbus. Weather-beaten, crumbling, and faded by
the late Thirties, it had once been the most impressive
structure on the Exposition's Avenue of the States.
After it was moved and left to the elements, it came to
be called the "Queen of the Mudflats."

It was two stories high, 130 feet long and 80 feet
wide, and had soaring Doric columns. The huge building, weighing over a thousand tons, had been barged
on the Bay down to Steinberger Slough on the San
Carlos shoreline. A get-rich-quick promoter had purchased it from Ohio at the end of the Exposition run.
He planned to convert it into the "Colonial Club
House" for the elite of the Peninsula. The San
Francisco housemover he hired managed, after great
difficulty, to float the building up on pilings at the

*This is a hillside cabbage field on the site of the present West-
lake housing development, looking down at the town of
Colma, in 1917.*

Courtesy of the San Francisco Public Library

Thoroughbreds parade in front of the clubhouse before a race at Tanforan. In the background is a crowded grandstand. (Probably Thirties.)

Courtesy of the San Francisco Examiner

slough. However, the entrepreneur's idea of dredging the adjacent marsh land to create a yacht harbor for the club never materialized. He found no support or financing for his ambitious scheme. The housemover, who had accomplished what many considered an impossible engineering feat, was never paid.

The building remained deserted until the early Prohibition years. Then it became the Babylon Club, a nightclub which soon gained a reputation as the scene of wild parties, a hideout for bootlegging rum-runners, and a habitat where "ladies of the night" were available. Visitors walked a plank from the beached building's ornate portico to a scow where they could buy drinks. When federal law enforcement agents showed up, the whiskey and gin stock was dumped into the slough.

After standing empty for several years, the building housed a movie company and, later, a machine shop which turned out radar equipment. Abandoned again, it was eventually burned down in 1956 by its owner to make way for an asphalt plant. Dismantling of its hardwood beams and other vestiges of fine building materials and workmanship was judged to be too expensive.

Just off of El Camino Real in the flatlands near Southern Pacific's San Carlos stop was a short-lived "million dollar" auto racetrack. The steeply banked board track was "shaped like the inside of a derby hat, more oval than round." It was called the Greater San Francisco Speedway at San Carlos, and was built by famous U.S. racetrack designer Jack Prince. The track opened in December, 1921, with a $25,000, 250-mile International Sweepstakes. Many of the outstanding drivers in the country, such as Tommy Milton, Harry Hartz, and Peter De Paolo, competed in the Sweepstakes. The press reported that between thirty and forty thousand people saw the race. San Francisco's own Jimmy Murphy won the race, setting a new world's record of 111.8 miles per hour in his Duesenberg. The night before the event, an elaborate dinner was held for the drivers, car owners, and invited local guests at the Ohio Building down on the Bay shore.

Approximately six months after it opened, on June 18, 1922, a fire destroyed a great part of the new mile-and-a-quarter track. Three San Francisco fire companies were called in to help local firefighters put out the flames. "Thousands of automobilists had stopped their machines to watch the great blaze, and from them a tremendous cheer went up when the San Francisco

This was the San Francisco Municipal Airport, then known as Mills Field, in San Bruno in September, 1927. Tanforan was near. The Bayshore Highway was still to be completed to Palo Alto.

Courtesy of the San Francisco Public Works Department

fire fighters, aided by those from the peninsula towns, first put a stream of water on the blazing grandstand,'' reported the *San Francisco Chronicle*. Only four races, including the opening event and a card of motorcycle races, had been held at the track. It never was rebuilt or used again.

At Redwood City, between El Camino Real and the new Bayshore Highway extension to be built in the Twenties, were a couple of small air fields, the Alfred Varney Flying Field and an air strip owned by Cy Cristofferson. Where Broadway ran into El Camino Real, the archway reading "Redwood City Climate Best By Government Test" spanned the highway. The glass dome of the old courthouse could be seen for

many miles. A few miles past Redwood City was the venerable Fly Trap Inn, a favorite restaurant and bootleg bar during Prohibition days.

Atherton had not been incorporated until 1923, but even then it was known, along with Hillsborough, as an affluent enclave of swanky estates. On the east side of the highway was a more modest real estate development known as Valparaiso Park.

At Menlo Park you could first spot the landmark Palo Alto tree, standing guard over the college town, on the east side of the highway. We usually went right through Palo Alto and then proceeded with caution, because we would be coming to Mayfield, not a part of Palo Alto until 1925 when the voters of both towns approved annexation.

Mayfield was a stagecoach stop for San Francisco-San Jose passengers in the 1850s. It had a notorious reputation as a "speed trap" for unwary motorists. My father had too many friends who had been nailed for just barely exceeding the speed limit of fifteen miles per hour through the minute town. Fines were stiff and the snaring of cars to augment the town's revenues was practiced fervently by the town police.

Mayfield was also known to be a traffic bottleneck with "5,000 feet of bumps." The *Palo Alto Times* referred to the six blocks of two lanes of tar-surfaced road which cooked in the hot summer sun as "approximately a mile of miserable roadway."

After Stanford Stadium was built in 1921, jam-ups of Saturday afternoon traffic on the three-lane El Camino Real were extremely serious. For a few years after 1924, when more automobiles were on the road, the thirty-mile return trip to San Francisco after a football game at Stanford could take up to three nerve-jangling hours. A good slice of that time would be consumed at the Colma cemetery strip. For those going south, the Mayfield traffic squeeze, only a few miles away, was not broken until 1934 when El Camino Real was widened to four macadam lanes.

Until 1933, electric streetcar service and trackage of the old Peninsular Railway ran between Palo Alto and Mayfield on the west side of El Camino Real. The metal tracks and red-trimmed cars made a sweeping right turn at University Avenue in Palo Alto when they came out of their terminal at Southern Pacific's Palo Alto station. They then ran directly across El Camino Real to just off the shoulder of the highway and did another curving turn to the left, south, toward Mayfield. Both north and south auto traffic had to stay alert for the big electric cars crossing the highway. There were no signals and no traffic directors, only the clang of the pull-cord and foot-stomping bells by the electric car motormen. It was all reminiscent of a Mack Sennett silent movie scenario including the potential of a smash-up. Traffic would often momentarily back up in both directions while the bulky cars, sometimes with only a few passengers aboard, made their Toonerville Trolley crossing of California's principal north-south highway.

The El Camino auto traffic had still another delay ahead in Mayfield. There Southern Pacific tracks made the same right turn and east-to-west crossing of El Camino Real on its route to Santa Cruz, Del Monte, and points south. This crossing, about 500 yards south of Page Mill Road, had some safety features, such as a wig-wag semaphore signal and up-and-down gates. The tracks, the signal, and the gates are still there with a slight gradual elevation across the path of the El Camino Real auto traffic. A Southern Pacific engine occasionally still crosses, delaying the autos, but it is only pulling freight cars for a customer nearby.

Between Palo Alto and San Jose, a city of some 50,000 by the early Thirties, everything was agriculture. There were no shopping centers, no markets of any substantial size, no lines of stores and shops except for the few clustered at Mayfield and Mountain View. The businesses you saw were occasional fruit stands and cold drink stands on the highway edges along the mile after mile of orchards, and an occasional gas station. There were also several isolated restaurants.

Beginning in 1932, if you were riding on El Camino Real past Palo Alto, you could look east toward the Bay and see the newest landmark in the area

Uncle Tom's Cabin restaurant at San Bruno on El Camino Real in 1923.

Courtesy of the San Francisco Chronicle

UNCLE TOM'S CABIN

This is not a shady back road. It is U.S. 101, El Camino Real, at Millbrae in 1933.

Courtesy of the San Francisco Chronicle

taking shape. This was the gigantic Hangar One at the new Naval Air Station on the Bay front at Sunnyvale. The hangar was built as a second base for the Navy's new lighter-than-air craft program. The other one was at Lakehurst, New Jersey. The seventeen hundred acres for the base, part of them an old Indian burial ground, were given to the Navy for one dollar after Santa Clara residents had raised $750,000 to purchase the land for that purpose.

In June, 1932, if you were riding on El Camino Real or on the Bayshore Highway, you could have seen the Navy's *USS Akron* airship at the Sunnyvale field. It was there for maneuvers with the Pacific Fleet.

In 1933, the new Sunnyvale base was opened eight

days after the *Akron* had crashed into the Atlantic Ocean. Only three of seventy-six men aboard survived. Five weeks after the field was commissioned, it was renamed Moffett Field in memory of Rear Admiral William A. Moffett, who had died in the crash of the *Akron*.

Later that year, the *USS Macon*, described by one writer as a "giant silver cigar gliding effortlessly among the clouds," arrived at the Sunnyvale base, its "permanent" home. During the next fifteen months, the big airship became a familiar sight to motorists. Then on February 12, 1935, it crashed into the Pacific off of Point Sur. This finished off the Navy's airship program. The *Macon* crew were luckier than that aboard the *Akron*. Only two of the eighty-one men aboard were lost. Hangar One remains on Moffett Field to this day. While Navy patrol blimps used Hangar One during World War II, it has since served principally for storage of various types of military planes. The north half of the hangar is now partitioned off for classrooms, offices, and training facilities.

From Palo Alto to Santa Clara and San Jose, El Camino Real was bordered with orchards of apricots, peaches, pears, and cherries. In the spring, white blossoms of prune tree orchards spread out over the Santa Clara Valley. For at least seven months of the year, fruit in the valley was ripening and flowers were blooming. In April red strawberries formed on the vines. In May, the cherry pickers would be up on their ladders. In July, pears, plums, and apricots were going into the baskets, and motorists could buy the fresh fruit at the roadside stands. The prunes were ready in August and grapes hung heavy on the ground stakes in September. October meant apples. In November, with fields a soft brown in color before the coming rains, the large English walnuts would be shaken from the weighted branches.

The largest fruit canneries and fruit drying houses in the world were in the Santa Clara Valley to receive the abundant harvests. The valley is about sixty miles long and thirty miles wide, and contains more than 850,000 acres. It raised more prunes, cherries, and apricots than any similar area in the country. Fruits were shipped to Covent Garden in London and other discriminating markets to yield the highest prices anywhere. The Valley's dried prunes, apricots, and pears commanded the world's markets. Champagne was made in San Jose. In the low hills and canyons surrounding the tableland orchards and farms were thick stands of redwood, oak, and madrone trees.

ON A SUNDAY AFTERNOON

In the mid-1920s, when I can first remember driving to San Jose with my folks, it seemed that there weren't too many people or buildings around the Santa Clara Valley. Just to make sure, I looked it up. "Each inhabitant of this Valley may have about eight acres of space to move about in," Sam Evans wrote in a *Motorland* article in 1926 called "Blossom Time in the Valley of Heart's Delight." In the sixty mile valley, there are "a scant 100,000 or so who live there," Evans noted. Then he described almost poetically the delights of being away from it all around San Jose:

Maybe it will be an unpopular thing to say, but the principal charm of the West, of California and of the Valley of Heart's Delight is that there aren't too many people in it. . . .

From almost any point on the hills surrounding the Santa Clara Valley, you will not be able to see any of the towns or cities that are spread on the floor of the valley. Even San Jose disappears beneath a bower of green. It is as though you were looking down on a vast garden. A few of the higher buildings that have marked the advance of San Jose are visible above the tree tops, but that is all. . . .

The skyline of the Valley of Heart's Delight is a line of purple mountains with only the blue sky above and a carpet of green and gold below. And through that garden run wide roads between well-kept orchards and vineyards where there is plenty of room for children to play and where one may get his feet again on the soft earth.

"Big Jim" Leary, the San Francisco City Hall figure and baseball fan, has typical mellow memories of what drives through the Santa Clara Valley meant in those years to a San Francisco city resident.

"Every year they had the Santa Clara Blossom Festival," Leary reminisces. "You'd drive for miles and see nothing but blossoms of different colors. And the perfume from the blossoming trees. That was something you never forget. It was like going through a rose garden. But now you see nothing but hamburger stands, and pizza and taco emporiums."

Before land costs, taxes and operating expenses rose, before eager housing and industrial tract subdividers appeared to chip away at agriculture in the Santa Clara Valley, and before the aging of orchards had become an important consideration, farmers and their families doggedly managed to survive in farming, even during the Depression years. During the 1930s,

school kids helped to pick prunes and apricots or cut the "cots" for drying. Picking usually started at 6 A.M. and continued until dark. All the members of a farm family had to pitch in and they had to help their neighbors too.

Wages for picking were twenty cents an hour, or five cents a box. On a good day of ten working hours, a picker could earn two dollars. Usually, pickers worked a six-day week. On Sunday, many of the workers went off to the beach at Santa Cruz, an hour away. When no picking was going on, the orchard brush had to be cleaned up with pitchforks, at fifteen and twenty cents an hour.

If you drove by the orchards in the evening, you might see students who went to school in the daytime working at the irrigation of walnut and apricot orchards. It was often said in the valley that a person was not really from Santa Clara County if he or she hadn't picked prunes or worked in a cannery. In the summer, masses of apricots would dry on acres of trays under the bright sun, covering the valley floor with large splotches of yellow, orange, and, later when the prunes were brought in, blue. If the heavy rains came when the prunes were on the ground, the entire valley smelled like a distillery.

If the weather in San Jose was hot when we arrived there, and it usually was, the old-fashioned San Jose Creamery on South First Street downtown, with pro-

The Ohio Building being barged on the Bay from its site at the 1915 Panama Pacific International Exposition to its mudflat destination on the San Carlos shore.

There weren't too many people in the Santa Clara Valley then.

peller-bladed ceiling fans whirring overhead, was a favorite stop for us. The milk shakes there were cold and creamy and rich. The sundaes were huge and came with liberal portions of chopped nuts and thick, real whipped cream topping the smooth and flavorful ice cream. The creamery seemed to have the same prestige that a lone ice cream parlor had in a small town. Everyone knew about it and recommended it. And San Jose seemed to be like a small town in the Twenties, with its languid pace and easy familiarity.

After we had made our San Jose stops and visits, we would usually drive out seven miles on East Santa Clara Avenue to Alum Rock Park in the hills under the Mount Hamilton range. The park took its name from a massive, smooth-faced monolith that dominated the entrance. The park was overrun with families and picnickers on Sunday, and you had to get there well before noon to get a decent table. My relatives used to try to get me to drink some of the smelly sulphur waters that came from mineral springs scattered around the park, mostly in the upper section. More than twenty rock grottos, many of them under cupolas, gushed waters that were supposed to be medicinal. You could bring your own cup, and there was no charge for the waters. Penny Dixie Cup machines were installed at the springs also, in case you hadn't brought your own cup. Not all the springs smelled bad. Some had plain spring water and others plain soda water. The springs containing sulphur and iron were reputed to have marvelous curative or pain-relieving effects for such maladies as gallstones.

Groups of people, sometimes entire families, would stroll casually from spring to spring, patiently waiting to thrust a cup under a spigot and partake of the reputed

Much of the Santa Clara Valley floor used to be covered with drying fruit.

Courtesy of the San Francisco Examiner

qualities of that particular variety of water. A visit to the park was a social event of a sort, also. Friends met and gossiped there, or just sat together on a bench for a while to soak up some of the sunshine. Although the park was essentially a picnic ground, many wore their best Sunday clothes because it was their one chance to do so all week.

There was also an indoor swimming pool in the park known as the Natatorium. It had a steep "death-defying" slide that was a little scary for most kids. Also, sulphur and mud baths with tubs set in white tile stalls, built before 1920, were well-maintained and popular with adults.

Penitencia Creek flowed through a part of the more than six hundred acres that made up the park. The

An Alum Rock Park scene. The mineral spring cupola is still in the park.

Courtesy of the San Francisco Public Library

El Camino Real at Palo Alto in 1930, looking north toward Menlo Park from University Avenue. The Stanford Shopping Center now occupies the site on the left.

Courtesy of the Palo Alto Historical Association

burbling water, rolling slowly through the canyon bottom, where practically all the activity and improvements were concentrated, seemed to add the rustic touch that proved we were really in the country.

Two street railway lines ran from downtown San Jose into the park, and a good part of the heavy weekend attendance came from San Jose crowds armed with picnic baskets and boxes who piled off the cars arriving every half hour. The park claimed to be able to accommodate fifty thousand people, and the picnic facilities were extensive. There were a lot of stone barbecue pits and tables and benches on which to spread the food and beverages you had brought down for the day. Before and after lunch the tables would be used for the inevitable card games—usually separate poker tables for men and women players, and a pinochle table or two.

A merry-go-round, a deer paddock, and two children's playgrounds with swings were other park attractions. The usual concession booths and refreshment stands were concentrated in the same flat central core of the park, and two dance floors, one indoors and one outside, completed the facilities.

Birds whirred through a wide assortment of trees, flowers, and plants. Hiking and saddle trails spread out from the lower end of the park and there were some open areas for softball games.

When the shadows started to creep down into the canyon and the evening chill began to come on, baskets would be packed, blankets folded, and the family clans would gather, spurred on by shouts of "Get ready to go; we're leaving right away."

Driving back to San Francisco at night, you were even more conscious that you were in the country. When you left Santa Clara for home, there was almost absolute darkness on El Camino Real. The stars overhead shone in a clear sky and the silhouettes of the orchards stood out sharply on each side of the three-lane road. A service station, or late-closing fruit and vegetable roadside stand, would occasionally emerge glowingly along the edges of the road. The only illumination visible on some long stretches of the highway were the overhead lamps that played on Foster and Kleiser billboards alongside the highway.

The weather cooled off considerably at night in the valley, and the touch of evening cold in the air seemed fitting for the rather lonely drive back. There were no car radios then, so usually the ride began with an animated exchange of comments by my parents about the vagaries and oddities of the relatives we had just visited. After that came a soft, soothing silence. The end-of-the-day mental and physical weariness set in and you could hear the sizz of the tires on the road, and even the crickets. It was peaceful and quiet.

The lamps and bulbs of Mountain View and Mayfield, just off the road as you passed through, were sparse and dim because it was Sunday night. Dinah's Shack restaurant, just before Palo Alto with its rows of parked cars, lights, and movement, was perhaps the liveliest spot you saw. After Palo Alto the traffic would increase as the road passed through residential areas. Until you came to Redwood City, El Camino Real was still mainly a night drive in the darkened country. From then on, glare on your windshield, traffic, and noise became even more intense, and it took longer to get back to the City because it seemed that everyone in the Bay Area was trying to get through Colma on Sunday night. Finally, you rolled into the sea of light filtering through the welcoming fog of the City—and you were home.

ACKNOWLEDGMENTS

My sincere appreciation goes to many persons and several organizations who not only cooperated with me, but in many instances shared my enthusiasm in attempting to bring back some of the pleasant memories of life in the Bay Area in the Twenties and Thirties. I have attempted to make my recollections as accurate as possible. If some errors do appear, they are innocent ones, and I assume full responsibility for them. Memories more than fifty years old understandably tend to blur around the edges.

Listed below are some of these people who contributed to this project. Some have been especially generous with their time; their names are listed in italics. Following the individuals is a list of the institutions which generously made materials available to me. And following that list is a brief bibliography of sources I found helpful. Earlier versions of "Fillmore in the 1920s" and "Remember the Rose Bowl?" chapters appeared in the pages of the *California Living* section of the *San Francisco Sunday Examiner & Chronicle*.

Martin Abaurria
Barney Apfel
Clyde Arbuckle
Doug Archer
Earle Behrens
Dante Benedetti
Eugene Block
Bill Brown
Suzanne Caster
Rene Cazanave
Dick Chase
Jack Chow
Nate Cohen
Nate Cohn
Merv Coleman
Jerry Connolly
June Dellapa
Louis De Martini
Virginia Dennison
Don Denton
Dick Dobbins
Mrs. R. C. Doherty
Dick Dyer
Al Erle
Doris McLeod Evon
Frank Finney
Edna Fischer
David Flamm
Esther Flamm
Willie Frizzi
Sue Gallup

Elmer Gavello
Daniel Goldberg
Dr. Milton Gordon
Roland Gotti
Victor Gotti
Newton Hale
Dick Halligan
Norman Hanley
Mrs. Gladys Hansen
Tommy Harris
Ernie Hecksher
Marion Holmes
Andy Hynes
John Jellincich
Willie Kamm
Jack Kavanaugh
Hermie King
Richard F. Kline
Max Kniesche, Jr.
Jack Kramer
S. K. Lai
Jimmy Leonard
Jim Leary
Ray Leavitt
Ralph Lintner
Joe Lerner
Tommy Maloney
Sister Mary Clement Manion
George Mardikian
Marshall Maslin
Jack McDonald

Jimmy McFadden
Jimmy McGee
Paul Mechetti
Adolph Motta
Marshall Moxon
George Mullany
Eddie Murphy
Ted Needham
Frank O'Mea
Ernest O'Hair
Richard Osicka
Adolph Parodi
Gordon Peters
Bill Phelps
Al Pollack
Ollie Quillanin
Stu Rasmussen
Mel Rifkin
Mrs. Reuben Rinder
Sid Tait
Charles Sava
John Shackleton
Joe Sprinz
Lou Stein, Jr.
Fred Stindt
Larry Storbo
Arthur Strehlow
Robert Strehlow, Jr.
Gus Suhr
Prescott Sullivan
Peter Tamony

Myron Tatarian
George Taylor
Cy Trobbe
Lynn Vermillion
Reuben Waxman
Mrs. Ruth Wilson
Harvey Wing
Bill Weiss

AC Transit
Bancroft Library, University of California
California Historical Society
California State Automobile Association
Naval Air Station, Moffett Field
Oakland Museum
Oakland Tribune
Palo Alto Historical Association
San Francisco Chronicle
San Francisco Examiner
San Francisco Maritime Museum
San Francisco Public Library,
    California Section and Newspaper Room
San Mateo Times
San Mateo Historical Association
San Jose City Library
San Rafael Independent Journal
Southern Pacific
The Daily Californian

Index

169

INDEX

INDEX

INDEX

BIBLIOGRAPHY

Berkeley. Bancroft Library, University of California. C-B 816. "Writings and Articles on Chinese and on Narcotics" [by J. H. Manion].

Bruce, John. *The Gaudy Century*. New York: Random House, 1948.

Buxton, Frank, and Owens, Bill. *The Big Broadcast 1920-1950*. New York: Viking Press, 1966.

Chandler, Samuel C. *Gateway to the Peninsula: A History of the City of Daly City*. Daly City, Calif., 1973.

Coffman, Arthur. *An Illustrated History of Palo Alto*. Palo Alto, Calif., 1969.

Ennis, Earle. "Ferry Tales." *San Francisco Chronicle*, 1932-33.

Fillmore Street, Past, Present and Future. San Francisco: J. W. Treadwell Realty Co., 1913.

Scoop: Annual Yearbook of the Press Club. San Francisco Press and Union Club Library.

Wells, Evelyn, *Fremont Older*. New York and London: D. Appleton Century, 1936.

Works Progress Administration, Writers' Program. *San Francisco—The Bay and Its Cities*. New York: Hastings House, 1947.